INVESTOR'S GUIDE

How the Stock Market Really Works

The Guerrilla Investor's Secret Handbook

LEO GOUGH

FINANCIAL TIMES
PITMAN PUBLISHING

LONDON · HONG KONG · JOHANNESBURG
MELBOURNE · SINGAPORE · WASHINGTON DC

FINANCIAL TIMES MANAGEMENT
128 Long Acre, London WC2E 9AN
Tel: +44 (0)171 447 2000
Fax: +44 (0)171 240 5771
Website: www.ftmanagement.com

A Division of Financial Times Professional Limited

First published in Great Britain in 1994
This edition 1997
© Leo Gough, 1997

Figs. 7.5 & 7.6 reproduced from A Random Walk Down Wall Street, Fifth Edition,

Including 'A Life-Cycle guide to Personal Investing', by Burton G. Malkiel,
by permission of W. W. Norton & Company, Inc.

Copyright © 1990, 1985, 1981, 1975, 1973 by W. W. Norton & Company Inc.

ISBN 0 273 62685 X

British Library Cataloguing in Publication Data
A CIP catalogue record for this book can be obtained from the British Library

This publication is designed to provide accurate and authoritative information in
regard to the subject matter covered. It is sold with the understanding that neither
the author nor the publisher is engaged in rendering legal, investing, or any other
professional service. If legal advice or other expert assistance is required, the
services of a competent professional person should be sought.

The publishers make no representation, express or implied, with regard to the
accuracy of the information contained in this book and cannot accept any legal
responsibility or liability for any errors or omissions that may be made.

10 9 8 7 6 5 4

Typeset by Northern Phototypesetting Co. Ltd, Bolton
Printed and bound in Great Britain by Bell and Bain Ltd, Glasgow

The Publishers' policy is to use paper manufactured from sustainable forests.

Contents

To Rob Ormsby

The first thing to do is to take stock of yourself and your circumstances, and to develop a capacity for clear-mindedness and good judgement.

Introduction

If you were living in Europe during World War 2, you probably have little difficulty in entertaining the notion that the authorities are not always fair or honest; if, however, you were brought up in post-war Britain – or in many other European countries, for that matter – you might well have trouble with this idea.

Now you want to be an investor. The first thing to do is to take stock of yourself and your circumstances, and to develop a capacity for clear-mindedness and good judgement. As a small investor, you will find that governments, the institutions, financial advisers and the professional classes are not your friends – if you do as they urge, and leave the decisions about your money to them, you are likely to end up with less of it than you had before. It is not simply a question of fraud, although as we will see in this book, the financial world is an adventure playground for fraudsters, with ludicrously mild punishments in the unlikely event of their conviction. It is also that the rules of the game are weighted against you.

> **Many of the savings and investment 'opportunities' available to the public are designed to prevent you from getting rich.**

Many of the savings and investment 'opportunities' available to the public are designed to prevent you from getting rich. Inflation, fluctuating interest rates and exchange rates, government regulation and taxes have a tendency to catch out the individual. In this book I have tried to explain how the financial markets work, and to suggest strategies for increasing and preserving capital. It is possible to do this, but only, unless you are unusually lucky, by taking investment seriously and learning as much as you can about it – like life, investment really is a 'do-it-yourself' project.

Here's what the book covers:

Chapter 1: The guerrilla investor

- The guerrilla investor concept – strategy and tactics.
- Net worth – why you should monitor your net worth.
- Income and expenditure.
- Employment – using your income to get ahead.
- Educating yourself about money.

Chapter 2: Shares

Chapter 3: Bonds

- The Barlow Clowes scandal.
- Convertible bonds.
- Ex dividend and cum dividend bonds.
- The US bond rating system
- Bonds for the guerrilla investor.

Chapter 4: The life cycle of a company – from launches to liquidations

- New issues – how companies are floated on the stock market.
- The offer for sale.
- Stagging and application tactics.
- Private placing.
- Offers for subscription.
- Tenders and introductions.
- Rights issues, calculating the value of rights and clawbacks.
- Scrip issues.
- Takeover bids.
- How to choose companies that may be subject to takeover bids.
- The Monopolies and Mergers Commission.
- Why companies bid for other ones.
- When companies go bust …
- Gauging solvency.
- Suspensions and liquidations.

Chapter 5: Banks

- Money – why and how it works.
- The money stock and the money supply.
- The role of central banks.
- The Bank of England.
- UK monetary policy.
- The Federal Reserve.
- Types of bank.
- Interest rates.
- The BCCI story.

- How banks lend to individuals.
- Guerrilla borrowing tactics.
- Banking and Big Brother.

Chapter 6: The money markets

- Bills of exchange.
- Certificates of deposit.
- The discount market.
- The local authority market.
- The inter-bank market.
- The finance house, inter-company and commercial paper markets.
- The certificate of deposit market.
- The Euromarkets – Eurodeposits and Eurobonds.
- Interest rate and currency swaps.

Chapter 7: Investment theories

- Probability, and why some people are just lucky.
- The Kondratiev wave, an unproven economic cycle lasting 60 years or so.
- Technical analysis, or 'chartism', for the fortune-tellers of the stock market.
- Fundamental analysis, the science of evaluating companies, and why it tends to cancel itself out.
- The efficient market theory, which explains why most strategies don't work for long, and why 'buy and hold' does.
- Risk.
- MPT (modern portfolio theory), which describes the virtues of diversification.
- CAPM (capital-asset pricing theory), which gives a measurement of risk, called 'beta', and APT (arbitrage pricing theory).
- GARCH, chaos theory and computer models, which are newer ways of trying to predict price movements.

Chapter 8: Commodities, futures and options – for gamblers only?

- Commodities – what they are and how they work.
- Futures – how they developed. The difference between hedgers and speculators.
- Financial futures – how money is treated as a commodity.
- The London International Financial Futures and Options Exchange (LIFFE).
- Chicago and other US futures markets.
- Tokyo futures.
- Far East futures markets.
- The smaller futures markets.
- Options and traded options – what they are and why you should avoid them. Calls, puts, hedging and option writing.

Chapter 9: Foreign Exchange

- The Bretton Woods system – why it was set up after World War 2, how it worked and why it has ended.
- The floating rate system – how it emerged and why it is good news for private investors.
- The Euromarkets.
- The foreign exchange market. How currencies are traded.
- Exchange rates – how to calculate them, and how to hedge in currencies. Arbitrage and speculation, and how to predict exchange rates.
- The special drawing right (SDR).
- The European Monetary System (EMS).
- The future of the yen.

Chapter 10: Lloyd's of London

- The origins of Lloyd's.
- Lloyd's structure – the agents, Names and its governing body.
- The syndicates – how they work.
- The underwriters and brokers – how Lloyd's chooses what to insure.
- How to become a Name – deposits and premium limits.

- The down side – excess of loss and the LMX spiral. Open years.
- The problems of asbestos, pollution and catastrophe claims.
- The Names' rebellion.
- Is it still worth becoming a Name?

Chapter 11: Fraud and the regulatory bodies

- The Securities and Investments Board (SIB).
- The Self-Regulatory Organisations (SROs) – IMRO, LAUTRO, FIMBRA, PIA and SFA.
- The Department of Trade and Industry.
- The Securities and Exchange Commission (SEC) in the United States.
- Two perennial scams: The hard sell and Conning the law breakers.
- Insider trading in the 1980s – Boesky, Milken and Levine.

Chapter 12: Overseas investments

- Why you should invest overseas.
- The companies and individuals that do so.
- Tax havens, what they are and how they work.
- Offshore trusts and corporations.
- How to avoid the sharks.
- How to minimise risk.

Chapter 13: Other investments

- Property – its advantages, how to profit from its unique qualities and the varieties of property.
- Collectibles – why most people fail to make money in 'things', what you must do to have a fighting chance and the dangers of the collectibles market.
- The Enterprise Investment Scheme (EIS) – the successor to BES (the Business Enterprise Scheme), this is a new tax incentive programme in the UK designed to attract higher-rate taxpayers to invest in new companies. Its advantages are, as yet, doubtful.
- Cash – where to keep it and how safe it is.
- Annuities – why they are bad news for retired people.

- Pensions – why you don't have to have a pension.
- Life insurance – the varieties on offer and how to profit from the trade in second-hand policies.

Chapter 14: Tax

- Tax avoidance and tax evasion – why avoidance is legal and desirable.
- Residence, ordinary residence and domicile – how these different categories affect your tax status.
- Income tax – the current allowances and reliefs in the UK.
- Capital Gains Tax (CGT) – how to reduce your liability.
- Inheritance Tax – why it is never too early to make a will, and some ideas on how to plan for passing on your estate.
- Trusts – the varieties of trust and their uses.
- Tax avoidance through starting a limited company.
- Working abroad.

You may find some of the views expressed in this book controversial. This is intended. To develop the capacity to discriminate, which all successful investors must have, you must allow yourself to be exposed to new and different ideas that may conflict with what you already know, or what you are constantly being told on radio and television. Investing combines theory and practice in a complex and imperfect world; you may not always get it right, but that should not be your objective. Prosperity and coming out 'on top' in the long run is far more important. May you achieve this worthy goal!

> To develop the capacity to discriminate, which all successful investors must have, you must allow yourself to be exposed to new and different ideas

Please note that since new legislation and financial products are being introduced all the time, some of the details in this book may be out of date by the time you read them; these will be rectified in future editions. In the meantime, remember that while you should always check the precise details of an investment before committing yourself, you can be confident that the basic principles of investment will not change.

I would like to thank Phyllis Reed, Simon Reed, Tony Jay, Trevor Pepperell, Barry Riley and Nick Henderson for their valuable help and advice. The opinions and any mistakes herein are mine, not theirs.

You must adopt a survival strategy
entirely different from the way the
big boys operate

1

The guerrilla investor

This book is for people who want to make money. If you think that having money is wrong, or unfair, this book is not for you. Don't despair, though, if you don't have any money yet; it is possible to accumulate capital if you are determined to do so, whatever your disadvantages. In this chapter we will look at the basic things you need to do before investing. The topics are:

- The 'guerrilla investor' concept – strategy and tactics.
- Net worth.
- Income and expenditure.
- Employment.
- Educating yourself about money.
- Should you own your own home?
- Preparing for the stock market.
- Risk and diversification.
- Choosing a financial adviser.
- Gough's five golden rules for guerrillas.
- Some financial maths – present value (PV) and net present value (NPV).
- Simple and compound interest.

THE 'GUERRILLA INVESTOR' CONCEPT

The private investor has vastly superior forces arrayed against him in the struggle for wealth – they have better information, better equipment, more experience, incomparably more money, and political influence. In this respect, the private investor is in a similar position to a real guerrilla; the way to fight back is to exploit the opportunities that being small gives. In the Vietnam War, the North Vietnamese forces had, on paper, no chance against the overwhelming US military, yet they fought on until the enemy left. After a battle, the guerrillas were trained to pick up every usable cartridge case. A black market trade in US arms grew up. By the end of the war, almost all of the equipment used by the North Vietnamese forces was American, stolen, captured and bought from the opposition. The guerrilla soldiers were expected to live off the land, on a tiny amount of food; they were prepared to sit in a tree for a week waiting for the enemy to pass by. They were determined not to give up, and they used their greater flexibility to move faster than the cumbersome organisation they opposed.

So it is with the private investor: what would be a small gain to, say, a merchant bank is large gain for an individual. You cannot compete on the same terms as the huge financial institutions and companies that dominate the world's economy. You must adopt a survival strategy entirely different from the way that the big boys operate.

Guerrilla strategy and tactics

Traditionally, investors are supposed to fall into two categories: those who want capital growth (i.e. to get more money) and those who want to live on the income they get from investing the money they already have. The notion of 'widows and orphans', middle-class people with no job but a little capital, used to be used as a symbol for the investors who wanted income – advisers felt that it was their duty to keep such individuals in the safest possible investments because they were unlikely to be able to recover if they suffered a serious loss. With the advent of social welfare, the situation has changed – widows and orphans will not starve in the gutter if they lose their capital – so I believe that these traditional categories are no longer helpful. After all, we all want capital growth if we can get it.

Here is a list of questions you should ask yourself regularly:

- *What is my net worth?*
- *What is my total income and expenditure?*
- *Am I getting richer or poorer? Why?*
- *What are my future employment prospects?*

Net worth

Net worth is simply the difference between the value of all the things that you have and all the money that you owe. Most people on this planet have no net worth. Even in the richest countries of the world, most people only have some clothes, a car and a few sticks of furniture – not much to show for a lifetime's toil. The reason why this is so is that the system is constantly ripping them off. They buy life assurance and then give it up after a couple of years, making a loss. They buy consumer goods at retail prices and borrow money at high interest rates to do so. They run up expensive overdrafts and live off credit cards. They buy things to make themselves feel they are richer than they really are. They borrow too much money in boom times to buy houses and fail to anticipate the inevitable bust. On and on it goes. Financially speaking, most people are abused and pushed around all their lives. The guerrilla fights back!

> To fight back, you have to be in command of your own resources; first and foremost this means knowing what you've got and how much it is worth.

To fight back, you have to be in command of your own resources; first and foremost this means knowing what you've got and how much it is worth. Naturally, it is hard to estimate the value of some things, particularly houses, so take the trouble to get realistic valuations and be conservative. If you had a house worth £150,000 in 1988, it might only be worth £100,000 now, so don't kid yourself. The market value of assets go up and down all the time, which is why you must frequently take a 'snapshot' of how you are doing. Make your net worth the benchmark by which you measure your performance.

Income and expenditure

Working out how much you earn and how much you spend is a mundane housekeeping activity that most people practise. However, they don't usually go far enough. Simply aiming to cover your bills leaves you exposed, although it is a cardinal principle for accumulating capital. Engrave this on your mind:

Don't consume more than you earn

Most people waste their money on things they don't need. By all means buy the best you can afford – the best quality is usually the best value in the long run – but look for bargains and ways of reducing your expenditure. Examine each category in your regular budget, and try to think of ways of cutting it down. A guerrilla has few resources, and must put them to the best use. Don't worry if you don't buy things that your peers do. Your job must be to generate regular savings out of your income.

Employment

The world of employment is uncertain. If you have a good salary, there is no excuse not to save, but many high earners manage to get into debt nevertheless. In old age you may not be able to get a job – don't rely on your pension, start saving!

Many of us don't earn as much as we'd like. Re-train, and get a better job. Self-employment is an option, and has tax advantages, but it is not something to be taken on lightly. The whole mentality of the self-employed is different: it's lonely, you must bear more responsibility, it is uncertain, and it often takes years of struggle to get established. If you get it right, though, it is very rewarding.

Educate yourself about money

Sportsmen often say that people's general unfitness and lack of body awareness is as great a form of ignorance as not being able to read and write. I believe that the same holds true for financial matters: if you were not fortunate enough to have been born into a business-minded family, you will have to learn it all for yourself. Talk to people who are richer than you are and know something about the subject. Read widely. When you have run though your local library, try using university libraries (you don't normally have to join) and talk to academics, who will be scrupulously careful to give you a balanced view. There are uncertainties and unanswered questions in the world of investment; developing a deep appreciation of this will help your judgement.

Should you own your own home?

Buying a property is usually a good investment in the long term. We all have to live somewhere, and if the alternative is renting at market rates, you should find that the cost of servicing a mortgage is equivalent to the rent you would otherwise pay. In the long term, property has been a good hedge against inflation, and if prices go up you are using the 'leverage' of your mortgage to increase the value of your equity.

> **✳ EXAMPLE**　If you buy a £60,000 flat with a £40,000 mortgage and £20,000 of savings, and the flat's value increases to £90,000, your equity will increase from £20,000 to £50,000. If you had bought the flat entirely with your own money, your equity would have increased by a lower percentage – from £60,000 to £90,000.

People in the UK are nervous about property at present because of the problems of the recent property crash (this is discussed in detail in Chapter 13). You really have only to do two things:

- Don't borrow more than you can afford, taking into account possible interest rate hikes.
- Don't buy 'consumer' homes; buy well-built bargains. Buying a brand new house from one of the big construction companies is not usually a good deal.

Preparing for the stock market

Let's assume that you have a regular income, a house of your own, and that by saving regularly you have accumulated a capital sum. You have practised all the bourgeois virtues and now you feel ready to spread your wings. Investing in the stock market will probably give you a better return on your money than any other kind of passive investment; but try not to be greedy. Trying to 'beat the market' almost always means taking more risk, so you are much more likely to lose money. The safest way to invest in shares is to buy good ones and hold them for a long time; constantly buying and selling is expensive because of the commissions you pay.

Risk and diversification

The concept of risk is dealt with in detail in Chapter 7. The first thing to realise about any investment is that it is always risky; that is to say, since no one can predict the future with complete accuracy, you cannot say that an investment has 0 per cent risk. If the world blew up tomorrow, all investments would be worthless. It is very important, however, to try to assign a degree of risk to investments. Powerful, stable governments want to support the system, and provide many kinds of guarantees for certain kinds of investments. It takes study, experience, good judgement and a good adviser to pick the best investments.

CHOOSING A FINANCIAL ADVISER

Your best financial adviser is yourself – you care more than anyone else what will happen to your money. Before seeking professional advice on a matter, read everything you can about it and try to understand it. This will help you to get the best out of your advisers. A very experienced businessman once told me that there are two kinds of customers who get the best treatment: the ones who spend a lot of money, and the 'difficult' ones who never stop badgering, looking for a bargain, insisting on their rights and making demands. Be a difficult customer – it's your money, and you are the person who cares most about it. Don't be afraid to be rude or pushy if necessary, and don't let yourself be pushed around – there is always someone else if your adviser doesn't want your business. As with most things, the personal recommendation from someone whose business judgement you really respect is the best way to find a good adviser.

> It takes study, experience, good judgement and a good adviser to pick the best investments.

Nevertheless, there are general points about financial advisers that are worth considering. They are basically of two kinds, the 'tied agents' and the 'independent financial advisers' (IFAs).

Tied agents

Tied agents represent a company, most often an insurance company, and only sell the products offered by that company. They don't have to tell you how much commission they are making, but they do have to tell you that they are tied. The high street banks and most building societies are tied agents, since they will only sell financial products offered by a particular company. Before dismissing tied agents out of hand, you should recognise that, since they are backed by large companies, they are unlikely to go bust, and they may, sometimes, be able to give you the best deal on a particular product. Never sign an agreement that contains a penalty clause specifying that if you allow, say, an insurance policy or mortgage to lapse you will pay a percentage of the sum to the agent.

Independent financial advisers (IFAs)

IFAs can be stockbrokers, accountants, insurance brokers, solicitors and some building society managers. They may also be individuals without professional qualifications other than having passed the Financial Planning Certificate exams. IFAs have to tell you about their charges and any commissions they make, if you ask them, and are obliged by law to give you the best advice for your circumstances. IFAs that live on commissions are arguably less independent than ones that only charge fees. The latter type may rebate any commissions they earn to you. Never rely on the regulation of IFAs to give you complete protection; check them out very thoroughly before you part with any money. Such checks would include getting references, confirming that they are members of the relevant regulatory bodies, making sure that you have obtained, and understood, all the relevant paperwork, and verifying that they are insured against professional negligence.

GOUGH'S FIVE GOLDEN RULES FOR GUERRILLAS

It is said that one can't be taken seriously these days unless one propounds laws, so here are 'Gough's five golden rules' for achieving prosperity:

- Put not your faith in governments or their minions.
- Don't spend more than you earn.
- If a deal looks too good to be true, it IS too good to be true.
- Get rich slowly.
- Trust yourself.

If these rules seem a bit simple-minded, think about the people you know who have grown rich through their own efforts. They are often not particularly clever or well-educated, and their methods are often surprisingly unsophisticated. In my view, succeeding as an investor is not so much about trying to outsmart everyone else as it is about steadiness, common sense and self-reliance.

A LITTLE FINANCIAL MATHS

People don't like doing sums, but if you are going to be a successful investor you will have to learn how. This section introduces a few important notions which you need to be familiar with.

Net present value (NPV)

Suppose that your house has burned down and that the land where it once stood is worth £40,000. You have received £160,000 from your insurance company to build a new house, but you think that if you build shops instead you will be able to sell them for £300,000 in a year's time. It will cost you £200,000 to build the shops, and you want to know whether this is a good investment compared with the other ways you could use the money. One way to work this out is by using the concepts of 'present value' (PV) and 'net present value' (NPV). The present value of the shops, if you start building now, is the amount you will receive when you sell, adjusted for the interest you would earn if you kept the money in cash or bonds. This adjustment is calculated by using the 'discount factor', thus:

> Succeeding as an investor is not so much about trying to outsmart everyone else as it is about steadiness, common sense and self-reliance.

Discount factor = 1 ÷ (1 + rate of return)

Suppose you can get 10 per cent on your money if you leave it on deposit. The discount factor would be:

$$\text{Discount factor} = 1 \div (1 + 0.10)$$

$$= 1 \div 1.10$$

$$= 0.909$$

This is incorporated into the formula for working out the present value:

Present value = Discount factor x future payoff

Thus, the present value of the shops project is:

$$PV = 0.909 \times 300{,}000$$
$$= 272{,}700$$

Assuming that your estimate of the sale value of the shops in one year's time is correct, the present value of the sum you would get by selling is £272,000; this is the amount of money you would have to put in a bank deposit to have £300,000 in a year from now. If you start work, and are then approached by someone who wants to buy the whole project right away, the present value is the figure that represents a fair price to sell at. The rate of return, 10 per cent in this example, that you would get in a safe investment, is also known as the 'opportunity cost', since it is the return that you are giving up by investing in the building project rather than putting the money on deposit in a bank.

Suppose that you decide not to sell to the first buyer and continue with the construction work. You believe that the present value of the site is £272,000, but you have invested £40,000's worth of land, £160,000 in cash from the insurance company and borrowed another £40,000 (let's assume this was from a relative who charges no interest). You now work out the 'net present value' (NPV) of your investment:

$$\textbf{NPV} = \textbf{PV} - \textbf{amount invested}$$
$$= 272{,}000 - (40{,}000 + 160{,}000 + 40{,}000)$$
$$= 32{,}000$$

The net present value of £32,000 represents the profit you are making (in today's money) over and above the return you would have got if you had kept the money on deposit.

Building a row of shops is not the same as putting money on deposit, though. Most people would say that it is riskier. Problems with the local council, regulations and builders might slow things down, and you might find that it took longer to sell the buildings than you originally anticipated. Suppose you decide that the project is as risky as investing in shares, and that the forecast for the average return on shares in the coming year is 14 per cent. The discount factor would be:

$$\text{Discount factor} = 1 \div (1 + 0.14)$$
$$= 1 \div 1.14$$
$$= 0.877$$

the present value would be:

$$PV = 0.877 \times 300{,}000$$
$$= 263{,}100$$

and the net present value would be:

NPV = PV – amount invested
$$= 263{,}100 - (40{,}000 + 160{,}000 + 40{,}000)$$

$$= 23{,}100$$

Another way of looking at this is to work out the rate of return you are getting from your project:

Rate of return = profit ÷ amount invested
$$= (300{,}000 - 240{,}000) \div 240{,}000$$

$$= 60{,}000 \div 240{,}000$$

$$= 0.25$$

The rate of return is 0.25, or 25 per cent. This beats the 10 per cent you can get from depositing the cash, and the 14 per cent you could get by investing in shares. Nevertheless, you cannot be sure these figures are accurate – they are assumptions, and the most doubtful of them is your assumption that you will be able to sell the shops for £300,000 in one year's time. For this reason, you would probably do further calculations adjusting your assumed figures to see what would happen if, say, it took you two years to sell the shops, or if the average return on shares was lower.

Discounted cash flows

Suppose that you believed that after a year you would only be able to sell some of your shops, for a total of £100,000, and that you would sell the rest at the end of the second year for £200,000. You decide to work out the present value assuming a rate of return of 10 per cent in both years as being the opportunity cost. The discount factor for the first year is 0.909, and for the second is:

Year 2 discount factor $= 1 \div (1 + \text{rate of return})^2$
$$= 1 \div 1.10^2$$

$$= 0.826$$

The discount factor for any particular year in a series is found in the same way, i.e. by raising '1 plus the rate of return' term to the power that is the same number as the year number. For instance, in Year 5 it would be $(1 + \text{rate of return})^5$, in Year 6 it would be $(1 + \text{rate of return})^6$ and so on.

The present value is worked out by calculating the PV for each of the years and adding them together:

PV = (Discount factor Year 1 x future payoff Year 1) +

(Discount factor Year 2 x future payoff Year 2)

= (0.909 x 100,000) + (0.826 x 200,000)

= 90,900 + 165,200

= 256,100

and the net present value is:

NPV = PV – amount invested

= 256,100 – (40,000 + 160,000 + 40,000)

= 16,100

The NPV is a positive number, so in this scenario the project would perform better than if you had kept your cash on deposit. Adding together the PVs of several years in a series is called the 'discounted cash flow' method.

Many of the ideas associated with NPV are quite complex and are beyond the scope of this book. However, you should be aware that the principles of NPV can be applied to all types of investment, including shares and bonds, and that it is probably the best of several methods currently in use.

Future value (FV) is the sum obtained at the end of a specified investment period. To work out the future value of a stream of payments, for example when you are saving a regular amount, use the formula:

$$FV = [p \times <1 + i) - 1>]/i$$

where p is the amount invested per period, n is the number of periods and i is the rate of interest per period.

SIMPLE AND COMPOUND INTEREST

Interest is the amount that you pay when you borrow money from someone else for a certain length of time, and the amount that someone will pay you for borrowing your money. If you put money into a bank or a building society, you are lending it money so make sure that you receive some interest. Since the amount of interest paid is related to the length of time that the money is borrowed, interest is calculated as a percentage of the sum borrowed per a fixed time period, usually a year. Thus, if you lent a building society £1,000 and it is paying 10 per cent interest per annum, you could get your money back at the end of the year with the interest as well: 10 per cent of £1,000 is 100, so you would have £1,100.

If only life were so simple! Unfortunately, governments have found out about interest, and like to take some of it in tax, so your building society might have to offer a gross rate of interest of 10 per cent, which only non-taxpayers can get, and a net rate of 7.5 per cent for most taxpayers. The remaining 2.5 per cent is taken by the government directly from the building society.

Another complication is that your £1,000 might not buy as much at the end of the year as it could have done at the beginning – this is because of inflation. The 10 per cent interest that you earned should compensate you for the reduced buying power of your £1,000, but the inflation has taken another bite out of your profit. Out of the gross interest of 10 per cent, you might have made only 2 per cent profit after tax and inflation on your original £1,000. The £1,000, by the way, is the 'capital' that you have lent.

Obviously, governments and financial institutions know all about this, so the interest rate offered to you will vary, taking tax and inflation into account. A point to notice is:

Interest rates are usually quoted as the interest you will get or give for a year's lending or borrowing, but not always, so you should check.

The kind of interest we are talking about at the moment is called 'simple interest'.

✻ EXAMPLE If you lent £1,000 for five years at 10 per cent simple interest p.a. (per annum), you would earn £100 per year:

	10 per cent interest
Year 1	100
Year 2	100
Year 3	100
Year 4	100
Year 5	100
Total	500

At the end of the fifth year you would have your original £1,000 back, plus the £500 interest, totalling £1,500. The value of what you lent at the beginning (£1,000) is the 'present value', and what you will get at the end of five years (£1,500) is the 'future value'.

Fixed term investments

It is important to compare the terms of different investments because you can make more or less money depending on the terms, even if the annual interest rates are the same. Let us look at an example:

Suppose you can lend £1,000 to a bank for a year for 8 per cent interest, or to another bank for six months at the same rate. Which is better? If you had no other way of lending the money, you would have to consider the following:

- Can you withdraw the money before the period is up? Are there 'penalties' (e.g. loss of interest) for doing so?

- Do you think that interest rates are likely to change during the period in which you invest the money? You probably won't know for certain but you might be able to make a guess if you read the financial pages regularly. If you are experienced, you may be able to make quite an accurate guess.

If both the investments are for fixed terms and you can't take the money out again before the end of the period, it might be better to lend for six months rather than for a year, so that you could do something else with the money after six months. If, however, you thought that by the end of the six months banks would only be paying 6 per cent interest on new deposits, you would be better off lending for a year since for the second half of the year you would be getting 2 per cent more than the going rate.

Many investments let you take out money whenever you want, but it is an advantage for which you often get a lower interest rate than if you tie up your investment for a fixed term.

Compound interest

If you were getting £100 in simple interest every year, you could also lend that, and get interest on it.

Earlier we saw that if you lent a bank £1,000 for five years and **EXAMPLE ✳** received 10 per cent interest a year, you could re-invest the 10 per cent (£100) each year and earn interest on that too. If you did this by leaving the interest in a deposit account, the £100 that you received in the first year would earn £10 in the second year, so by the end of the second year you would have:

The capital	£1,000
10% interest on capital in Year 1	£100
10% interest on capital in Year 2	£100
Interest in Year 2 on Year 1's interest	£10
Total	£1,210

Interest plus the interest on the interest is called 'compound interest'. How much compound interest you get depends on how often the bank gives you the interest. If you deposit £2 million in a bank at 10 per cent p.a. and it only gives you the interest at the end of the year, you would have £200,000 in interest at the end of the year, but what if it calculated the interest every six months? The annual interest rate would be the same, but the interest you earned in the first six months, (half of £200,000 = £100,000), would earn interest in the second half. You would earn an extra £5,000, which is half of 10 per cent of £100,000. The intervals between the times when the bank calculates the interest is called the 'conversion period'. The shorter the conversion period, the more the interest will be compounded, and the more money you will make for a given annual rate.

Accumulation factor

When you look at interest rates offered for deposits, you need to know the conversion period as well as the rate. If the interest rate is 10 per cent p.a.

with two conversion periods it means that the interest is calculated every six months. For each of those six months, the total of capital and interest on every £1 invested is $1 + (0.1 \div 2) = 1.05$. This is called the 'accumulation factor'. If you invest £1,000, you multiply it by the accumulation factor to get the total you will have at the end of one conversion period: $1,000 \times 1.05 = 1,050$. To work out the total at the end of two conversion periods (in this case, two 6 month periods), you multiply the sum invested by the accumulation factor twice: $1,000 \times 1.05 \times 1.05 = 1,102.50$.

✳ EXAMPLE Suppose there are twelve conversion periods: the accumulation factor is $1 + (0.1 \div 12) = 1.00833$ per month. At the end of six months, the £1,000 will be worth $1,000 \times 1.00833 \times 1.00833 \times 1.00833 \times 1.00833 \times 1.00833 \times 1.00833$. This is a bit long-winded, but the sum is easier if we write it in the form $1,000 \times 1.00833^6$. We write the accumulation factor to the power of 6 because we are multiplying it by itself 6 times: $1,000 \times 1.00833^6 = 1,051.03$.

1,051.03 may not seem much more than the 1,050 we got when we worked out the total for a six-month conversion period, but if you were investing millions, it would be a significant amount.

The limit to conversion periods

So, if you make more compound interest the more conversion periods there are in a year, is there any limit to the amount of interest you can earn as the number of conversion periods per year increases? Pure maths says that there is, and gives the formula

$$e^i - 1$$

(where e = 2.71828 and i = interest rate)

for the total interest you will get in a year 'in the limit' where you have conversion periods at every moment in time. Thus, if the interest rate is 10 per cent, the maximum interest you can earn, however many conversion periods there are in a year, is

$$2.71828^{0.1} - 1 = 10.52\%$$

Comparing different conversion periods

If you are comparing several investments with different conversion periods, you need to convert them all to the same period, which is usually taken as being the rate with one conversion period (i.e. paying the interest once a year only). This is called the 'effective interest rate'. To work it out, you can use the formula

$$i_e = [1 + (i \div k)]^k - 1$$

(where i = the rate of interest as a proportion of the sum invested, e = the effective interest rate and k = the number of conversion periods in the year).

EXAMPLE ✻

To calculate the effective interest rate of an investment of £1,000 at 10 per cent with two conversion periods,

$$\begin{aligned} \text{effective rate} &= 1 + (0.1 \div 2)]^2 - 1 \\ &= (1 + 0.05)^2 - 1 \\ &= 1.05^2 - 1 \\ &= 1.1025 - 1 \\ &= 0.1025 \end{aligned}$$

The effective rate is 10.25 per cent.

As we've seen, there are traps for the unwary in the comparison of interest rates: £1,000 at 10 per cent interest a year with twelve conversion periods gives 10.47 per cent interest (the 'effective rate'), while two conversion periods would only produce a 10.25 per cent effective rate, so the former is the better rate.

Laws have been introduced in many countries to help consumers compare rates more easily.

Lenders have profited from the public's lack of awareness of this phenomenon, so laws have been introduced in many countries to help consumers compare rates more easily. In the US, the law says that the effective rate must always be stated. In the UK, interest rates must usually be given in two forms: a rate of the advertiser's choice, such as the 'flat rate', which calculates interest on the whole sum lent, even after part of it has been repaid; and the APR, or annual percentage rate, which adds hidden extras such as commissions, charges for documents and maintenance to the effective rate. The APRs on credit cards, for instance, are often quite a shock when compared with the other rate quoted.

> ▶ The price of a share changes all the
> time: it may bear little relation to
> the value of the company if you
> were to sell all its assets.

2

Shares

In this chapter we will look at the basics of share ownership and stock markets. If you are a UK taxpayer you should read the latter part of the chapter, which examines Personal Equity Plans (PEPs), carefully. These are currently a very attractive way to invest in shares. The topics covered in this chapter are:

- What are shares?
- The London Stock Exchange.
- Stock indices.
- Stock markets across the world: New York, Tokyo, Europe and the Far East.
- Buying and selling shares.
- Yields and price/earnings ratios.
- Net asset value (NAV).
- Investment strategies.
- Unit trusts.
- Investment trusts.
- PEPs.
- Choosing a broker.
- The CREST system.

WHAT ARE SHARES?

A company that is quoted on a stock exchange offers shares in its owner-ship to anyone who wants to buy them. A large company may have issued millions of shares. If you buy one, you are a part owner, or shareholder, in the company, with the right to share in its profits, to attend board meet-ings and to vote on key issues and appointments. You can sell your shares if someone is willing to buy them.

The price of a share changes all the time: it may bear little relation to the value of the company if you were to sell all its assets. There have been many cases, for instance, where the buildings owned by a company were grossly undervalued and its share price was much lower than it 'should' have been.

Shares are volatile – they go up and down all the time as people buy and sell them. All sorts of factors influence the prices of shares, including company analyses, political change, natural disas-ters, wars, and economic fluctuations, but one of the main influences is the behaviour of people who buy shares, or, as some would have it, 'the madness of crowds'. If many investors think that the price of a share is going to go up and buy it, the price of the share will go up until they stop buying. This may have nothing to do with the essential soundness of the company. As we will see, this kind of volatility is temporary. In the long term, shares in good com-panies are thought to be better investments than those in bad ones.

> In the long term, shares in good companies are thought to be better investments than those in bad ones.

This capitalist system of financing big business is fundamental to the world's present economic system. Following the collapse of the USSR, there is no other system that is a serious contender with it. Thus, like it or not, people who want to increase or preserve their assets must learn about how it works, and will probably decide to participate in it at some time in their lives.

Shares are also called 'equities'. Outside the UK, shares are often called 'stocks'. This can cause confusion since, in the UK bonds are traditionally referred to as 'stocks'.

How shareholders make profits

There are two ways:

- by selling their shares at a higher price than they paid for them; and secondly,
- by receiving 'dividends', which are a distribution of profits that the company has made.

The quality of shares

The soundest, best-established companies are known as 'blue chips'. The term 'blue chip' comes from the world of the casino, where blue chips are those with the highest value. Next come the 'secondary issues', which are shares in solid companies. These receive slightly less confidence than the blue chips. 'Growth stocks' are shares in newer companies which are expected to do well in the future, but which may not do so. Finally, there are 'penny shares' which are those of companies with a low value, but which may increase for some reason.

Kinds of shares

> .... **Most shares are 'ordinary' shares, putting the shareholders at the back of the queue of creditors if the company goes bust.** .....

Companies usually start out by being privately owned. When they get big enough the owners may decide to 'go public' and sell part of the shares of their company on a stock market. The rules for going public are quite strict, to make sure that the company is worth buying. The advantage to the original owners of selling their shares is that, if the offering is successful, they can realise very large sums of cash. Some owners, however, prefer to keep control by staying private, while others have been known to buy back all the shares and return the company to private ownership.

Companies can issue several kinds of shares, usually labelled 'A', 'B', 'C', and so on. Each class of share will have different rules, different market prices and different dividends.

Most shares are 'ordinary' shares, putting the shareholders at the back of the queue of creditors if the company goes bust, and giving them equal voting rights and dividends to all other holders of ordinary shares in a company. Less common are 'preference' shares, which give the holder a slightly better chance of recovering some money in the event of a liquidation, often pay a fixed dividend, and usually don't give voting rights. The rights of preference shares vary from company to company, so you should always examine the rules in detail before buying. 'Convertible' preference shares give the holder the option to change them to ordinary shares at a fixed future price and date.

Companies sometimes issue warrants. These give the holder the right to 'subscribe' for shares at a fixed price at some point in the future. If the share price then rises higher than the subscription price, the warrant can be sold in the market. People who buy company bonds (see Chapter 3) are sometimes given warrants as an inducement to hold on to their bonds, thus helping the company to prosper.

> When considering the purchase of obscure shares, always investigate the number of market makers in the share and its marketability before investing.

When considering the purchase of obscure shares, always investigate the number of market makers in the share and its marketability before investing. A share with only one market maker may be very expensive, in terms of the 'spread', to buy and sell, and it may not be possible to sell the share at all for long periods of time.

THE LONDON STOCK EXCHANGE

Since the 'Big Bang' reform in 1986, groups of financial services have been formed, combining several kinds of business that used to be kept separate:

- *Market making* – this means dealing in certain shares 'wholesale', guaranteeing to buy or sell these shares at all times, which ensures that investors can trade with them whenever they want to. Market makers sell shares at more than they buy them for in order to make a profit. The difference between the price at which they will buy ('bid') and the price at which they will sell ('offer') is called the bid/offer spread. On popular shares in large companies the spread is quite small, while on less popular companies the spread gets wider.

- *Broker/dealing* – this is the business of buying shares on the behalf of investors.

- *Investment analysis* – this is the detailed study of the performance and prospects of companies and industries.

- *Merchant banking* – principally, this involves bringing new companies to the market, arranging rights issues and advising companies on takeover bids and defences.

These groups are called securities houses. The different parts of the organisation often have access to privileged information which, in order to keep the market fair, they are not supposed share with other parts of the group. For example, if the merchant banking part of a securities house is privately advising a company on a planned takeover bid, it is not supposed to tell the broker/dealers or the others because they would use this 'inside' information by buying shares in the company targeted for takeover in the hope of a quick profit. In order to prevent this kind of conflict of interest, 'Chinese Walls' exist between the various arms of the securities houses. They are intended to keep sensitive information secret. Often, the different arms are housed in separate buildings. A much repeated joke about Chinese Walls is that they are full of chinks – in other words, many people feel that Chinese Walls don't really work. Since the Big Bang, shares have been dealt via computer. The only places where dealers actually crowd together waving bits of paper are in the futures and options markets (see Chapter 8); everyone else sits in front of a computer screen.

▮ STOCK INDICES

A stock index is a mathematical measurement of the performance of a number as a group. The most widely known indices are:

- The *Major Market Index*, produced by the American Stock Exchange, which follows 30 of the most important industrial shares quoted on the New York Stock Exchange.

- The *Standard and Poor's 500 Index* (S&P 500) follows 500 shares quoted on the New York Stock Exchange, American Stock Exchange and the over-the-counter market in the United States.

- The *FTSE 100* (Financial Times Stock Exchange 100 Share Index) measures 100 of the largest companies quoted in London and was introduced principally for options and futures trading.

- The *FT-30 Share Index* (also known as the Financial Times Ordinary Share Index) measures 30 blue chip companies quoted on the London stock market.

- The *FT Actuaries Indices* which examine the performances of different industrial sectors so you can judge the relative performance of, say, shipping and energy.

There are many more indices, and they are a very helpful tool against which to compare the performance of individual companies. Anyone can run an index, and you may see obscure indices advertised by private investment firms.

> **Anyone can run an index, and you may see obscure indices advertised by private investment firms.**

In Chapter 7, stock market indices are shown to be extremely important in the analysis and measurement of the risks of investment. Indices provide strong evidence that shares are a good investment over the long term, and fund managers are always trying to get their funds to 'beat' the performance of the indices. There are even funds and portfolios that are tied to an index, and move up and down with it, the idea being to reduce risk. Investing in funds that 'track' the indices, by spreading money in the same proportions as the index uses to produce its measurements, is more popular in the United States than here, possibly because the realities of the risk/reward relationship are better understood there.

The role of the institutions

In important stock markets, such as those of New York and London, most of the investing is done by pension funds, unit and investment trusts and insurance companies. Along with banks and building societies, they are known as the 'institutions'. Most of the money in these funds is owned indirectly by ordinary people so, in effect, the institutions are middlemen. The funds are run by managers who decide how the money is invested. These managers are under enormous pressure to 'outperform' the averages of the market, as indicated by the market indices – this is principally because they want to do well in their personal careers, and the way to do well as a fund manager is to think in the short term and try to produce spectacular results. The net result is that most of these funds don't outperform the market. In fact, since they make up such a large proportion of the market's capital, one could say that they are the market, and can't outperform themselves – they are just too big.

THE WORLD'S STOCK MARKETS

There are now more than 60 countries in the world with stock exchanges. The biggest one of all is the New York Stock Exchange where about a third of the total value of the world's shares are traded. Many of the newer stock exchanges are tiny, such as the one in Croatia which trades only a handful of stocks and shares. Some countries, such as Germany, finance their industries more by bank lending than through shares, and their stock markets are smaller than you might expect. Then there are the highly internationalised stock markets, such as London and Hong Kong, where the total value of shares far exceeds the country's gross domestic product (GDP). Different countries have different rules for managing their stock exchanges. Most of the big ones now allow unrestricted foreign investment. Dealing costs and tax arrangements vary considerably, and if you buy or sell shares worth less than £10,000 in some markets you may be hit with a wide bid/offer spread.

The United States

The most important stock exchanges in the United States are based in New York.

The New York Stock Exchange (NYSE)

The NYSE is the best-known of the New York stock exchanges, trading tens of billions of shares in nearly 2,000 companies. It is well-regulated by the Securities and Exchange Commission (SEC), and individual investors get preferential treatment over institutions when buying and selling thanks to the Individual Investor Express Delivery Service (IIEDS). The main index used is the Dow Jones Industrial Average, which is the arithmetic mean of the share price movements of 30 important companies listed on the NYSE.

The American Stock Exchange (AMEX)

Until 1921, brokers who didn't have a seat on the NYSE would trade in the street. Eventually, they were organised into a proper exchange where companies not large enough to qualify for listing on the NYSE are listed.

National Association of Securities Dealers Automated Quotations (NASDAQ)

NASDAQ began in 1971. It has no central dealing floor, but works as an international system of trading in shares and bonds via computer screens. It has information links with the London Stock Exchange and was the first foreign exchange to be recognised by the Department of Trade and Industry in the UK.

The Tokyo Stock Exchange (TSE)

There are eight stock exchanges in Japan but the TSE is the largest, rivalling the NYSE for the title of 'world's biggest'. Companies are listed in three sections, the first for over 1,000 of the biggest issues, the second for a few hundred smaller companies, and the third for non-Japanese companies. There is also an over-the-counter market which is separate from the TSE. The main Japanese index is the Nikkei Stock Average, which is price-weighted and includes over 200 Japanese companies from the first section of the TSE. Although there are still some limitations to foreign buying on the TSE, it is possible for a small investor to buy and sell quite freely.

Continental Europe

Shares have been traditionally regarded with some suspicion by Europeans, and not without reason. Nevertheless markets have existed for centuries in most countries. The world trend towards liberalisation has encouraged European governments to reduce taxes on dealing and to move towards standardising their regulations.

The Paris Bourse

The Paris Bourse is the largest continental exchange after Germany's. It is highly advanced in its use of technology and there is virtually no floor trading. Trading is done through the 45 members of the exchange, some of whom are foreign-owned.

Germany

There are eight regional stock exchanges in Germany which together make Germany the next biggest market after New York, Tokyo and London. The biggest of these regional centres is Frankfurt. Only banks are allowed to deal in shares on the behalf of investors – there are no brokers as there are elsewhere. German shares are usually issued in bearer form, meaning they can be passed around almost as easily as cash. Dealing commissions are comparable to those in the UK and United States.

The Far East

Eastern Asia is the fastest growing area in the world and is likely to remain so for many decades. Japan is the most powerful economy, but the 'Tigers' (Hong Kong, Taiwan, Singapore and South Korea) are catching up. Not far behind are the 'Dragons' (Thailand, the Philippines, Malaysia and Indonesia). People in these countries tend to save a large proportion of their incomes which is one of the reasons why economists believe that their growth is sound and will continue. The Dragons are rapidly moving from being producers of commodities into heavy industries, such as car and machine manufacturing.

The Stock Exchange of Hong Kong (SEHK)

Hong Kong has had a stock exchange since the last century but it wasn't until the 1970s that the market began its rapid expansion. It suffered badly in the 1987 crash and its regulation has subsequently been tightened. It has two main indexes, the famous Hang Seng Index and the broader Hong Kong Stock Index. Hong Kong was leased from China by the British in the imperial era and will be handed back in 1997; while it seems that China will try to maintain Hong Kong as a world financial centre, long-term investment in the market looks risky. At present, though, there are no restrictions on foreign investment in shares.

Korea Stock Exchange (KSE)

South Korea's exchange is large and modern but foreigners' access to it is still restricted to a few funds and bonds.

Stock Exchange of Singapore (SES)

This market is almost entirely open to foreign participation – only large stakes in certain important companies are prohibited. The SES has trading links with US dealers and many Malaysian companies are quoted on it.

Taiwan Stock Exchange

Trade in shares grew in Taiwan after a land reform in the 1950s gave owners stocks and shares in government-run companies. The market is very liquid and dominated by a few investors. Foreigners are allowed to invest in some mutual funds.

Jakarta Stock Exchange

The larger of the Indonesia's two exchanges, the Jakarta Stock Exchange allows foreign investment in bonds, with some restrictions on share ownership. There are two main indices, one published by PT Jardine Fleming Nusantra Finance, and the other by BT Brokerage.

BUYING AND SELLING SHARES

Except for new issues, you must usually buy shares through a broker. Since the Big Bang, brokers have found that increased costs have made it difficult to offer an ideal service to everyone, so, unless you have £50,000 or more to invest, the best deal available is the 'execution only' service which means that the broker just does what you ask, without offering any advice. Not all brokers offer this service, so you will have to shop around. If you are investing £9,000 or less each year, you should use a PEP scheme, which limits the field further (see below for how these work).

Earnings per share

Earnings per share (EPS) is simply the total dividends paid out by the company in a year, divided by the total number of ordinary shares. This is not the same as profits, since some profits are not paid out as dividends.

Yields and p/e ratios

These are the two main ways that investors judge shares and both are published in the financial pages. The yield tells you the rate of income, as dividends, that you will get at the current share price. The p/e (price/earnings) ratio is the market price of the share divided by the company's earnings per share. It is a measure of how much the market is prepared to pay for the company, given the profits that it makes. It is often said that the actual number of a p/e ratio is irrelevant, and that it is whether that number is right that is important. For a more detailed discussion of p/e ratios, see Chapter 7.

Net asset value (NAV)

Unlike yields and p/e ratios, which can mislead those of us who are not maestros at the art of analysis, the net asset value of a share is a 'real' measurement. The NAV is calculated by adding up all the company's assets, subtracting all its liabilities, and dividing the result by the number of ordinary shares in the company. This gives you a number which is a theoretical value of a share in the company if it was broken up and sold off. The value is only theoretical because in practice the money that would be raised from selling assets is likely to be different from the valuation of those assets in the accounts. NAVs shed an interesting light on the stock market, though, because it is often the case that they are considerably lower than the market price of the shares. For instance, the NAV of a share might be $2 and its market price might be $6. If you are the kind of investor who is brave enough to buy shares during a crash and when there is 'blood in the streets', finding NAVs which were higher than the market price of the relevant shares could be a good guide to choosing which companies to invest in, the rationale being that you would be buying into the companies cheaply, and that their share prices would be likely to rise above their NAVs when times improved.

Investment strategies

Try this exercise when considering which shares to invest in. Obtain the prospectuses of a number of very successful investment and unit trusts that look for long-term growth and see which shares they hold. Make a list of these companies and organise them into their various industries. Now obtain annual reports for all these companies, and try to get to know them a little better. Look for companies that have good growth rates, a strong position in their own market and that sell something for which you believe there will be a continuing and growing demand. Now get in-depth studies for each of the companies on this shorter list – you may have to pay for these and do some detective work to find them, but they do exist. Try to understand these studies as fully as possible. Now list all the pros and cons for each of these companies and narrow down your list of companies. Pretend to invest in each of the companies in your short list and watch what happens for a year. By the end of this process, you will not only be well-acquainted with some of the best companies available, but you will also have learned a great deal about the interface between the stock market and business in general – you will be much better qualified to make your investment decisions.

Here are some strategies you may want to consider:

- If you have invested in a share that has increased dramatically, sell off

enough to get back the original investment and
hold on to the rest. This helps you to stay calm
– losing a profit is not so bad as losing your
capital.

**Don't spread
yourself too thin.**

- Look for companies that are worth a lot more than their share price. You
  can find this out by looking at their accounts and reading studies on
  them.

- Look for companies that have good growth potential but a share price
  that is still low.

- Look for companies that are likely to be taken over (see Chapter 4).

- If the market crashes in a big way, buy good quality shares – they will
  probably go up again.

  Here are my pet 'don'ts':

- Don't believe in technical analysis, which is the prediction of future
  prices on the basis of past patterns. It is supposed to work because of
  the 'psychology' of investors, but it has a rather less rational basis than
  astrology or the study of UFOs. See Chapter 7 for a more detailed
  discussion of this strange cult.

- Don't spread yourself too thin. Specialise in certain areas and get to
  know them well.

- Don't be forever jumping in and out of shares in the hope of a quick
  buck. This will cost you money. Have the guts to hold on to companies
  which you believe in, having done the hard work of studying them
  before you bought.

UNIT TRUSTS

Before we look at what unit trusts are, you should be aware of these
points:

- Unit trusts which are closely linked to stock market indices are one of
  the safest ways to invest in shares; the reasons for this are examined in
  detail in Chapter 7.

- I believe that investment trusts generally offer better value than unit
  trusts.

- Unit trusts are heavily marketed financial products aimed at the
  general public. Their literature and sales approach is designed to put
  fearful savers at their ease and is generally bland; the image projected

is paternalistic and reassuring. You pay for all this 'service' in the charges.

- You hear a lot about how advantageous it is for you to put your money into the hands of the professional unit trust manager who will invest it so much better than you can. As will be discussed in Chapter 7, there is considerable evidence that this is not really the case.

Unit trusts were introduced into the UK from America, where they are known as 'mutual funds', in the 1930s. The idea is that a large number of investors put their money into a fund, for which they receive 'units'. The fund is then professionally managed and spread across a range of investments, including shares and bonds in the UK and in foreign markets. Each investor can buy and sell units in the trust and the value of the units fluctuates with the value of the investments of the funds. Since you pay charges to buy and hold units, they are medium to long-term investments. In other words, you should expect to hold them for at least three years. Traditionally, the main advantages of unit trusts are considered to be:

- Good diversification for the small investor – possibly better than you could do on your own.
- Less worry, and less work, than holding your own portfolio.
- At times it has been difficult for small investors to find brokers to handle their business. In such conditions, which do not exist currently, unit trusts were virtually the only way a small investor could get into the stock market.
- Unit trusts have been well-regulated and far freer from scandal than other investments.

The money is held by a trustee, such as a bank or an insurance company, and not by the unit trust company itself. The trust is regulated by a Trust Deed, which lays down all the rules of how the money is to be handled.

Types of unit trust

There are different categories of unit trusts, specialising in different kinds of investments. Here are the main ones:

- UK general trusts.
- UK growth trusts.
- UK equity income trusts.
- Gilt and fixed-interest trusts – these trusts invest in bonds, not shares,

and are intended to provide safety, a higher income and low growth.

- Growth trusts spread across shares in particular countries or areas of the world, such as the Far East, Europe, Japan and the United States. They are designed to increase the capital value and are thus more risky than income-oriented funds.

- Financial trusts – these specialise in buying the shares of banks and insurance companies.

Offshore trusts

This is a British definition meaning a trust which is not an 'authorised unit trust' in the UK. Many of them are run from places like the Channel Islands, Bermuda and the Cayman Islands, and are run on the same lines as 'onshore' unit trusts. They are harder to buy and sell in the UK, and are, in some cases, less well regulated, so you should check the companies out very carefully before investing. Their charges tend to be higher and there are no direct tax advantages for UK taxpayers.

Savings schemes

Many trusts allow you to pay in a monthly sum, and you can miss a few months, or reduce or increase your payment without any penalties. Such schemes should outperform financial products such as endowment and unit-linked insurance policies.

Managed funds

The difference between an ordinary unit trust and a managed fund is that the latter uses an independent professional to decide how the money should be invested. The idea is that since the manager is independent and can be dismissed easily, he or she will have no motive to 'churn' (needlessly buy and sell) the investments held by the trust.

Umbrella funds

These are offshore trusts which have separate funds in different parts of the world, allowing you to switch from one fund to another at low cost.

Buying and selling unit trusts

There are many ways to buy unit trusts; you can buy through a newspaper advertisement, a bank, a solicitor, an accountant, a stock broker or an insurance broker. If you buy through an intermediary, you will be expected to hand over a cheque once the units have been bought. You will then receive a contract note recording your purchase. Some weeks later you should receive a unit trust certificate which is your proof of ownership. As with all business documents, you should always check both the contract note and the certificate to see that the right type of unit trust is recorded, that the number of units are the same on the contract note and the certificate, and that your name and address appear correctly. If all is well, you should then store the documents somewhere safe where they will not be lost or destroyed.

> ..... The majority of unit trusts quote prices every day, but some may do so once a week or even once a month. .....

When you come to sell, you contact the organisation from whom you bought the units, and send them the certificate, having signed it first. Normally you should get the money within ten days. If you lose the certificate, you must apply for a new one, which will take several weeks. You can still sell units in the meantime, but you won't receive the money until you have surrendered the duplicate certificate.

Check newspapers for the bid and offer prices; remember that the higher one, the offer, is the one you must pay when buying, and the lower one, or bid, is the one you get when selling. Check the difference between the bid and offer prices; normally they are around 6 per cent, but they can be more than double this. The majority of unit trusts quote prices every day, but some may do so once a week or even once a month. You may find that the trust has rounded up a buying price or rounded down a selling price by 1.25p or 1 per cent, whichever is the smaller; they are allowed to do this.

The charges

The two main charges are the 'front-end load' or fee that you pay when you buy, and an annual management fee. The front-end load is included in the published offer price. If you buy into a unit trust and sell soon after, you will probably lose 5 per cent or so. The idea is to hang on until the units grow enough to cover the front-end load. These charges are in addition to the bid/offer spread discussed above.

Check the annual management fee before you buy. It is usually 1 per cent or less, but VAT is added. This fee is usually taken from investment income automatically by the management.

Exchanges

If you have good quality shares, you can exchange them for units in many unit trusts. The cost of doing this is usually lower than if you sold the shares in the normal way and then bought units, because the trusts want you to join their scheme. You can do such swaps if your shares are worth more than around £500.

Tax

Income Tax is deducted from your dividends at the basic rate and you will have to pay Capital Gains Tax (CGT) on profits over your annual exemption. However, there is no CGT on gains made within the fund, if, for instance, the manager switches investments.

Unit trust advisory services (UTAS)

There are over a thousand unit trusts available in the UK, managed by nearly 200 groups, and the trusts are in many categories. In order to expedite the process of picking the ones you want, there are unit trust advisory services (UTAS) available that monitor most or all of the trusts in the marketplace and will give detailed reports on them. Often the first report is free, after which, if you invest through a UTAS, you will continue to get advice for an annual fee of 0.75 per cent. If you like paying people to hold your hand, then this scheme may have some value. Personally, I'd get the free report, then save the money and do my own research.

INVESTMENT TRUSTS

Investment trusts are similar to unit trusts in that they are pooled funds which are professionally invested in a wide range of shares. They are not trusts, however, but companies whose shares are quoted on the stock market; you buy shares, rather than units, in an investment trust. They are taxed in much the same way, and offer a similar variety of categories, including monthly savings schemes. Generally, they are better value than unit trusts because the buying costs are often lower and the shares can

> **You can expect investment trusts to do better than unit trusts in the future.**

often be bought at a discount to the value of the fund. The bid/offer spread is around 2 per cent, as opposed to 5 per cent in unit trusts, annual management fees are about half, and the initial charges are lower too. Another feature is that, unlike unit trusts, they are allowed to borrow money to invest; this makes them slightly riskier and more volatile than unit trusts. All this helps to boost their performance, and you can expect investment trusts to do better than unit trusts in the future.

PERSONAL EQUITY PLANS (PEPS)

If you do not pay any tax in the UK and do not expect to in the future you can skip this section. PEPs are a tax break for British taxpayers designed to encourage wider share ownership. To emphasise the point, please note that if you are a British resident but are not liable for tax (e.g. if you have a low income), then you should stay out of PEPs. Astonishingly, there have been several cases recently of financial advisers putting non-taxpayers into PEPs.

When PEPs were introduced in 1986, they got off to a slow start, partly due to the hideously complicated rules which required a lot of administration and provoked resistance to the scheme in the City. Since then, the restrictions and administrative burden on PEPs have been reduced and they are now an attractive proposition to UK taxpayers.

The background

In the 1950s, the majority of shares in the UK were held by private investors. After two decades of social and political change, many private investors dropped out of the stock market, and new generations of people grew up who never considered the possibility of owning shares. Important factors causing this decline were Capital Gains Tax (CGT) on shares (which initially taxed gains from inflation as well as 'real' gains), an investment income surcharge and the increase of tax breaks for house mortgages, pensions and insurance schemes. Private individuals' money was still ending up on the stock market, but as part of the huge institutional funds which now began to dominate the City. By the late 1970s, small private investors had diffi-

> **Astonishingly, there have been several cases recently of financial advisers putting non-taxpayers into PEPs.**

culty in finding a broker to act for them – the only real chance they had of owning shares was through unit trusts. Another reason for the decline of the private investor was a decline in confidence, particularly during the industrial unrest of the 1970s when restrictions on movement of money overseas, the oil crisis and labour problems combined to make the private investor feel that only unit trusts were safe investment vehicles.

With the advent of Thatcherism in 1979, the tide turned. The investment income surcharge was abolished, and CGT was indexed to take inflation into account. Tax breaks on life assurance were abolished, making this alternative less attractive. Slowly, industries that had been nationalised during the socialist reforms following World War 2 were 'privatised', having their shares sold to the public at a substantial discount. Finally, after the Big Bang and the introduction of PEPs, a new era for private shareholders began.

The way PEPs work

Anyone who is resident in the UK and over eighteen may invest in a PEP. The PEP has to be managed by a person who is authorised to do so under the Financial Services Act. Currently, you can invest up to £6,000 a year in a 'General' PEP and up to a further £3,000 a year in a 'Single Company' PEP. Thus, a married couple can invest up to £18,000 per annum in PEPs – which is a substantial sum for most UK wage-earners.

PEPs are free of tax on their dividends and there is no CGT to pay on profits made from selling shares. Money held on deposit within a PEP is exempt from tax on the interest it earns, so long as the money is used to buy securities later.

You can invest in any of the following:

- UK shares quotes on the stock market
- European Community shares quoted on EU markets
- UK company bonds, preference shares and convertibles
- cash
- UK investment trusts
- UK unit trusts.

Although PEP dividends are tax free, 20 per cent of their value is paid to the Inland Revenue by the PEP manager, who subsequently reclaims the money on behalf of the investors and returns it to their PEP accounts. This is an administrative advantage which is sometimes overlooked –

> Following a relaxation of the PEP rules, investors may cash in their PEPs at any time and still retain their tax breaks.

small investors can avoid a large amount of paper-work by investing through a PEP.

Following a relaxation of the PEP rules, investors may cash in their PEPs at any time and still retain their tax breaks; some managers make a charge for early withdrawal, but this is still far less than the equivalent charges for early surrender of such things as endowment policies.

You don't have to put a lump sum into a PEP. You can make a monthly payment into a scheme. The only restriction is that you cannot make regular payments into more than one scheme at a time.

There are a variety of PEPs on offer:

Self-select PEPs

In this kind of scheme an investor decides how the money is invested. The manager of the plan takes a small fee and executes the investor's trading instructions without giving advice.

Advisory PEPs

A little more expensive than Self-select PEPs, these are where the plan manager does give some advice on investments. Often these schemes are only available to a broker's well-established clients.

Managed or discretionary PEPs

This is where the investment decisions are made by the plan manager, not the individual.

Corporate PEPs

These usually are for shares in one company and are most often used as part of an incentive scheme for employees of that company.

Single Company PEPs

These are restricted to shares in one company, with fewer restrictions than Corporate PEPs. They are useful to investors who have already invested the annual maximum of £6,000 in a General PEP and wish to invest up to £3,000 more.

Unit trust and investment trust PEPs

These PEPs invest exclusively in unit trusts or investment trusts from a list chosen by the plan manager. Managed and Self-select plans are available.

More on the tax advantages

The two big advantages of PEPs for the private investor are:

- A big reduction in costly and time-consuming paperwork.
- The tax concessions.

Despite reductions, income tax is still a substantial burden for British residents, particularly those who pay the higher rate of 40 per cent. Those paying tax at the basic or lower rate may find that the tax saving is small in the early years after the deduction of set-up charges, say £20, and annual management fees, say 1 per cent, but if the value of the investment grows, the savings will too.

Capital Gains Tax (CGT) is levied on gains in one year over a certain figure, currently £6,300. The rates of tax are constantly changing, and although CGT is now indexed against the Retail Price Index (RPI), it is difficult to calculate how much the CGT will be if you sell a particular investment. Capital losses can be set off against future gains.

Since PEPs are exempt from CGT, they are clearly essential for any investor who already pays CGT. Those who do not currently pay CGT may have their savings sunk into other CGT-exempt vehicles, such as their own homes, pensions schemes, gilts and insurance policies. PEPs offer a chance for such individuals to invest in the stock market while still enjoying CGT exemption.

PEP rules in more detail

Despite the increased flexibility of PEPs, there are some restrictions that you should be aware of.

Maximum allowances

As already mentioned, the maximum annual investments allowed are £6,000 into a General PEP and £3,000 into a Single Company PEP. Generally, PEP managers charge their fees on top, so the whole £9,000 can be invested. There are no minimum limits, but you probably won't find a manager who will let you invest less than £50 a month, except for unit trust and corporate PEPs. The annual allowances cannot be taken forward into future years, so, for example, if you only invest £8,000 in one year, you cannot bring forward the unused £1,000 of the allowance to the following year and add it to the £9,000 pound allowance for that year.

Another point to remember is that if you want to make up your allowances towards the end of a financial year (which ends on 5 April), you need to invest at least a fortnight before the year end to give PEP managers time to do the necessary paperwork for setting up, or topping up, the PEP.

Cash deposits within a PEP

Self-select PEP holders can hold cash deposits within a PEP and buy and sell shares at any time. Deposits must be held in designated sterling deposit accounts, which pay interest gross of tax. Any cash held on deposit must eventually be used to buy securities. An investor wanting tax breaks on permanent cash deposits should use the TESSA scheme (see page 234).

Investment trusts and unit trusts

General PEPs may invest in 'qualifying' unit trusts and investment trusts. To qualify, the trusts must have at least 50 per cent of their total funds invested in ordinary shares of UK or EC companies quoted on a stock market. Additionally, up to £1,500 of the £6,000 allowance may be invested in 'non-qualifying' trusts which invest elsewhere in the world, and these must have more than 50 per cent in quoted ordinary shares. The rules allow you to hold QITS and NQITS together in the same PEP, and use the rest of your allowance on other qualifying investments.

What you can invest in

As we saw on page 39, you can invest in any of the following:

- UK shares quoted on the stock market
- European Community shares quoted on EU markets
- UK company bonds, preference shares and convertibles
- cash
- UK investment trusts
- UK unit trusts.

What you can't invest in through a PEP

Corporate bonds, preference shares and convertibles are eligible after 6 April 1995. After that time, the only non-eligible investments will be gilts and non European Union securities.

Changing from one PEP manager to another

You can move a PEP from one manager to another at any time, but you may incur charges. Some managers make no charge at all, while others make a small charge of £20 to £30. Always check on the penalties, though, since a few managers make high charges for early withdrawal to 'lock in' their clients.

Some managers make a small charge for incoming PEPs, while most charge nothing. Occasionally, discounts are offered for incoming PEPs.

Note that some managers do limit the number of investments within a PEP, or have a minimum amount for any particular holding.

The ease of transfer and withdrawal is probably the most attractive feature of the PEP scheme. It helps investors to protect themselves against their PEP managers and to take advantage of opportunities as they arise.

PEP dividends are tax free

Investors can withdraw their dividends tax free. Many plan managers distribute dividends every six months or annually, and investors in Self-select PEPs can usually retrieve dividends sooner. Alternatively, you can leave the dividends in the fund to benefit from further growth and compound interest.

Putting existing share holdings into a PEP

You are allowed to transfer shares and unit trusts into a PEP and various managers offer good terms for doing so.

Cashing in your PEP

You can cash in all or part of a PEP at any time, exempt of tax. What you can't do, is to withdraw cash from a PEP and then re-invest it in a PEP in the same year. Check plan managers' penalties for partial withdrawal or early withdrawal and avoid the ones with high charges.

PEP holders are politically vulnerable

British taxpayers are probably well-advised to use part or all of their PEP allowances at present. If a Labour government comes to power, the PEP rules are likely to change, so the current opportunities may be short-lived. Avoid putting all the funds which you have ear-marked for the stock market into PEP investments, though, since they are tied to EC companies. You should probably invest in some equities in other countries as well.

> Guerrilla investors should choose self-select PEPs, since charges are lower.

How to choose a PEP

There are over 700 PEPs on the market, managed by over 200 different managers. The variety of schemes available can be confusing, so the first thing to do is to ask yourself the following questions:

Do you want freedom to choose or professional advice?

The truly passive investor can use a unit/investment trust PEP or a managed PEP, while others may prefer a Self-select PEP. Guerrilla investors should choose the latter, since charges are lower. You can minimise your risk by investing in a spread of blue chip shares, and you have the freedom to take advantage of the opportunities you find.

Do you want growth or income?

It's probably best to look for funds which offer a better than average income and are mainly invested in shares, since these have a chance for good capital growth, rather than the funds which offer the highest income rates, since these will have restricted growth potential, having up to half of their portfolios in fixed-interest securities.

Should you diversify or concentrate your portfolio?

It depends on what proportion your PEP funds take up of your available funds for investment. If they are a small part, say less than 30 per cent, you can afford to concentrate on particular shares, perhaps even through a corporate PEP, which has very low charges, while diversifying your other investments elsewhere. Conversely, if your PEPs are a large part of your total investments, make sure they are well diversified, into at least 15 shares across a range of countries and industries.

What kind of manager do you want?

The ones you definitely don't want are the managers who reluctantly offer PEPs, either to keep existing clients, or because they want to offer a complete range of services. Choose your manager carefully, and remember that you can always switch to another manager if you are not satisfied. Many brokers, banks, building societies, insurance companies, solicitors and financial advisers manage PEPs. Pick one who will give good service and reasonable charges.

Managed PEPs

Managed PEPs advise clients to keep their portfolio to between ten and twenty shares, which is low for adequate diversification. There are four types of scheme:

Just shares

Some managed PEPs invest only in shares; these do not offer enough diversification and tend to have high charges. Possibly worthwhile for larger investors are the share-only schemes which have good portfolios and low charges.

Share and investment trusts

These invest in investment trusts as well as shares, offering wider diversification. You may be able to choose your trusts, but usually from a limited number offered by the manager.

Share and unit trusts

These combine unit trusts with shares, and operate like the previous scheme.

Combinations

These are schemes which invest in unit trusts, investment trusts and shares. They do not usually allow the investor any freedom of selection.

Unit and Investment Trust PEPs

It's easy to get confused between managed PEPs which mix investments between shares and/or unit and investment trusts, and another PEP category of Unit and Investment Trust PEPs which invest exclusively in unit and investment trusts. For an investor who really wants a professional manager to make the decisions, they are probably the most suitable form of PEP, being less restrictive than managed PEPs.

Unit trusts

More popular than investment trusts, their 'front-end' management charges can be steep. Although often quoted at around 6 per cent, these charges can be as high as 9.5 per cent, depending on demand, so timing is important.

> **To make a profit from unit trusts, your units have to grow more than the bid/offer spread.**

The bid/offer spread is the price difference between that at which the manager will buy, or 'bid', for units, and the price at which he or she will sell, or 'offer', them to you. To make a profit from unit trusts, your units have to grow more than the bid/offer spread.

You can opt for the power to select your own trusts from a list provided by the manager. If you want to do this, it is better to choose a PEP that is managed by a large group which offers a wide range of trusts to choose from. You should also check whether you are charged for switching between trusts, or whether you can do so at a discount (up to 5 per cent). Check whether the manager lets you hold more than one trust at a time within the PEP.

Most managers do not charge management fees on top of the already high unit trust fees, or offer a discount on the trusts to balance their fees. In this second case, there is often a penalty for withdrawing funds in the first two or three years.

Investment trust PEPs

These are less common than unit trust schemes and, like them, you can find schemes which let you choose the trusts from a list provided by the manager. Initial charges can be as high as 4 per cent, which makes such schemes uncompetitive, but some make very low charges.

Unit and investment trust schemes

These are less common, but operate in a similar way.

Which one to choose?

Unit trusts invest in a large number of shares, carefully diversified. The price of a unit to an investor is found by dividing the value of the trust's portfolio by the number of units already issued, after taking into account the 'bid/offer spread' (see page 25) of about 6 per cent. This spread includes initial charges and dealing costs, but there is usually an annual charge of around 1.5 per cent in addition; this charge is taken out of dividends paid to the investor.

> **Unit trusts are better known because they are more widely marketed.**

Investment trusts are actually limited companies which invest in shares and other securities. The trust's own shares are quoted on the Stock Exchange and can sometimes be bought at a discount to the value of the trust's portfolio – they are thus more volatile than unit trusts, but can do better. There are no initial charges and the annual management fee should be about 0.5 per cent.

Generally speaking, investment trusts are a better deal than unit trusts because of the lower charges and the possibility of the 'net asset value' or 'NAV' (see page 31), of the shares being greater than the price at which you can buy them. Unit trusts are better known because they are more widely marketed.

Self-select PEPs

This is the PEP option that gives you the most freedom. You can invest in any share quoted in London and many others quoted in continental Europe. You can mix shares with trusts, or stick completely to trusts. Managers give no advice and should make very low charges.

- Watch out for dealing charges; 1.25–1.5 per cent (plus VAT) is average, but they can be much lower. If they are very low, check the manager's charging system for higher charges elsewhere.
- Most managers charge £20 or less as a minimum commission on dealing – don't accept a higher rate than this.

What you can't do

Some Self-select PEPs make you choose shares from a limited range, often just the shares in the FTSE 100 index. Others give you a limit on the number of different shares you can hold within a single PEP. If you will be investing in PEPs for several years, this second restriction is not necessarily harsh, since you can build a well-diversified portfolio over a few years by investing in combinations of different shares each year.

Watch out for management charges for sending you company reports or attending meetings – they should be free. 'Dividend collection fees', levied each time you receive a dividend into your PEP, should be avoided.

Advisory PEPs

The main difference between advisory PEPs and Self-select PEPs is that advisory PEP managers do give advice on trading in shares, as well as on more general matters such as financial planning. They are hard to find, and are usually run by small stockbrokers in the provinces. Minimum commissions can be high. Small brokers can offer a good personal service, but they need clients who either trade frequently or who invest large amounts.

> 'Dividend collection fees', levied each time you receive a dividend into your PEP, should be avoided.

Single Company PEPs

As we saw on page 39, Single Company PEPs have a £3,000 annual limit and are intended for investors who have already invested £6,000 in a General PEP. They can be run by a different manager, but you may find that your General PEP manager offers no initial charges and other inducements to encourage you to remain loyal.

You must invest in the shares of only one company at any one time, but you are allowed to switch to another share as often as you wish. If you sell the shares, you must re-invest the money within 42 days, which means that even if the market as a whole is going bad, you cannot stay out of it for very long. There is no point in using a Single Company PEP if you have £6,000 or less to invest in a particular year – you get more flexibility in a Self-select PEP.

Self-select PEPs for guerrillas

UK taxpayers who want to invest in equities should certainly use their PEP allowances. Guerrilla investors will want to take advantage of the control over their own destinies offered by Self-select PEPs, remembering that they can still play safe by investing in unit or investment trusts. Every effort should be made to keep charges and dealing costs down. If, and when, a Labour government comes to power, it is thought likely that the benefits of

PEPs will be reduced, particularly to those who pay tax at the higher rate. However, given that the civil service dislikes retroactive legislation as being unfair, it would seem probable that existing PEP schemes would be allowed to continue unaltered. As with all investments, don't sign up with the first PEP manager you see standing on a street corner. Take the trouble to find one who offers you a good deal.

> .... **As with all investments, don't sign up with the first PEP manager you see standing on a street corner.** ....

CHOOSING A BROKER

If you are sticking to PEPs, you won't need a broker, but if you are in the fortunate position to have more than £9,000 a year to invest in the stock market you will need to find one. As with PEP schemes, you can choose between execution only services (the cheapest form of dealing), advisory services (the same principle as an advisory PEP) and discretionary services. Discretionary services ask you, the investor, to give the broker a free hand to buy and sell as he or she thinks fit. This can be expensive, and is probably only attractive to investors with large portfolios, say over £100,000, who are too busy to manage their own investments.

> .... **Like any service, the quality of brokers vary.** ....

Like any service, the quality of brokers vary. Some are large organisations with big research departments that are constantly analysing market movements and developments within quoted companies, while others are virtually 'one man and a dog' outfits. Choosing the right broker is a matter of personal taste, but here are a few points to be aware of:

- Watch out for the 'half-commission men' who work with brokerage firms on a kind of freelance basis – some of them are good, but they are, perhaps, under more pressure than their salaried colleagues to get you to trade frequently.

- Resist any attempt on the part of your broker to sell you securities that he is simply trying to get rid of. For example, some brokers are under pressure to sell issues that their group has underwritten and funds that are managed in-house. Examine anything you are offered very carefully.

- There is a trend towards clients' investments being put into 'nominee accounts' operated by the broker. Resist this if you can, since you are giving up a degree of control.

- Using an execution only service doesn't mean you can't get access to information. The *Investor's Chronicle*, the Extel card system (which is available in some major libraries) and the financial press are all valuable sources of information and ideas.

THE CREST SYSTEM

Since the summer of 1996, the London Stock Exchange has introduced a new computerised system, known as CREST, to handle the settlement process. As of the end of 1996, you still have a choice between still obtaining physical possession of share certificates or having the purchases registered electronically. Electronic registration requires you to keep your shares in a nominee account which is managed by a broker or other qualified person. The system reduces the time allowed for payment to three days, and brings London into line with most of the other major stock markets.

Use bonds as a balancer to your investments, rather than as a means of trying to accumulate wealth.

3

Bonds

A bond is an IOU issued by a government, local authority or a company in return for the loan of cash. In most cases, a fixed rate of interest is payable to the bond holder, and the bond issuer promises to pay back the amount borrowed (the face value of the bond) at a certain time in the future. Most bonds are registered, so if a bond is sold by one holder to another, legal title is only transferred when the ownership is re-registered. There is another kind of bond, the bearer bond, for which there is no register of ownership. Thus bearer bonds are similar to cash – whoever has physical possession of a bearer bond is its owner.

In this chapter we will look at:

- Auctioning new issues.
- Gilts.
- The price of bonds.
- Buying and selling gilts.
- The best way to buy.
- How gilts are taxed.
- Futures and options.
- Index-linked gilts.
- Undated bonds.
- The Barlow Clowes scandal.
- Convertible bonds.
- Ex dividend and cum dividend bonds.
- The US bond rating system.
- Bonds for the guerrilla investor.

In the UK, bonds are traditionally called 'stocks' and equities are called 'shares'; in the United States, fixed-interest securities are called 'bonds' and equities, 'stocks'.

AUCTIONING NEW ISSUES

When a state body or a company wants to borrow money by selling bonds, it 'brings an issue'. In the United States, the government issues bonds to a regular timetable using the auction method. Individuals can obtain a tender form from a bank and apply for the bonds (usually Treasury bills which have a life of a year or less) at a set price, enclosing a cheque. Private individuals are classed as 'non-competitive bidders'. What happens is that institutions bid for large amounts of the bonds, at any price they choose, but usually quite close to the set price of $10,000 per bond. The US Treasury then accepts the highest bids to fulfil its quota and takes the average price of the accepted bids as the price to the non-competitive bidders, who are then refunded the difference between the average of the accepted bids and the price they paid when they applied for the bonds. In the UK, the practice of auctioning government securities has been adopted relatively recently, and purchasers don't know what kind of bond will be offered until about a week before the auction.

> In the UK, the practice of auctioning government securities has been adopted relatively recently, and purchasers don't know what kind of bond will be offered until about a week before the auction.

GILTS

'Gilts' or 'gilt-edged securities' are bonds issued by the British government. They get their name from their reputation for a very high degree of safety. It is thought, justifiably, that if you lend the British government money by buying gilts, it is extremely unlikely that it will default on the loan. The British government has issued gilts for hundreds of years without ever having failed to meet payments on the due dates. About two-thirds of the British National Debt is funded by the issuance of gilts; at times, it has been as high as 80 per cent.

Gilts are issued either for a fixed length of time, such as five years, or, more unusually, for an indefinite period. They pay interest half-yearly, and repay the capital at the end of the bond's life.

The return on gilts is generally lower than you can get by investing in more risky propositions, such as shares, but is often better than the interest rate you can get by simply keeping your money in a bank or building society. It is also possible to make a capital gain on the sale of gilts that is currently tax free in the UK. There are about 90 gilts in issue at the time of writing, of which 12 are index-linked. The interest payable (called 'the coupon') can be as little as 2 per cent on some bonds, and as high as 15 per cent on others. Most gilts are very liquid, meaning that they are easily bought and sold.

> **Most gilts are very liquid, meaning that they are easily bought and sold.**

The price of bonds

The price of a bond varies according to macro-economic factors, of which inflation is the most important. If the interest rate in the market goes higher than the interest rate payable on a bond, the price you can get if you sell the bond goes down. Conversely, if the market interests rates go below a bond's interest rate, you can sell the bond for more than its face value.

Every day information on bonds is published in the Financial Times and elsewhere; you are given the current market price of the bond (which is usually different from its face value), the high and low of the market price in the current year (which gives you an idea of its volatility), and then two figures for 'yields'. Market prices quoted are the middle of the bid/offer spread, as with shares. The 'interest yield' simply tells you what percentage of your money you would get if you bought the bonds at the current market price. It is a simple calculation.

✳ EXAMPLE Suppose the bond in question is 'Treasury 7 1/4 pc 1998': the 7 1/4 pc is the coupon rate for the bond, '1998' is the year when the government pays back the capital invested. Since you must buy the gilt for more than its face value, the 7 1/4 pc coupon does not tell you the interest rate you are getting, so you divide the coupon by the market price and multiply the result by 100:

$$(7.25 \div 102.188) \times 100 = 7.1 \text{ per cent}$$

7.1 per cent is the interest rate, or interest yield, that you will get at the moment. Since the market price is higher than the face value of the bond, its interest yield is lower than its coupon, and if the market price rises, the yield will go even lower.

To pick the best deal available between comparable bonds (remember that company bonds are more risky than gilts, so you would expect a better rate on them in compensation) it is better to use the 'redemption yield', which is also given in the financial pages. The redemption yield tries to account for the difference between the price you pay for the bond and what you will get for it on redemption, which may give you a capital gain or a loss, depending on the price at which you bought, as well as for the interest rate. It's a complicated sum which in practice is not worth calculating yourself, but in principle it works as follows:

Suppose you buy Treasury 7 1/4 pc 1998 for 102 3/16 in 1994. **EXAMPLE ✳** You know that if you hold the gilt until 1998, when it will be redeemed, you will make a capital loss of 2 3/16 over four years, making an annual loss of 2.188 ÷ 4 = 0.547, which is 0.5 per cent of 102 3/16. Subtracting this loss from the interest yield gives you the redemption yield:

$$7.1 - 0.5 = 6.6$$

Redemption yields are useful for comparisons, but they don't remove all uncertainty, since the underlying market prices on which they are based will fluctuate, and the figures only tell you what return you would get if you held the bond to redemption, not what will happen if you sell before.

When comparing the redemption yields, say of different gilts, you will notice that some are higher than others. Usually, the longer that the gilt has to run, the higher the redemption yield because investors expect a reward for tying up their money for a longer time. This effect is called the 'normal yield curve'. When there is uncertainty about interest rates, the market distorts the normal yield curve both by trying to guess what long-term interest rates will be and also by moving in and out of bonds in response to changes in interest rates elsewhere. Banks mainly buy short-term bonds ('shorts'), while the institutions tend to buy long-term ones ('longs'), leaving medium-term bonds (5–15 years) out in the cold, which can cause them to have a better yield than longs. When short-term interest rates are up, yields on short-term bonds improve. Uncertainty about interest rates can cause longs to have lower yields than the shorts, in which case the yield curve is inverted.

> **Redemption yields are useful for comparisons, but they don't remove all uncertainty**

Gilts are free of Capital Gains Tax, so if higher-rate taxpayers expect the market price to improve they often invest in low coupon gilts, which may give a good capital gain. Since yields are constantly fluctuating in the opposite direction of the market prices, you are taking a risk in gilts if you don't keep them until redemption; making a gain or loss depends on when you buy.

Buying and selling gilts

The gilt-edged market makers (GEMMs) must quote bid and offer prices on demand for gilts at all times, thus ensuring that gilts are always liquid (i.e. that you can always buy or sell them). There are about 20 GEMMs, many of which are foreign-owned. The institutions can buy gilts directly from GEMMs; but many of them, like many private investors, buy gilts through a broker, who buys them from a GEMM. The GEMMs make their money on the 'spread' between their bid and offer prices, not by charging commission, except in certain special cases.

> Since yields are constantly fluctuating in the opposite direction of the market prices, you are taking a risk in gilts if you don't keep them until redemption.

Brokers, known in the gilts market as 'broker/dealers' are regulated by the Securities and Futures Authority (SFA). They have a duty to get the best prices when buying and selling for a client. The broker charges the investor commission for this service. Brokers can also sell their clients gilts which they have bought themselves, but in this case the rules say that they must give as good a price as the best price currently being offered by a GEMM.

As a private investor, you can also buy gilts through some accountants and solicitors, or through share shops. It is legal for you to sell a gilt to another private investor, provided that the transaction is properly registered.

The best way to buy

By far and away the best way to buy and sell gilts if you are a small investor is at a Post Office. The commission is low – you only pay £1 commission if you buy up to £250's worth of gilts, and a further 50p for every £125 above this. Sales commissions are 10p for every £10's worth of gilts up to £100, £1 for sales of between £100 and £250, and a further 50p for every £125 over this. The interest is paid gross, but you must declare it to the Inland Revenue and pay tax on it later.

This system is run by the National Savings Stock Register (NSSR). You are allowed to buy up to £25,000's worth of any one gilt on any one day, and you can transfer up to £5,000 in gilts from the NSSR to the Bank of England Register free of charge.

How gilts are taxed

UK taxpayers must pay tax on the interest they receive from a gilt at source (in other words, the tax is deducted from the interest before it is paid), unless they buy through the NSSR system, in which case it is paid gross and taxed later. Overseas investors should be careful to invest in those gilts which are defined as 'free of tax to residents abroad' (FOTRA) – this will enable them to receive the interest gross.

Futures and options

You can gamble on gilts by buying and selling futures and options on them on the London International Financial Futures and Options Exchange (LIFFE, pronounced 'life'). For a detailed explanation of how futures and options work, see Chapter 8.

Index-linked gilts

These pay a rate of interest linked to the official inflation figures and the face value of the bond is adjusted for inflation when it is repaid. If you buy such a bond for its face value and keep it to redemption, you are therefore guaranteed to make a profit in real terms.

Undated bonds

Some gilts have no redemption date; the government simply goes on paying the interest for ever, unless it chooses to redeem. Others have a range of years (e.g. 1995–1999) within which the government can decide to redeem the gilt at any point. Others give a redemption date followed by the words 'or after' (e.g. '1990 or after'), meaning that the government can choose when it wants to redeem the gilt at any time after the redemption date.

> The point is that gilts are safe – it's the middlemen who may not be.

The Barlow Clowes scandal

If you've heard of Barlow Clowes, you may be wondering why gilts are said to be so safe, when thousands of people who invested in gilts through Barlow Clowes narrowly escaped losing their life-savings when the firm collapsed and two of its directors were jailed for theft. The point is that gilts are safe – it's the middlemen who may not be. Many of the victims of

Barlow Clowes had invested through financial intermediaries, creating two unnecessary layers between themselves and the brokers. It is a classic example of how investors can get caught by believing printed lies: it seemed so unlikely that a company would actually dare to make false statements in their literature and on consumer radio programmes on the BBC that investors assumed that it must be alright. The Department of Trade and Industry's role in the affair was far from glorious – they knew about irregularities with Barlow Clowes for years before the collapse, and did nothing.

Convertible bonds

Convertible bonds offer the investor the chance to exchange bonds at some pre-agreed time for shares in the issuing company. Whether this is worth doing depends upon the market value of the shares when you convert. Obviously, if the shares have gone up you will make a capital gain by converting to shares and then selling them. The price of these bonds usually rise and fall with the share price but at a lower rate. Usually the price at which you can convert to shares is set higher than the market price of the shares when the bonds are issued.

Ex dividend and cum dividend bonds

Interest on bonds is usually paid every six months, so when you buy a bond in the market you will want to know if a dividend is just about to be paid. Approximately five weeks before the interest is paid the bond is declared to be 'ex dividend', meaning that if you buy it, the seller keeps the imminent dividend and the first dividend that you receive will be the subsequent one – this is indicated in the financial pages by 'xd'. Ex dividend bonds are cheaper than 'cum dividend' (meaning 'with dividend') bonds to compensate for the longer wait for the first dividend. Cum dividend bonds require the purchaser to pay for the 'accrued interest' since the last time the interest was paid.

The US bond rating system

The main rating systems for US bonds are Moody's and Standard and Poor's.

They are as follows:

	Standard and Poor's	Moody's
Top quality bonds	AAA	Aaa
High quality bonds	AA	Aa
Good bonds	A	A
Medium quality bonds which may be insecure in the long term	BBB	Baa
Bonds with only moderate security	BB	Ba

The following categories are for bonds which are generally considered to be bad investments for small investors:

Standard and Poor's	Moody's
B	B

The 'C' categories are for bonds which have sometimes defaulted or are in danger of doing so:

	Standard and Poor's	Moody's
	CCC	Caa
	CC	Ca
	C	C
In default	D	–

Bonds for the guerrilla investor

If you buy a bond just before market interest rates take a dive, you can make a substantial tax-free capital gain, as the market value of the bond will rise. Buying gilts through the Post Office will save you a fortune in broker's fees. Buying bonds outside your own country in other currencies can be a good bet if you think the value of your own currency is falling. For those who don't want to become specialists in the field, bonds are basically safe and boring. If you live in the UK or another country where the government perpetually fiddles with interest rates, you will have to keep a weather eye on the economy at all times if you hold long bonds unless you hold them to redemption, and even then you may find that inflation has taken a bite out of them. Personally, I find speculation on interest rates unappealing – it is so easy to get it wrong. Use bonds as a balancer to your other investments, rather than as a means of trying to accumulate wealth.

> **▶** If you are tempted to stay, watch the Press, what the brokers say and the grey market. If you feel confident, take the gamble.

4

The life cycle of a company – from launches to liquidations

In this chapter we will look at:

- New issues – how companies are floated on the stock market.
- The offer for sale.
- Stagging and application tactics.
- Private placing.
- Offers for subscription.
- Tenders and introductions.
- Rights issues, calculating the value of rights and clawbacks.
- Scrip issues.
- Takeover bids.
- How to choose companies that may be subject to takeover bids.
- The Monopolies and Mergers Commission.
- Why companies bid for other ones.
- When companies go bust …
- Gauging solvency.
- Suspensions and liquidations.

NEW ISSUES

Private companies seek to offer their shares through the stock market either to raise extra money cheaply, or so that the owners can get a lot of money out, or for a combination of both reasons. Doing this costs the company a fortune in fees to City professionals which you, the new investor, are paying for. This process is known as a 'new issue'. There are three main kinds:

- The *introduction*. This is where there are already many shareholders in the company. Additional money is not sought, and the company's shares simply become officially part of the stock market.
- The *private placing*. This is where shares are sold to big institutions without other investors getting a look-in, except in certain circumstances which are examined below.
- The *offer for sale*. This is where shares are offered to anyone who wants to buy them.

The company can choose which kind of issue it is going to offer, whether it wants to sell all or just some of its shares, and can also combine different kinds of issue at once. Because of the particularly high costs of an offer for sale, many smaller companies prefer a private placing, if they can find institutions to buy their shares. The rules for a new issue are stringent, and the company must conform to the Stock Exchange's standards for accounting methods, nature of the business, financing, and so on.

THE OFFER FOR SALE

This is the method used by the big privatisation issues in the UK over the last few years. The government decided to float many of the big industries, state- owned since the post-war nationalisations, on the stock market as private sector companies. Politically, it was a gamble that the public's desire for profit would overcome its outrage at having industries which, in theory, it already owned being sold back to itself. To make sure that the issues worked, the government had to try to arrange things so that investors who were new to the stock market would do well out of the issue and be encouraged to take more interest in shares. Here's how it was done:

- Investors were sold shares which they paid for in instalments, so they did not have to find all the money for the shares at once. This is called issuing 'partly-paid' shares.

- There was a huge advertising campaign, and several prospectuses were published to make it easier for the unsophisticated investor to understand what was going on.

- Existing customers of the industry to be privatised were given incentives to invest, such as free shares and priority share applications.

- People were generally given a longer time than usual to consider whether or not to invest, and the time between the closing date for the applications and the commencement of share dealing was extended.

- To reduce 'stagging' (see page 70), there were special rules to stop people trying to get more shares than they were supposed to by making multiple applications for shares.

- The share price was set at a level designed to ensure that successful share applicants would see a rise in the value of their investment as soon as market dealing began. This attracted a lot of criticism along the lines that this was a deliberate undervaluing of the company, which was unfair on those members of the public who did not, or could not, invest, since they were indirectly beneficiaries of the proceeds that the government would get from the sale. However, the howls of protest following a BP share issue, when the market share price went down, were for the opposite argument – that it was unfair for the government not to provide an instant profit for the investors.

- To improve the profits of investors who wanted to sell when dealing in the market began, dealing costs were greatly reduced for a period. In addition, as with all new issues, there were no brokers' fees or stamp duty when you bought the shares.

The principles behind all this are clear enough; the government wanted to widen the number of stock market investors in the UK, and to do this it made efforts to ensure that the new investors' first experiences were happy ones.

When an ordinary company makes a new issue, the situation is rather different in that investors cannot be so certain of doing well as they have

been with the privatisation issues. The first thing
to check in the prospectus is what the company
intends to spend your money on – how much of it
is going to the people who presently own the company and how much of it is going to be spent on
improving the company itself. Investors like to see

> ...As with privatisations,
> these new issues will
> get pre-publicity,
> though on a
> smaller scale...........

their money being put to good use, rather than being siphoned off for
someone else's benefit, so they generally don't like to see more than 5 per
cent going to the original shareholders and another 5 per cent to the
employees.

The next thing to look at is how much of the money raised is going on
fees and expenses associated with the issue – these can be as high as 10 per
cent. You will hear all sorts of justifications for this but the fact remains
that it is a lot to pay middlemen for bringing the company to market.
Unless you feel that the fees are unusually high, even by City standards,
then you have to live with it and invest anyway – you don't have to like it,
though! As with privatisations, these new issues will get pre-publicity,
though on a smaller scale, so you won't see huge posters on roadside
hoardings, or nightly television commercials, extolling the issue's virtues.
The price of the share has to be set by the company. This is done in con-
sultation with the banks and other institutions who have agreed to
'underwrite' the issue – this means that they have agreed to buy all the
shares of the issue that the public don't want, thereby ensuring that all the
shares in the issue will be taken up. Setting the price can be tricky; it is a
fine balance between selling the company too cheaply by choosing a low
price and the risk of the issue 'flopping' by setting the price so high that
no one wants to invest. In the case of a flop, the underwriters must take up
the shares and sell them off slowly into the market as opportunities arise.
Naturally, underwriters hate flops, because they cost them money.

Once the price has been set, the prospectus is published, giving details
of the business, its accounts, its future plans and so on. Past dividend
yields and the p/e ratio of the offer price are given to help with rule-of-
thumb calculations of whether the share price is good value. The time
from the issue of the prospectus to the closing date for share applications
can be surprisingly short, often a matter of days. Once the closing date has
passed, all the applications are added up. If the number of shares applied
for exceeds the total number of shares to be issued, the offer is said to be
'oversubscribed'. This means that the company has to decide who gets
shares and how many they will get. Often there is no way of knowing for
certain how the company will allocate the shares – will it make sure that
the smaller investors get at least some of what they applied for, or will it

favour the institutions who want to buy large quantities of shares? Oversubscription is moderately good news to the investor since the share price will usually rise when market dealing starts.

'Undersubscription' is bad news if you have invested. You'll get all the shares that you asked for, but the left-over shares are taken up by the underwriters who generally don't want to hold on to them and will keep the share price down as they dribble their shares into the market.

FOR GUERRILLA INVESTORS – STAGGING AND OTHER POINTS

'Stagging' simply means applying for shares in a new issue in the hope that they will go up quickly and you can sell out at a profit. Applications usually close at 10.01 am on the morning of the closing date. Long queues form outside the applications office – usually a bank in the City of London – waiting for the doors to open. Applicants crowd in, frantically thrusting their forms and cheques across the counters until a halt is called at 10.01 am, and anyone who has been unable to get his or her application in has missed the boat. Better to get your application in early, you might think, but there is a good reason for leaving things to the last minute – market sentiment. There is a 'grey market' in new issue shares that trades before the closing date, and everyone watches its prices to guess what the price will be when dealing the shares officially begins. Don't be tempted to deal in the grey market yourself, though – it's a game for professionals. Read the Press and ask your broker for opinions on whether the issue will be a success.

> .....Oversubscription is moderately good news to the investor since the share price will usually rise when market dealing starts. ....

Suppose you decide to apply for shares on the morning of the closing date. You apply for the maximum number of shares you are allowed, or can afford, and wait to see how many you get. Because you have to put up part or all of the cash when you apply, you may have paid out more money than the price of the shares you actually receive, and you may have quite a long wait before you are sent back the balance. Many stags are keen to borrow money in order to apply for shares, in the hope that the profit they make from selling will more than cover the cost of borrowing. This can be worth doing if you are pretty sure of success, since you are borrowing the money for a short period of time.

Study the application form carefully. The rules are usually quite complicated and are strictly enforced.

For example, you may be allowed to apply for shares in amounts of **EXAMPLE ✳**
200 shares up to a total of 1,000 shares, then in amounts of 500
between 1,000 and 5,000 shares, and finally in amounts of 1,000 above 5,000
shares. If you apply for, say, 1,700 shares, you will get none at all – you would have
had to apply for 1,500 or 1,000 to qualify.

Sometimes these cut-off points (the 1,000 and 5,000 limits in the example) are used in deciding on share allocations when an issue is oversubscribed. For example, those who applied for more than 5,000 shares may get allocated proportionately more shares than those who applied for between 1,000 and 5,000 shares, who, in turn, will get a bigger percentage of their application than people who asked for less than 1,000 shares. If the market price is higher than the issue price, you can sell at a profit, so the more shares you have the better, but naturally the more shares you have when an issue flops, the more money you will lose if you sell, so you may have to hang on to the shares for a long time before you can get your money back.

Multiple applications are not allowed – several apparently respectable people were prosecuted for making multiple applications in privatisation issues. What some City folks do, though, is to get a large number of non-investors to apply for shares in their own names; all the shares ultimately go to the stag, who pays a small fee to his team of applicants. You can do this legally in a small way by getting your friends and relatives to apply, and giving them a piece of the action.

Clearly, if the City likes a new issue it is likely to do well. Look at the names of the brokers and banks who are sponsoring the issue. The top names, especially of the banks, are generally thought more likely to have got the issue price right, to avoid a flop. If you are tempted to stag, watch the Press, what the brokers say and the grey market. If you feel confident, take the gamble.

Tenders

Some new issues set a minimum price at which you can apply for shares and invite you to tender a higher figure. Once all the applications are in, the sponsors then decide on the 'striking price'. This is the price that everyone will be asked to pay for the shares. If you tendered at a price lower than the striking price, you don't get any shares. You can make multiple applications as long as each application is at a different price.

Another variety of tender is called 'pay what you bid'. In this case you pay the price that you tendered for the shares if you have bid higher than the striking price. Usually you receive all the shares that you asked for.

Private placing

This method is popular with many companies as well as with City institutions. The private investor doesn't usually get the chance to buy shares since the sponsors place most of the shares with big fund managers, and any other shares tend to go to the favoured clients of a broker. Companies like placings because the costs are lower and the flotation happens with less risk and more quickly. If the money to be raised is between £15 and £30 million, the sponsoring broker must allow at least one other broker to sell shares, and if more than £30 million is being raised then part of the issue must be offered to the public.

Offers by subscription

Often used to introduce brand new investment trusts to the stock market, offers by subscription set a minimum price at which you can apply for shares. If there are not enough investors willing to apply, the issue is cancelled since it is not fully underwritten.

Introductions

This method is often used by foreign companies which are already quoted on another stock exchange. There is no chance of stagging since no new shares are issued. The company's shares must already be widely held in the UK.

RIGHTS ISSUES

When a company whose shares are already listed on the Stock Exchange wants to raise more money, it can do so by a 'rights issue', offering new shares to the shareholders that it already has. In case not enough shareholders want to take up their rights, the company will often arrange for the issue to be underwritten by stockbrokers and banks who promise to buy shares in exchange for a commission. The problem is that if the rights issue flops, meaning that few shareholders want the new shares, the underwriters are stuck with them and have to dribble them out slowly onto the market; whenever the share price rises, the underwriters will sell more of the shares they are stuck with, and this will bring the price down again. 'Deep discount' rights issues are when the issuing company offers the shares at well below the market price.

As a shareholder, you have the choice of whether to take up your rights or not. You have to come up with the money to pay for them, so you need to be confident that the company is conducting the rights issue for a good reason (e.g. expansion), rather than to pay off debt. You will receive an 'offer document' explaining why the company wants to raise the money and giving its accounts so you will be able to make a judgement. However, even a 'rescue rights issue' by a company in trouble can sometimes result in an increase in the subsequent market price. If you decide not to exercise your rights, you may still be able to make a profit by selling the rights themselves. Once dealing begins after the issue, the price will, in theory, be between the old market price and the amount of discount on the issue price, so the effect for the shareholders is that their old shares will come down a little and the new shares will go up. If you sell your rights for more than the amount your original shares drop to, you make a profit.

You can estimate the price of the shares after the rights issue by multiplying the number of shares you are being offered by the offer price, adding the result to the total market value of the shares you already own, and dividing by the total number of shares. This figure represents the expected movement down from the old market price after the issue because of the discount on the new shares. It is called the 'ex-rights' price since it is, in theory, the price that the share will settle down to after the issue is over, when the shares would be sold in the market without the rights. The ex-rights price is used to work out the price you should get for selling your rights. You can do this either by not responding to the offer document, in which case the company will sell the rights for you and send you the money, or selling them in the stock market 'nil paid'.

Working out rights values

Suppose you own 22 shares in a company with a market value of 300p each, and a rights issue offers you the chance to buy 1 share for every 11 shares you already own at a price of 250p each. You can calculate the ex-rights price as follows:

EXAMPLE ✷

2 new shares x 250p = 500p

500p + (22 old shares x 300p) = 500p + 6600p = 7100p

7100p ÷ 24 shares = 296p per share

Thus, you estimate that by buying the two new shares at the discounted offer price, you will see the market price drop from the 300p of the old, 'rights-on' shares to the 296p of the ex-rights price. The value of the two new shares that you bought for 250p each will have gone up, however.

During the rights issue, there is a period between the time when you are notified of how many new shares you are being offered and the deadline for acceptance during which the old shares are traded in the market ex-rights. This means that the person selling them is keeping the rights and the rights are traded separately as 'nil paid' shares. In our example, the ex-rights price during this period should in theory be around 296p and the nil paid share price should be about 46p (the difference between the ex-rights price and the exercise price). In practice, though, the nil paid value will fluctuate.

Suppose you want to exercise your rights, but you don't have enough cash to do so. You could try to sell some of your rights and use the cash to exercise the rights you have left. You can work this out by multiplying the number of new shares you have been offered by the price you can get for the rights and then dividing the result by the actual ex-rights price.

✳ EXAMPLE   Suppose you owned 220 shares originally and have been offered the right to buy 20 shares:

(20 x 46p) ÷ 296p = 920p ÷ 296p = 3.1

This tells you that you can sell 17 shares nil paid (17 x 46 = 782p) and use the cash to buy three new shares (3 x 250 = 750p).

Clawbacks

Clawbacks are becoming more popular than rights issues. The company issues new shares to one or more institutions, but allows existing share-holders to buy some shares at the issue price, thus 'clawing back' the shares. The big difference for the shareholders is that if you don't want to exercise your clawback rights, you can't sell them in the market.

SCRIP ISSUES

'Free' scrip issues, also called capitalisation issues or bonus issues, are when a company offers new shares to shareholders in proportion to the number that they already own, but without asking for more money. This is done in order to make the total number of shares in the company larger, so that there are more shares in the market and they can be bought and sold more easily, and also so that the company can transfer some of its reserves into capital on its balance sheet, giving it various business advantages. The company needs the approval of its shareholders to conduct a scrip issue. The result will be that the company has more capital, though it is not worth more, and there are more shares, but with a lower nominal value to reflect the scrip issue. Generally, shareholders like scrip issues and share prices often increase at the announcement of one.

A similar method is 'share splitting', where a company splits each share into several more with lower nominal values that add up in total to the nominal value of the original share. Both these methods are often thought to make shares more attractive because investors don't like to buy shares that have a high market price; it is considered that it somehow 'feels' better to buy 800 shares for a pound each than 200 shares at four pounds each.

Some companies have annual scrip issues and increase the amount they distribute in dividends by keeping the dividend rate the same as before. They can also pay 'scrip dividends', which means that they pay you a dividend on your shares or free scrip shares. A variation on this is 'enhanced scrip dividends', which offer scrip shares of a considerably higher value than the alternative of a cash dividend.

TAKEOVER BIDS

While rights issues are generally regarded as a mixed blessing for share-holders, the news that a company is trying to take over your company by

> Sometimes a company does not want to be taken over and decides to fight the bids; it will produce strong arguments for rejecting

buying its shares is almost always good news. Often companies compete to take over a target, so its shareholders find themselves the focus of a stream of letters urging them to accept or reject increasingly higher bids for their shares. There then follows the enjoyable task of deciding which bid to accept, and when.

You usually have sixty days in which to decide whether to accept a bid. Once the bid has expired, if the bidding company has succeeded in buying over 90 per cent of the total number of shares in the target company, it can then force you to accept a price for your shares which is lower than the successful bid price. The bids for your shares may offer shares in the acquiring company, or a combination of such shares, fixed-interest securities and cash in exchange. These shares must be examined carefully – you may not feel that they represent a profitable exchange. Sometimes a company does not want to be taken over and decides to fight the bids; it will produce strong arguments for rejecting the offer.

As we have seen, if you own shares in a company that is the subject of a bidding war, you are likely to gain substantial profits, as long as you sell out to a bidder before your company is bought. The rules for takeovers say that bids cannot be called 'final' until very near the end of the war, so if you receive a bid that is not described as final you should wait for a better offer. The target company may try to find a 'white knight' investor to counter-bid in the hope that life under the white knight will be better than under the predator. Bidders can improve their offers up to the 46th day of the bid, and the defending company has until the 39th day to produce key financial arguments against the bids.

A bidding company doesn't have to own any shares in a company to bid for it, but often it tries to build up a stake in advance of bidding. The rules say that shareholdings of over 3 per cent in a company must be declared publicly so that people can have some warning of what may happen. Once a bidder controls over 50 per cent of the shares, he effectively controls the company. Predators sometimes buy up to 15 per cent of a company in a 'dawn raid' on the stock market, after which they may not buy any more shares for a week. They can then build their holdings to 25 per cent before waiting again. Once the shareholding has passed 30 per cent, they must bid for the company. If they can persuade people to sell them 20 per cent more of the company's shares, they can then announce that the bid is 'unconditional as to acceptances', which means that the rest of the shareholders have two weeks in which to make up their minds. If these shareholders refuse the offer, which is unusual, they keep their shares in the company, but it is now under the bidder's control (as mentioned earlier, if bidders manage to get 90 per cent of the shares, they can forcibly buy the remaining 10 per cent).

> ...... **Sometimes people prefer to take some shares in lieu of cash because there is no Capital Gains Tax to pay when you receive the shares.** ......

Once a bidder is in control of the company, it remains to be seen whether the predator has gauged its value correctly; companies engaging in a series of takeovers during a boom, doing their sums on the assumption of ever-increasing values, can be very badly caught out in a crash. Just because an acquiring company is willing to pay a high price for your shares does not necessarily mean that it is cannier than you are, so if you think that the cash you are being offered is a lot, take it – you may be glad that you did! Sometimes people prefer to take some shares in lieu of cash because there is no Capital Gains Tax to pay when you receive the shares. If you decide to do this, don't assume that these shares will rise, and consider when you want to dispose of them and what they will really be worth then. If you want to take the cash, check how much time you have in which to accept – sometimes you are only given 21 days from the date of the bid in which to decide on cash.

Buying after a winning bid

This is speculative. If you really think that the takeover is sound and you expect improved business results, then it may be worth investing after a takeover. However, make sure that other speculators haven't pushed the share so high that you are paying too much.

How to choose companies that may be subject to takeover bids

Some companies get a reputation for being likely to attract bids that lasts for decades without a bid ever actually emerging, so it is difficult to spot winners with certainty. The profile of a likely candidate for a takeover bid is a company with a large amount of assets, a broad shareholder base and a good underlying business. Sometimes they are found in the following situations:

● Companies that have been controlled by families for decades, if not for generations, may be amenable to takeover bids; it all turns on whether the major shareholders want to sell, perhaps in order to retire, or whether they are determined to hang on.

- Companies that produce a lower return on the capital employed than is normal in their industry can be the target of takeover bids from other more competitive companies in the same industry, the idea being that the acquirer will be able to make the company more profitable than it is at present. The same goes for trading profits; sometimes a famous name is going downhill, and is taken over by a company in the same business which hopes to increase margins through the power of the combined turnover.

- Companies in which a possible predator has bought a large number of shares can be the target of takeover bids. The share price will rise on this news but if you feel that the target company is an attractive one, it can be worth buying now and waiting for the bid. Sometimes the stakeholder sells the shares on to another bidder, so you must play a waiting game. The danger is that the stakeholder may simply withdraw.

- Although it is now illegal in the UK to buy shares because you have inside information, share prices have a curious tendency to rise before any news of the acquisition of a large stake appears. Company employees, their relatives and people in the City who know about the planned bid may buy shares without realising that it is illegal to do so – but even if the insider trading is deliberate, it is very hard to prove (see Chapter 11). Thus, some people invest on unexplained share price rises on the assumption that the insider traders know that a bid is the air. This may work sometimes, but it is a puny strategy, rather like being a builder who undercuts his competitors' quotations for work and finds himself making a loss because he hasn't done his own budgeting – after all, the share price increase may simply be the result of false rumours, so look at the company carefully to see if you think that a takeover is credible.

- Sometimes it is worth buying shares after a winning bid. If the acquiring company is actively pursuing other targets, or if the takeover is perceived to have been a very promising one, the share price may continue to rise. This can be dangerous, since rapid expansion may ultimately result in total collapse. More often, the share price stays quiet for at least a few months after a successful takeover.

The Monopolies and Mergers Commission and other authorities

There are laws to prevent companies buying up their competitors in order to create a monopoly, so there is a chance that a UK takeover bid may be referred to the Monopolies and Mergers Commission. Sell your shares if you think that the bid will be referred, as a failure can mean a large fall in the price. Although companies take a lot of advice to ensure that their bids will not be referred, some bids do fail. The British Takeover Panel is a City organisation which oversees the takeover process and tries to make sure that everybody plays by the rules. It is not a state-controlled body, and has attracted criticism from outsiders who feel that it does not have enough power to force people to play fair. The European Commission is also sticking its finger in the pie with the job of overseeing big European takeovers. The European Commission is expected to try to change the way that takeovers are conducted in the UK in the future.

> ..... As far as the private investor is concerned, takeovers represent an exciting and profitable process if you are fortunate enough to own shares in a target company. .....

In the United States the rules are different. The 'anti-trust' laws make it illegal for companies not only to monopolise markets, but also to 'tend' to create a monopoly, use unfair methods of competition or attempt to 'unreasonably' restrain trade. In practice, the bigger the companies, the more likely it is that a takeover bid will provoke anti-trust lawsuits. Such lawsuits have a political dimension. Under President Reagan, corporate America was given clear signals that there would be fewer government lawsuits against them and a greater freedom to seek profits wherever they could be found. In Chapter 11, pages 201–6, we will look at some of the scandals that emerged during a frenzy of takeovers (known as 'mergers' in the United States) in the 1980s.

Cycles of takeovers

Takeovers seem to come in waves. Around 1900 there was a flurry of takeovers, then another one in the boom of the 1920s, and others in the late 1960s and the 1980s. They are associated with bull markets, although one would expect to see takeovers in bear markets too, if the real motive was to pick up a bargain. Since many eager predators have come a cropper over the years, there is a general feeling that there is something wrong about takeovers, and that they are bad for the economy as a whole. As far as the private investor is concerned, they represent an exciting and profitable process if you are fortunate enough to own shares in a target company.

The reasons why companies bid

Takeovers can be divided into three kinds: 'horizontal', which is where both companies are in the same business; 'vertical', where the companies are in associated businesses at different points on the route from the production point to the point of sale; and 'conglomerate', where the companies are in unrelated businesses. The acquiring company may have sound business reasons for making the offer, such as the following:

- *Economies of scale*, where the combined buying power of the two companies can improve research and development and reduce costs. Horizontal takeovers are very often for reasons of economy of scale, but the same motive is sometimes claimed for conglomerate mergers. This is less convincing, because conglomerates tend to breed large bureaucracies which can outweigh the benefits of the takeover.

- *Vertical integration economies*. Taking over a supplier or a customer can help a company to become more powerful in the marketplace while substantially reducing costs. Sometimes a new method or product can be made more profitable in this way.

- *Improving efficiency*. If the target company is peopled by bad managers who are firmly entrenched, a takeover by a dynamic company which will sack the old regime and increase efficiency is sometimes the only practical way to save the company.

- *Tax losses and pension funds*. A company may have made substantial tax losses which it cannot use. If it takes over another company, it can benefit by setting off the tax losses against the other company's profits. Some companies hold large pension funds for their employees, which have been known to be an attraction to predators.

- *Taking over a smaller specialist company to market their products* better can often be cheaper for a big business than setting up competing products from scratch.

Here are some less convincing reasons for takeovers:

- *Diversification*, or the conglomerate-style takeover, is not thought to increase the value of the companies concerned. Buying a number of unrelated companies does not seem to be very good business in the long run, and often shares in diversified groups of companies are lower than their combined worth.

- *The 'chain letter' effect*. This is when a company with low earnings and high growth conducts a series of takeovers of high-earning, low-growth companies, financing the offers mainly with its own 'paper' (e.g. offering its own shares to shareholders in the target companies). There is nothing wrong about this in principle, but if the acquiring company fools the market into thinking that its rapid growth is for sound business reasons, rather than simply through the acquistions, it must then continue with the same rate of growth if it is to keep its share price up, and the temptation is to find further acquisitions. In the end there will be no more companies to buy, its growth will slow and its share price will collapse. Here's how it works.

EXAMPLE ✳

Suppose that Company A, the acquiring company, has total earnings of £300,000 and 1,000,000 shares, making its earnings per share 30p. Its p/e ratio is, say, 20, so its share price will be 600p. Now suppose that Company B, the target company, also has earnings of £300,000, 1,000,000 shares and earnings per share of 30p, but the lower p/e ratio of 10, making its share price 300p. Company A's market value is thus twice that of Company B's; if Company A can buy Company B by offering half of its own shares, it will then have total earnings of £600,000 and 1,500,000 shares, making the earnings per share 40p. If its share price stays the same, its p/e ratio falls to 15. If investors think that the increase in earnings per share is 'real' growth, they may invest, pushing up the p/e ratio as the share price rises.

- *Reduced borrowing costs.* This doesn't mean the genuine saving a company can get by making fewer and larger rights issues in the future after the takeover; it refers to the notion that corporate bonds can be issued at lower rates of interest because the increased value of the company gives lenders (bond buyers) more security. This may be true, but it is essentially an adjustment of risk rather than a real gain to the company.

WHEN COMPANIES GO BUST

If you invest in a company that is not listed on the stock market, you either know what you are doing or you are a brave soul indeed. In comparison with unquoted companies, the ones in the stock market don't go into liquidation very often. When they do, though, they often go in large numbers, as happened after the stock market crash of 1929, so one can never be complacent. We all hear about recessions causing companies to go under, but this doesn't mean much. A company that is going to survive will survive a recession, and one that is unsound can collapse even in times of prosperity.

Nevertheless, even top companies that are included in market indices have gone bust in the past, and will do so in the future. When this happens, you have to assume the worst. A liquidator is appointed to sell the company's assets in order to pay off its debts, and while you may have done sums to show that you will get back, say, 40p in the pound, in practice the insolvent company's assets tend to be sold off at rock bottom prices. The proceeds go to the 'secured creditors' and the shareholder, who is at the back of the queue, often gets nothing. The cautious investors will get out when danger signals appear, before the collapse happens. One way of watching out for trouble is regularly to check your investments' business ratios.

Using business ratios to gauge solvency

The 'gearing' or 'leverage' of a company is an important test. What you are looking at is how much the company is borrowing as a proportion of its own capital. To understand its significance, imagine you had friends who bought a house for £300,000 with £50,000 of their own money and borrowing the rest as a mortgage. Would you think they were wise? They might be able to service the debt on their current salaries, but what if one of them got ill, or lost their job, or if the property market went down, or interest rates doubled? What if all these things happened at once? We know from experience that bad things can happen to people; obviously, the same is true for companies too.

While it is true that some industries are more dangerous than others, any company which borrows more than £1 for every pound of its capital should be treated with caution. A high-borrowing company is called 'highly geared'. Companies can become highly geared when they expand very fast and borrow money to do so. In all the excitement the company's overheads have a tendency to grow very quickly too, and if the business subsequently gets into trouble, high overheads and interest payments can sink it like a stone.

Generally speaking, companies that borrow the equivalent of less than half of their capital are pretty stable, and ones which borrow the equivalent of between a half and all of their capital are usually okay. Another way of measuring a company's ability to pay its debts is to look at the proportion of trading profit which is being spent on paying the interest on loans. There is something wrong if most of the money is going in this way – after all, a company is supposed to be making money for you, not for the banks!

The next thing to do is to look at the company's 'liquidity'. In this context, liquidity means the ability of the company to pay off its current creditors, such as suppliers, the Inland Revenue and short-term lenders, with its current assets, such as its stock, the money owed by customers and its money in the bank. If the proportion of current debt to current assets is more than 2:3, it is a bad sign. Remember that current assets are sometimes valued rather optimistically, and may be worth far less than their book value if they have to be sold in an emergency. There are, however, vast, well-established companies that allow their current liabilities to exceed their current assets by a wide margin, confident in their power to keep their suppliers waiting for payment should the need arise. Indeed, quite a number of large companies are well-known for taking many months of credit from their smaller suppliers as a matter of course.

All kinds of things can kill a company, including regulatory changes, changes in the market and losing big court cases. Accountants know that something is wrong, after it has happened, by looking at the books, although the published accounts may not reveal the whole story. In published accounts, accountants use certain stock phrases to signal that they are unhappy; large 'extraordinary items' and a change in accounting practice should alert you to possible problems. The reason why you cannot take published accounts as the absolute truth is that it is very difficult to value things correctly, given the complexity of modern business and also that it is often in the directors' interests to distort the accounts in some way. Directors want to improve the look of profit figures for such motives as improving the chances of a sale of all or part of the company, to put off unwelcome bidders, or even to ensure their own bonuses, and they may try to lessen profit figures for reasons such as reducing the tax bill, avoiding public criticism and defending attacks from trade unions. When a company gets into trouble some directors react by trying to fight their way out by fair means or foul, and may juggle the accounts to put off the evil day when they must declare insolvency. Although the external accountants must, by law, audit the books each year, and will do their best to present an accurate picture, it is not impossible for directors to pull the wool over their eyes, for a few years at least. Interestingly, accountants feel happier about low valuations and profit estimates because they know that there may be unintentional overvaluations elsewhere, and also because they are far less likely to be sued if it turns out that the company is worth more than was thought, than if it emerges that the company was grossly overvalued.

> **When a company gets into trouble some directors react by trying to fight their way out by fair means or foul, and may juggle the accounts to put off the evil day when they must declare insolvency.**

Suspensions and liquidations

Suppose you wake up one morning to find that the shares in your favourite stock have been suspended. This does not necessarily spell disaster. 'Suspension' means that the trading of the shares in the market is stopped. The idea is that suspending shares when there is uncertainty about a company levels the playing field, giving time for all the investors to find out what is going on. The danger is that the suspension can last for years, which means that you are stuck with a dodgy shareholding that you cannot sell and that you cannot claim as a loss against Capital Gains Tax. However, suspensions are sometimes used in happy circumstances too, such as when a bid is in the air, to allow time for all the information to reach the investors.

Despite their comparative lack of access to information, small investors will usually get plenty of warning when a company gets into trouble. At the time of writing, Euro Disney, quoted on the Paris Bourse, has had its shares temporarily suspended. Trouble has been brewing for more than a year; this morning the shares fell by 10 per cent, were suspended for a short time, then began to rise and were suspended again in the afternoon. A British analyst was blamed for the fluctuation – he had suggested that the shares were worth less than the market price.

> The actions of its directors have a great bearing on what happens to a company once it starts to sink.

Whatever happens ultimately to Euro Disney – it may well survive, given its association with Disney in the United States – the point is that no one can say that they didn't have any warning that all was not well.

The actions of its directors have a great bearing on what happens to a company once it starts to sink. In many circumstances they can put the company into 'administration' before a creditor, or the law, forces them to relinquish control. An independent accountant is appointed by a court to manage the company for three months or more before creditors can take any action to recover their debts. This gives time for re-financing, cutting losses and raising cash by selling off businesses and assets. It is a courageous thing for the directors to do, since, as mentioned earlier, the money raised may not be enough to cover the debts, so the temptation is to go on trying to keep the company going, ignoring its slide into ruin. Creditors may object to an application to put the company into administration, and they can themselves apply to put the company into 'receivership'. This effectively takes all control out of the directors' hands. The 'official receiver' appoints a 'liquidator' to sell off what he can.

Guerrilla investors and insolvent companies

People who have had no experience of insolvent companies have a tendency to remain hopeful long after disaster has struck. It is a matter of judgement, but if you feel that a company is getting into trouble, get out while you still can. Once a company goes into administration or receivership you haven't really got a prayer.

▶ Work out your own defensive strategies and be tough – you can be sure the banks won't listen to reason if they have you over a barrel, so make sure that you hold the aces!

5

Banks

Many people think that anything to do with banking is deadly dull.
I disagree. Any subject that has such a directly significant affect on one's
life as the banking system does has to be of interest to the guerrilla
investor. In this chapter we will look at:

- Money – why and how it works.
- The money stock and the money supply.
- The role of central banks.
- The Bank of England.
- UK monetary policy.
- The Federal Reserve.
- Types of bank.
- Interest rates.
- The BCCI story.
- How banks lend to individuals.
- Guerrilla borrowing tactics.
- Banking and Big Brother.

MONEY

There is an alternative to money. If you live an isolated life and can obtain all that you need through your own physical work, you don't require money. This is the kind of life lived by most people in the far past. Money is an invention, like writing, which grew out of the increasingly complex needs of settled societies. In essence, money is a solution to the problems of barter. If I spend a week making a chair and I want to give it to you in exchange for your grapes, how many grapes should you give me? Perhaps I don't want very many grapes, because I don't want to spend time converting them into a form that won't spoil, so I ask you for 'change' – a

> Money makes exchange easier. It is a token that can be passed from hand to hand, and which most people will accept as payment.

few grapes and some other items in return for the chair – but all you want to give is grapes …. You can see how cumbersome bartering is! Anyone who has spent time in less developed countries can testify to the awkwardness and inefficiency of non-money economies. Money makes exchange easier. It is a token that can be passed from hand to hand, and which most people will accept as payment. It doesn't have to be in the form of coins and notes – even highly civilised nations have occasionally reverted to using other objects for money during periods of collapse, for instance when cigarettes were widely used for money in Europe at the end of World War 2.

The main characteristics of money are:

- It is generally accepted as payment for other things.
- It is a way of measuring the prices of other things.
- It can be saved, so you can keep the value it represents until later.
- It is relatively easy to transport.
- The units of money are, or should be, standard and easy to recognise.
- The supply of money must be controlled.

Gold and money

Gold and silver coins were once popular as money, since they had an intrinsic value to which their monetary value was related. However, they are vulnerable to tampering; people would clip off tiny bits of the metal before spending the coins, which were then worth slightly less than they were supposed to be. It is also possible to forge coins using a lower content of precious metal. This activity was popular with kings and governments who controlled the coinage. If a king minted coins with, say two-thirds of the official gold content, he could buy a third more goods and services with the coins. Eventually people would discover the trick and adjust prices accordingly (an inflationary process), but in the meantime the king had benefited by cheating his subjects. Nowadays governments are supposed to be more responsible and protective of their currencies, but this kind of thing still happens. For example, the horrific inflation in Germany during the inter-war years is thought to have been, in part, a tactic to reduce the unjust burden of war reparations imposed by the victorious Allies; Germany paid part of the huge debt in devalued currency while ordinary people saw their savings evaporate.

Because of the problems with coins, bank notes were introduced. These have no intrinsic value, but are guaranteed by the government that issues them. To operate such a system you need stable, organised bodies to run it, which is where banks come in. Banks developed from trusted groups, such as goldsmiths, who were able to issue receipts for money that they held in safekeeping for other people, and thus bank notes were born. In the nineteenth century British currency was tied to a gold standard. This meant that coins and notes could be exchanged for gold at the Bank of England on demand. The gold standard was abandoned during the upheavals of the two World Wars, and the international system which has replaced it is discussed in Chapter 9.

The money in circulation

We hear a great deal about the importance of the money supply; different political forces and economic theorists hold conflicting ideas about how, and how much, the money supply should be controlled, but it is clear that some degree of control is necessary. If, for example, anyone could print as much money as they liked, people would soon become very wary of accepting it as payment. Thus, it is in everyone's interest for the creation and movement of money to be regulated.

The world has become so complicated that it is actually quite difficult to keep tabs on the movement of money, even within a country, so in order to make analysis easier, various definitions of different parts of the total supply of money have been invented. In the UK they are:

- M0 (pronounced 'M nought') is the notes and coins in circulation, the notes and coins kept in banks for their daily operations, and the banks' balances at the Bank of England.

- M1 is the notes and coins in circulation, and non-interest-bearing bank deposits made by private sector companies and individuals repayable on demand (excluding deposits made by government-owned bodies).

- M2 is the notes and coins in circulation, and non-interest-bearing bank deposits made by private sector companies and individuals repayable on demand and certain interest-bearing private sector deposits.

- M3 includes the money defined in M1, plus all private sector deposits held by UK residents, including certificates of deposit, building society deposits and National Savings.

> **UK banks are allowed to lend around three-quarters of the total amount of the money that has been deposited with them for safekeeping.**

The amount of money in M1 is roughly ten times the amount of notes and coins in circulation, and the amount of money in M3 is about twenty times the amount of notes and coins in circulation. So where does all the extra money come from? Part of it is created by banks in the following way.

UK banks are allowed to lend around three-quarters of the total amount of the money that has been deposited with them for safekeeping. Suppose you borrow £1,000 from Bank X to buy a cheap car. You pay the money to the vendor, who deposits the £1,000 in Bank B; Bank B lends £750 of it to another customer, who pays it to Company A. Company A deposits the £750 in Bank C, who lends £537 of it to another customer, and on it goes. This process actually increases the amount of money in the banks' accounting systems several times over. In effect, they are creating extra money by giving credit, relying on the fact that not all their customers will want to withdraw their deposits at the same time. When this happens, there is a 'run on the banks' which we will examine later. The 25 per cent that the banks don't lend is called their 'reserves', and can vary, which leads directly to changes in the total amount of money in the system.

CENTRAL BANKS

Most countries have one central bank which acts on behalf of the government to control the banking system. In the UK, this role is performed by the Bank of England. Like most central banks, it is owned by its government and it acts as a state instrument rather than as a business undertaken for the profit of its shareholders. The main jobs of central banks are:

- To be the 'lender of last resort' (see page 109) for other banks in the country. This helps to give stability to the banking system and offers a limited guarantee to people using banks that they will not lose their money in a banking collapse.

- To oversee the activities of the other banks in the country.

- To exercise a degree of control on the money supply by regulating the amount of credit that the other banks are giving.

- To control the issue and circulation of notes and coins.

- To act as bankers to the state in the same way that other banks service their customers.

- To administer bonds issued by the government.

Every central bank has its own peculiarities, according to the character of its own country's system.

Government borrowing

In Chapter 3 we saw how governments borrow long-term money by issuing bonds. They also borrow funds in the short term, often using the banking system and the money markets (see Chapter 6), and this has a great affect on the money supply. If the total amount of money the government earns (mainly tax revenue) is less than the amount it spends in a certain period, the difference is called the Public Sector Borrowing Requirement (PSBR). The PSBR can be covered either by borrowing, or by selling assets. If the government borrows from banks by issuing Treasury bills in the Discount Market (see Chapter 6), the money supply is increased, which may have inflationary consequences, but if it borrows from the public, by issuing National Savings securities, it is thought that there is no effect on the money supply, since the money is raised to be spent, and thus returns to the banking system.

The Bank of England

As well as being the banker to the government, the Bank of England also provides banking services for a few private sector companies and individuals, the other banks and financial institutions in the UK, a few central banks from Commonwealth countries, the International Monetary Fund (IMF), the World Bank, the Bank for International Settlements, and members of its own staff.

The government holds many accounts with other banks, but by far its biggest ones are at the Bank of England. Taxes and other moneys go into the government's Exchequer account, and all the money that the government spends comes out of it. Other UK government accounts at the Bank of England include those necessary for the payment of interest on gilts. The Bank of England borrows money on behalf of the government by issuing bonds and Treasury bills (see Chapter 3), but only lends for very short periods (e.g. overnight). It also advises the government on what is happening in the market.

Most banks operating in the UK have to keep deposits of 0.45 per cent of their liabilities at the Bank of England. These earn no interest, and are called 'cash ratio deposits'. They also have accounts called 'operational balances' which are used for clearing all cheques through the system.

The Bank of England is the only bank allowed to issue bank notes in England and Wales. Bank notes get dirty and torn quite quickly, so the old ones have to be burned and millions of new ones are printed daily to replace them. As well as being the registrar for gilts, the Bank of England also handles bonds issued by some Commonwealth countries, UK local authorities and nationalised bodies. In Chapter 9 we will see how the Bank of England can act to influence the rate of exchange between sterling and other currencies. This is done through the 'Exchange Equalisation Account', which holds the government's gold reserves, special drawing rights (see Chapter 9) and foreign currency. If banks get into trouble, they can come to the Bank of England for a loan; this will cost more than the money market rates (see Chapter 6) and will be on terms that make sure that banks will only seek the loan if they have no other way of obtaining the money.

UK monetary policy

The Bank of England acts on behalf of the government to control bank lending in the following ways:

- *Interest rates.* The Bank of England can affect UK interest rates by setting its own rate of lending to the discount houses (see page 109). The idea is that if the Bank of England raises its interest rates, people will borrow less, but this does not always happen.

- *Special deposits.* The Bank of England can raise the amount of money that financial institutions must deposit with it. This reduces the amount of money in the system and forces banks to lend less.

- *Directives.* The Bank of England can tell banks what category of customer to lend to in order to influence the economy in different sectors. In the past it would also issue directives specifying that banks could lend up to a certain amount during a certain period – these are called quantitative directives, but they are not used at present.

- *Open market operations.* This is when the Bank of England buys or sells already issued gilts and Treasury bills in the marketplace, thereby reducing or increasing the money available to banks for lending.

The Federal Reserve: the central bank of the United States

The Federal Reserve, or the Fed, is actually twelve banks with 25 branches across the United States. Founded in 1913, it is run by a board of governors appointed by the President for 14-year terms to protect them against political vagaries. Like all central banks, its job is to oversee and stabilise the banking system. It is owned not by the government but by other banks. Apart from this important difference, the Fed operates on very similar lines to the Bank of England.

■ TYPES OF BANK

You are probably aware that there is more than one kind of bank; in this section we will look at the various kinds of bank to be found in the UK.

The banks that people are most familiar with are the *'retail'* banks, which have branches all over the UK, and clear people's cheques through the system. Until recently, the most important of these were the 'big four' clearing banks, (Lloyds, Midland, National Westminster and Barclays), the three Scottish banks (the Bank of Scotland, the Clydesdale Bank and the Royal Bank of Scotland (all three of which have the power to issue Scottish bank notes), and four banks in Northern Ireland. After regulations were relaxed, the TSB (Trustee Savings Bank), originally a non-prof-

it-making organisation, developed into an important retail bank which is able to offer services virtually identical to those of the big four. The
privatised Girobank, originally part of the Post
Office and now owned by the Alliance and Leices-
ter, has also become an important retail bank, with
a competitive advantage in its connections with
equivalent organisations abroad, allowing transfers and withdrawals from Post Offices in other
countries.

> ....Foreign-owned
> banks sometimes
> offer advantages to
> the guerrilla investor,
> mainly in lower costs
> and improved services
> when conducting
> international
> transactions. ....

The next category is that of the *merchant banks*, a variety that is peculiar
to the UK. Merchants banks arrange finance for companies, by issues of
shares and bonds, and manage large investment portfolios, principally for
institutional funds. They also accept interest-bearing deposits from companies, are involved in factoring (giving cash advances to companies
secured on money owed them by their customers), leasing and insurance
for companies, and are very active in the 'Euromarkets' (see Chapter 6).
They can be thought of as the wholesalers of banking services, operating
higher up the chain of the banking system. They have only a few branches and rarely deal with private individuals. There are also banks that are
owned jointly by a group of other banks, often from different countries,
and are not controlled by any one bank. These *'consortium' banks* are
involved in making large loans, too big for one bank to take the whole
risk, to companies and state organisations internationally, and are active
in the Euromarkets.

There are several hundred *foreign-owned* banks that have branches in
the UK. United States banks are keen to take part of the British retail market as well as to benefit from differences between the regulatory controls
of the United States and the UK, while others concentrate on serving businesses and consumers connected with their own countries. They sometimes offer advantages to the guerrilla investor, mainly in lower costs and
improved services when conducting international transactions. Occasionally you can find a foreign bank in the City that will change major currencies without commission, which is worth the effort if you are going on
holiday.

British overseas banks are the remnants of the imperial banking system,
the owners of banks in foreign countries, mainly in the Third World. Due
to nationalisations and the blocking of funds by the host countries, the
overseas banks have become progressively less profitable as Britain divest-
ed itself of its imperial territories during the last 60 years or so. New markets have been sought, including retail banking in the United States and

> **Bank customers are now bombarded with sales pitches for insurance and other financial products.**

Canada, the currency markets and the money markets (see Chapter 6).

The *National Savings Bank* used to be part of the Post Office but is now administered by the Department of National Savings. Its purpose is to offer facilities for saving to the public and is similar to a building society.

Finance houses are banks which specialise in lending money to companies and individuals for the purchase of large items on hire-purchase schemes. They also offer factoring and leasing services. More recently, they have opened retail outlets known as 'money shops'. The big banks have interests in the finance houses and they are carefully regulated to protect the consumer.

UK retail banking for guerrillas

In the 'good old days' the bank manager was a paternalistic friend to his customers; he was sometimes allowed to sell them insurance and take the commission personally, but in general he was able to offer relatively sound and independent advice to customers on their affairs and investments. The emphasis was on building long-term relationships, trust and integrity. The situation has changed. Bank customers are now bombarded with sales pitches for insurance and other financial products, their 'personal banking officers' change every six months, such advice as they get is far from impartial, charges (until very recently) are imposed without notice, and they are generally treated in an adversarial manner. Minimise the business that you do with them and don't inform them of your affairs unless it is absolutely necessary.

Interest rates

Interest rates vary, as most of us know, and the variations are caused by a number of factors:

- *Supply and demand.* If the public is saving a lot by depositing money in banks, the banks will have more to lend. Since they are in competition with one another, the interest rate they demand will tend to drop to attract borrowers. The amount that the government borrows or lends has a similar effect on the total supply of money available.

- *Risk.* Borrowers who are regarded as good risks can generally borrow money at a lower rate of interest than a 'bad risk' borrower.

- *Inflation.* As money becomes worth less through inflation, so lenders ask for higher interest rates to compensate. You can compare rates by subtracting the inflation component from the interest rates, but since the rate of inflation can only ever be an estimate, the figures will never be exact.

These factors affect all lenders and borrowers however large the sum involved. In addition, rates vary according to your own position in the marketplace. Banks set a 'base rate' which represents the minimum interest it is prepared to charge to the majority of its consumer and commercial customers. The base rate is set higher than LIBOR, the London Inter-Bank Offered Rate (see page 110), which is what banks charge each other for loans. Most consumers borrow from their banks at rates much higher than the base rate.

In the longer term, the interest rates in any particular country are affected by the exchange rate of its currency against the currencies of other countries, and by interest rates in the world's biggest economies. UK interest rates tend to follow US rates quite closely.

Banks are not lily-white – BCCI and others

Where there is money, there is fraud, and the banking community has its fair share of villains. What many people do not realise is that banks are, by their nature, involved in the grey world that lies between politics and commerce.

When Iraq invaded Kuwait its forces seized a vast amount of **EXAMPLE ✳**
Kuwaiti dinars held in cash by Kuwaiti banks. After the liberation of
Kuwait, its government changed the currency in order to prevent the looted currency being spent; anyone holding the old currency legitimately could apply to change it for the new money. To my personal knowledge, at least one London branch of a foreign-owned bank assisted in the changing of old money captured by Iraqis, using Kuwaiti middlemen as a cover. Was a crime committed? Presumably some Kuwaiti laws were broken, though, perhaps, British ones weren't.

This kind of thing goes on all the time, but is very rarely reported.

The collapse of BCCI, the Bank of Credit and Commerce International, brought to light examples of fraud and of what might be called 'political crime'.

✳ EXAMPLE BCCI had knowingly operated accounts for terrorist organisations, laundered drug money on a large scale and also, it was claimed, had assisted the CIA, Britain's secret services, and those of several Islamic countries in covert operations. It has even been suggested that civil servants in the regulatory bodies were actually afraid to do anything about BCCI because of its intelligence connections. The bank was started in the late 1960s by Pakistani bankers using oil money from the Gulf. Its operational headquarters were in London, though it was legally based in Luxembourg and the Cayman Islands, and it had branches all over the world. In the early 1970s it opened more than 40 retail branches in the UK, mainly serving customers who had recently immigrated to Britain. By the late 1970s, the Bank of America, which had increased its shareholding in BCCI from 25 per cent to almost 50 per cent in 1973, was eager to sell out, which it managed to do in 1980.

In 1979, the Banking Act in the UK tightened the rules on what kind of bodies could call themselves banks, and BCCI found itself awarded the lowly status of 'licenced deposit taker'. Because it had overseas branches, it could still use the word 'bank' in its name, but it had to display a sign reading 'licenced deposit taker' at its branches to tell customers that it was not as safe as a bank. In fact, ill-informed customers were told that this meant that BCCI was a more stable and important bank than the others with high street branches. Major losses followed, and BCCI began to pay out old depositors with the new ones' money.

In 1985 the Bank of England forced BCCI to move its money market operations to Abu Dhabi, and soon afterwards the authorities in Luxembourg asked the Bank of England to take over the supervision of the bank, which it refused to do. In 1987 a compromise was reached in which the central banks of several countries, including the Bank of England, formed a 'College of Regulators' to supervise BCCI. The following year several senior BCCI employees were arrested for drug money laundering in Florida. While banks acted to reduce their exposure to BCCI, customers kept on coming, in the touching belief that an international bank of its size (it had assets of $20 billion) would be properly controlled by the governments in whose countries it operated.

In 1991 the Bank of England finally made its move, leading some 69 regulators across the world in closing down BCCI. Unhappy customers mobbed its branches and a succession of court cases followed. The chief Sheikh of Abu Dhabi, as the majority shareholder of the bank, has promised to give compensation, but the row trundles on. Perhaps the whole story of what happened, and why the regulatory authorities took so long to act, will never emerge.

HOW BANKS LEND TO INDIVIDUALS

Most people don't really understand how banks think, which leads to a lot of public resentment. The first thing to appreciate is that in the UK, as well as in most other developed countries, banks are heavily regulated by the government.

The kind of borrowing we are considering at the moment is called the 'consumer loan'. The key word is 'consumer'. Banks behave very different-ly towards consumers than they do towards com-mercial customers. By law, and inclination, banks 'baby' consumers. If you want a loan, the banker will want to know several things:

> **By law, and inclination, banks 'baby' consumers.**

- How much?
- What for?
- How long for?
- What is the repayment schedule?

In asking how much you want to borrow, the banker really wants to know how much you have got. If, say, you have a house worth £100,000, no mortgage and no other debts, banks will be happy to lend you a smallish proportion of your £100,000 net worth without too much difficulty. If you have no money at all, the bank will be much less happy with a request for an overdraft. This is obvious once you understand it, but many peo-ple don't; they think that banks are being unfair, and are discriminating against people with no money.

> **In asking what the money is for, the bank wants to be sure that the amount borrowed will actually be enough to cover the proposed expenditure.**

In asking what the money is for, the bank wants to be sure that the amount borrowed will actually be enough to cover the proposed expendi-ture. No banker wants you to come back later and ask for more because you didn't get enough the first time.

The length of the loan is important for accounting reasons – the bank wants to control the proportions of money it lends for different periods.

The repayment schedule may come as more of a surprise; surely, you think, it doesn't make any difference to the bank how the money is repaid as long as it gets it back with interest at the end of the loan term. It does matter, though, because the banker looks upon you as a unit capable of producing a stream of future earnings (your wages). The banker wants to take regular sums out of your wages towards the repayment of the loan –

he or she may suspect, perhaps rightly, that you hope to find a lump sum for repayment by borrowing elsewhere, which may not be as easy as you think.

Security

The next think the banker thinks about is security for the loan. This is not because the bank wants to sell your property in order to recover the money lent (this is considered bad for business, particularly where consumers are concerned), but because he wants to be able to do so if he has to. Bonds and shares are acceptable as security since they are easy to value and to transfer from one owner to another. Shares in unquoted companies are generally unacceptable because they will be difficult to sell. Bankers keep a close eye on the market price of shares that they hold as security to make sure that their value still covers the loan.

Banks are stickier about life policies. They want to read all the fine print to make sure that the insurance company isn't going to wriggle out of paying. Nevertheless, whole life and endowment policies are generally acceptable.

Houses and land are also often used as security, usually by the banks taking a charge on the equity in the property. UK banks hate to repossess – it makes them look very bad when they throw people out on the street – which is worth bearing in mind if you ever have to negotiate an extension of the repayment schedule.

For guerrilla borrowers – don't be a nice guy

✳ EXAMPLE Suppose there are two entrepreneures, Sally and Jane. They both borrow from banks to acquire investment property, using the buildings as security. Sally has £500,000's worth of property and bank loans of £400,000. Jane was advised that she should keep her gearing low, so she owns £140,000's worth of property and owes banks £70,000. In both cases, income from rents service the loans. Suddenly the property market crashes by 50 per cent and rents drop too. Sally's properties are now worth only £250,000, but she still owes £400,000, while Jane's properties are worth £70,000, which is what she owes. Neither of them can service their loans fully, so they go to their bank to ask for a change in the terms of the loan.

Guess what? Sally gets terms she can live with, and stays in business, but the bank re-possesses Jane's property, giving her a bad credit record. After a few years property values creep up again and Sally is back in profit. Jane was wiped out and stays out of the business. This happens because the bank doesn't want to make a loss of £150,000 by re-possessing Sally's properties, so, believing that she is a competent businesswoman and that the market will bounce back, it gives her a chance to keep going. The bank may believe that Jane is equally competent, but it doesn't have to give her a chance because it can get all its money back right away.

The moral of the story is not to be nice to banks. Work out your own defensive strategies in case everything goes wrong, and be tough – you can be sure that banks won't listen to reason if they have you over a barrel, so make sure that you hold the aces!

Banking and Big Brother

In recent years a disturbing pattern has emerged of increasing state interference with banking privacy. Like most modern tyrannies masquerading as a moral crusade, this started in the United States, a country where ordinary people are prosecuted under anti-racketeering laws and innocent individuals have their property seized in the 'war on drugs'. Many so-called democratic countries are following suit. This catch-all legislation is being used by tax authorities to conduct 'fishing expeditions' in search of possible wrong-doers. Almost every financial organisation must report 'unusual' transactions, the registry of safe-deposit boxes and so on. The justification is that if you have done nothing wrong, then you have nothing to hide, but in a world where government departments exceed their briefs, break the law, and deceive and pressurise the innocent, this argument plainly does not hold water. Chapter 12 on overseas investing suggests a strategy for countering this trend, but realistically you need a net worth of £200,000 or more before it can be effective. Until then, you must just grin and bear it!

The future for banking

With the advent of information technology, the speed of clerical processing, and of communications, is increasing rapidly. Soon, we are told, a truly global marketplace will be possible, with individuals and companies holding 'wealth accounts' in databanks which are debited and credited automatically.

Transaction costs should drop, and derivatives (see Chapter 8) will increase in variety and sophistication as any credit risk can be bundled with any other and traded by banks.

Many organisations have large sums of cash which they want to lend for a very short time (as short as overnight) and still earn interest.

6

The money markets

In this chapter we will look at:

- Bills of exchange.
- Certificates of deposit.
- The discount market.
- The local authority market.
- The inter-bank market.
- The finance house, inter-company and commercial paper markets.
- The certificate of deposit market.
- The Euromarkets – Eurodeposits and Eurobonds.
- Interest rate and currency swaps.

The money markets are not places but simply the name for the 'whole-sale' trade in large sums of money that are lent and borrowed for short periods of time. It is important to understand something about them, but only investors with large amounts of cash can participate in them directly. In order to understand how these markets work we should first examine two financial instruments which are used to move money around – 'bills of exchange' and 'certificates of deposit'.

BILLS OF EXCHANGE

There is one kind of bill of exchange which is familiar to all of us – the cheque – but there are others too. In essence, they are written IOUs promising payment at a future date. Bills of exchange are negotiable, so the recipient can sell it on to someone else who can claim payment on the due date. The issuer of the bill of exchange either promises to pay the bill himself, noting this on the bill, or addresses it to a bank, which will provide the money. The origins of these bills were in the eighteenth century when businesses frequently settled debts with one another by the use of bills, usually dated for payment in three months' time. If the recipient wanted to be paid sooner, he could present it to a bill broker, who would pay the face value of the bill less a certain percentage and then re-sell the bill to a bank that wanted to invest money for a short period. The brokers began to hold bills themselves and developed into the 'discount houses' which are discussed below.

When a bill is issued, it has to be sent to the bank on which the money is to be drawn for 'acceptance'. This means that the bank signs the bill and agrees to pay the money on the due date. The law says that anyone signing a bill can be sued if it is not paid, so the safety of a bill of exchange depends upon who has 'accepted' it. For this reason certain banks, called 'accepting houses', specialise in accepting bills, and such bills are generally recognised as secure instruments.

CERTIFICATES OF DEPOSIT

Certificates of deposit, or CDs, are issued by banks and other financial organisations as evidence that a deposit has been made with them for a fixed period of time at a fixed interest rate. Like bills of exchange, they are negotiable, so a company can deposit money, receiving a CD in return, which they can sell to another party. The life of a CD varies between three months and five years. If they are issued for less than a year, the interest is paid on the expiry of the CD, and if they are for more than a year the interest is paid annually. CDs are popular with organisations with large amounts of money to be invested for short periods because they give flexibility. If you simply make a fixed-term deposit, you cannot get your money out before the end of the term, but with a CD you can sell at any time. For CDs denominated in sterling, the smallest sum of money you can deposit is £50,000.

THE DISCOUNT MARKET

Many organisations have large sums of cash which they want to lend for a very short time (as short as overnight), but still earn interest. The discount houses and discount brokers, members of the London Discount Market Association (LDMA), are the middlemen between borrowers and lenders. The main instruments that they deal in are bills of exchange, certificates of deposits, gilts and bonds. One of the most important of these are Treasury bills, which are issued every week by the British government and have a life of 91 days. They don't carry interest, but are instead issued and traded at a discount to their face value. The discount houses have a deal with the government to buy all the Treasury bills it issues and in return the Bank of England agrees to act as the lender of last resort to the discount houses. Other bills of exchange fall into two categories: 'eligible' and 'non-eligible' bills. These are a measure of how sure one can be that the bill will be paid, as the Bank of England will only take eligible bills as security for loans. Eligible bills are ones which have been 'accepted' by big banks in good standing, while non-eligible bills have been accepted by smaller banks. Bills are used by large businesses that borrow money from banks and financial institutions, issuing a bill in return which promises to repay the money. The rate of interest is usually better than they can get elsewhere.

> **CDs** are popular with organisations with large amounts of money to be invested for short periods because they give flexibility.

Gilts with a maturity date within five years are also held by discount houses, as are bonds and bills issued by local authorities in the UK, and certificates of deposit issued by banks.

Discount houses are institutions which are unique to Britain, and exist for historical reasons. Their relationship with the Bank of England enables the government to tinker with the money supply by varying the amount of Treasury bills that are issued each week; the discount of the Treasury bills are a good predictor of short-term interest rates generally available in the UK. If the discount houses cannot borrow money elsewhere, they can borrow from the Bank of England, which will set a rate higher than those prevailing in the market and take Treasury bills and eligible bills from the discount houses as security. This mechanism ensures that the discount houses only borrow from the Bank of England as a last resort and, when they do, it has the effect of driving up the

> ....**An important difference between the discount market and the parallel markets is that the parallel markets have no lender of last resort, and so are less stable**.............

market interest rates. If the Bank of England wants to lower the rates of interest in the market, it buys Treasury bills from the discount houses, thus releasing more money into the system and causing the cost of money (interest rates) to become cheaper.

Surrounding the discount market interface between government and banking are all the other banks and financial institutions, all eager to borrow and lend large sums for short periods. This is done in various ways which are collectively described as the 'parallel money markets', meaning that they work in parallel to the discount market and one another. An important difference between the discount market and the parallel markets is that the parallel markets have no lender of last resort, and so are less stable, although they are supervised by the Bank of England. Deals are done either directly between the banks and other organisations in the market, or through money brokers who act as middlemen.

THE LOCAL AUTHORITY MARKET

It is cheaper for a local authority to borrow through the government than directly from the markets but, because of financial restrictions that the government places on them, local authorities are often driven to borrow money elsewhere. Generally they borrow for two or seven days, but they can borrow for three months or more in amounts of £25,000 upwards. Lenders include big companies as well as banks and other financial institutions.

THE INTER-BANK MARKET

This market grew up as banks started to lend to each other instead of through the discount market. Most of the money is lent overnight, but loan periods can be for up to five years. The interest rates fluctuate according to supply and demand; the going market rate at any particular time is called the London Inter-Bank Offered Rate (LIBOR). The amounts lent are always over £250,000 and no security is asked for – the banks rely on one another's good faith and ability to repay. The LIBOR rate is usually the cheapest short-term rate to be had outside the discount market, and thus other rates are linked to it.

THE FINANCE HOUSE, INTER-COMPANY AND COMMERCIAL PAPER MARKETS

Finance houses, that provide money for hire-purchase and leasing, borrow their funds from banks, usually via the inter-bank market. Large companies sometimes lend directly to one another, cutting out the banks – the sums involved start at £50,000, and are lent through money brokers. Security is required, usually taking the form of a bank guarantee, and the sums are lent from between three months and five years.

A newer option for larger companies is to use the commercial paper market, in which they exchange promissory notes ('paper') for money. The minimum amount borrowed is £500,000. The paper is owned by the bearer and is sold at a discount in the same way as Treasury bills.

THE CERTIFICATE OF DEPOSIT MARKET

We saw earlier that certificates of deposit (CDs) are issued by banks and other financial organisations and that they are negotiable bearer securities. Companies, and even individuals, can invest in CDs which are more flexible than a fixed-term deposit because they can be sold in the market if required.

All the parallel markets are inter-linked and a transaction in one market leads to more transactions in the others. The liquidity of the money markets allows large sums to flow freely around the system to wherever they are needed without delay. The money that is borrowed and lent by ordinary people ultimately goes through the money markets, but in between are the retail banks, insurance companies and building societies.

The building societies began as non-profit-making societies set up to help people of modest means borrow to buy a home. Originally, all the

money that was lent by a building society came
from the people who saved with it, but more
recently they became able to borrow on the money
markets. There is tax relief on the first £30,000 of a
mortgage, so building society finance is cheap.

> **An important feature
> is that Eurobonds are
> issued in
> 'bearer form'.**

They are becoming more and more like banks, offering an ever-widening
range of services to the consumer. A series of mergers are in train and
banks are also expected to attempt takeovers of building societies. Since
some types of depositor are members of the building society (the equivalent of shareholders) they should receive a windfall upon a successful
takeover, so it could be worth depositing a few hundred in ten or fifteen
building societies in the hope of getting several pay offs.

THE EUROMARKETS

For historical reasons large amounts of the major currencies are held outside the jurisdiction of their home country. The prefix 'Euro' does not
mean that they are all European currencies, nor that they are held in
Europe.

The Eurodeposit market

Companies and private individuals are able to hold foreign Eurocurren-
cies on deposit in British banks, each currency earning interest at a rate
related to those prevailing in its home country. Originally looked down
upon by traditionalists, the relaxation of exchange controls has caused
this market to mushroom, and it has become so respectable that even
countries borrow in the market.

The Eurobond market

Despite its name, the market for Eurobonds is truly international; both
issuers of the bonds and investors can come from any country, and while
most of the banks involved in the market base their Eurobond offices in
London, they, too, are from all over the world. Some $7 billions' worth of
Eurobonds are traded every day over the telephone across the world.
Eurobonds can be denominated in any currency and are usually issued
outside the country of the borrower (issuer). An important feature is that
they are issued in 'bearer form'. This means that whoever is holding the

bond owns it, giving a great degree of discretion and anonymity to the investor. If Eurobonds ever lose their bearer status, the market is likely to shrink dramatically.

How Eurobonds started

After World War 2, the United States poured dollars into Europe to assist reconstruction. These dollars came to be known as 'Eurodollars'. In the 1960s, US legislation made it increasingly difficult for American lenders to provide dollars for foreign borrowers. The Eurodollar pool of capital, which was outside US control, then became the obvious place to go to borrow dollars. Banks in London jumped at the chance of earning fees and had a more sophisticated infrastructure than elsewhere in Europe at the time. Thus, London became the focus of the Eurobond market. The market has now grown to include all currencies, not just dollars. Eurobonds can even be denominated in ECUs, the EC's currency unit based on its member countries' currencies.

The Eurobond market really came into its own in the late 1960s, with the introduction of a clearing system. In fact, there are two: Euroclear in Belgium and Cedel in Luxembourg. Euroclear is the bigger system, having an annual turnover of trillions of dollars' worth of bonds and holding hundreds of billions of dollars' worth of bonds for their owners.

Who issues Eurobonds?

Banks, large companies, governments, quasi-governmental bodies and organisations such as the EC (European Community) all issue Eurobonds. Banks are the most active issuers.

Who invests in Eurobonds?

Banks, insurance companies, pension funds, government organisations and large companies all invest in Eurobonds, as can private investors. Unsurprisingly, most investment is done by institutions.

Interest and the credit rating of Eurobonds

Interest is paid gross, with no withholding tax deducted. Common maturity dates are five, seven, ten and twelve years. Like other bonds, most Eurobonds are rated by Moody's and Standard and Poor's, the best quality being rated as 'triple A' (see page 61). Curiously, corporate bond issuers with household names are often more popular with investors, and can thus offer a lower rate of interest than obscure companies with higher credit ratings.

Fixed-rate bonds

This is the most common kind of Eurobond, having a final maturity date and paying a fixed rate of interest. As with other kinds of bonds (see Chapter 3), if interest rates elsewhere rise above the fixed rate of the bond at some time during its life, the re-sale value of the bond goes down, and if rates fall, the bond's value will rise.

Floating-rate bonds

This variety ties the rate of interest to LIBOR (see page 110) or some other short-term interest rate by means of a stated formula.

Convertible bonds

An investor can exchange a convertible bond for shares in the issuing company at a predetermined price.

Interest rate and currency swaps

As with other bonds, it is possible for two Eurobond issuers to 'swap' (exchange) interest rates on their bonds, or even to swap the principal from one currency to another. The exchange is usually between a fixed-rate bond and a floating-rate bond, and gives both issuers an 'arbitrage' benefit (see page 166). Local authorities in the UK got into this in a big way in the 1980s and some began to speculate wildly on interest rates. Hammersmith and Fulham were the worst culprits with Hammersmith swapping interest on some £7 billion which it didn't have. When interest rates doubled it was in serious trouble, but after courts ruled that local authorities were not allowed to make swaps and that the deals were invalid, the financial institutions who had dealt with Hammersmith had to take the losses.

As yet, there is no complete, all-encompassing model to explain how all the mechanisms of the market intermesh, but this does not mean we have to resort to superstition, since there is sound evidence that certain strategies will produce a good return over the long term.

7

Investment theories

Some people have very odd ideas about how the stock market works and still make money from their investments, while others have beautifully rational theories but lose money. The reason for this is the extraordinary complexity of the markets. As yet there is no complete, all-encompassing model to explain how all the mechanisms of the market intermesh, but this does not mean that we must resort to superstition, since there is sound evidence that certain strategies will produce a good return over the long term. Millions are spent on predicting stock movements, yet as soon as a method seems to be working the market seems to adjust itself back to unpredictability. In this chapter, we look at the methods used by professionals:

- Probability, and why some people are just lucky.

- The Kondratiev wave, an unproven economic cycle lasting 60 years or so.

- Technical analysis, or 'chartism', for the fortune-tellers of the stock market.

- Fundamental analysis, the science of evaluating companies, and why it tends to cancel itself out.

- The efficient market theory, which explains why most strategies don't work for long, and why 'buy and hold' does.

- Risk.

- MPT (modern portfolio theory), which describes the virtues of diversification.

- CAPM (capital-asset pricing theory), which gives a measurement of risk, called 'beta', and APT (arbitrage pricing theory).

- GARCH, chaos theory and computer models, which are newer ways of trying to predict price movements.

INTRODUCTION

Mathematically speaking, the stock market is, as yet, full of unsolved problems. Many attempts have been made to describe and predict the market, but none have been completely successful. In this chapter we will review some of these theories and examine ways in which they are unsatisfactory. Much of the mathematics is too complicated to be dealt with in this book, but we will be able to cover some of the basic calculations.

Before we look at some of the techniques and theories used by market players, it's worth considering two general points: first, even in a completely random stock market there will be some winners; second, it is always possible for the unscrupulous to look as though they are winners.

WINNERS

We all hear the stories and meet the people – they can't do anything wrong, they always make money, they have the Midas touch. Naturally, we want to know what they've got that we don't. How is it that they have become 'winners'? We should be aware that it may simply be a function of probability; in any race, someone has to 'win'.

Suppose you eat out regularly with a colleague for many years, and always flip a coin at the end of the meal to see who will pay. After you've done it thousands of times, one of you is going to be seriously out of pocket, despite the fact that overall, the ratio of heads to tails gets closer and closer to 1:1 the more often you do it. This is because the monetary value of the difference between your wins and your colleague's wins is likely to be greater the more you play, even if the difference itself is getting smaller as a proportion of the total cost of all the meals. In addition, the person who gets ahead is quite likely to stay ahead for a very long time – it might take a lifetime for the lead to swap to the other per-

> In the stock market, there may be individuals who are highly successful simply because of random events – no special significance should be attached to their success.

son. Thus, if you've played the game for ten years, the winner at the end is quite likely to have been ahead 90 per cent of the time – is this person a 'winner' who has special knowledge, or a magic touch? Obviously not. The winner is simply benefiting from chance. In the stock market, there may be individuals who are highly successful simply because of random events – no special significance should be attached to their success.

A simple confidence trick

✳ EXAMPLE The following example illustrates an illegal confidence trick that illustrates the need for scepticism in following the advice of a successful predictor. Suppose you are an investment adviser and you write to 100,000 investors predicting the change in the value of a stock index. You tell 50,000 investors that the value will rise in a month, and the other 50,000 that it will fall. A month later, you write to the 50,000 who received the correct prediction, making a further prediction, again telling 25,000 the value will rise and the other 25,000 that it will fall. In the third month you have 25,000 people to whom you have made two correct predictions. Apply the same technique three more times, and you will have 3,250 people to whom you have given five correct predictions. Now you write to them asking for money, say £800, to continue sending them your information which has 'proven' its value. If half of them pay up, you've just made £1,300,000. Naturally, you will have supported your predictions with spurious claims about the techniques and theories you have employed. It is now time to disappear with the loot before you are caught.

Let's examine some of the techniques that are really used by stock market professionals. The rationale behind some of them contradicts that behind others, and one or two seem quite unreasonable, but they have all been used to invest large sums in the markets.

THE KONDRATIEV WAVE

Also known as the 'long wave', this is, on the face of it, an implausible idea – that there are recurring cycles of boom and slump in the world economy. It has also been an unpopular idea, because it is so directly opposed to the grand vision of an ever-growing world economy upon which so much policy has been based.

The long wave is said to take between 45 and 60 years to go from peak to peak. The post-war economic boom from 1948 to 1973 is considered to be the 'upswing' of a wave that was going down during the depression of the 1930s. We are now considered to be in a 'downswing' due to last until around the end of the century.

> **The existence of the long wave has not been proved.**

The existence of the long wave has not been proved. It is difficult to prove that any economic cycle exists without showing that it has repeated itself many times. If you go back four long waves (say 200 years) from the present, you get to the beginning of the Industrial Revolution, which is arguably the starting point of modern economies, and four waves is a small sample. Another difficulty is the lack of trustworthy data before about 1870. Figure 7.1 shows one interpretation of the figures for world economic growth since the mid nineteenth century.

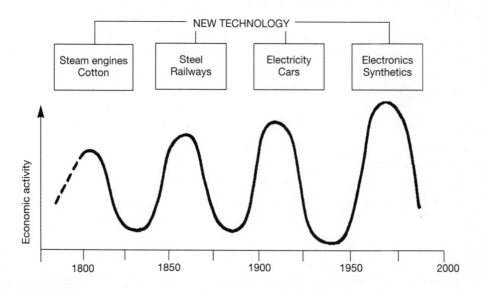

Figure 7.1 **The Kondriatev Wave**

Kondratiev was a Russian economist who gave his name to this cycle: Western economists became interested in his work after he successfully predicted the depression of the 1930s and the subsequent boom. His ideas cost him his life – he died in a Stalinist labour camp in the late 1920s.

More than one explanation has been offered for how the long wave might work. Briefly, Kondratiev himself thought that during the upswing industrial economies expanded as fast as they could until the primary producing countries were unable to keep up with the demand for raw materials. The downswing then began, driving capital and labour abroad to 'new' countries (e.g. Australia and America), and stimulating inventions and discoveries which would be exploited in the next upswing as the 'new' countries increased their supply of raw materials.

Whether or not you choose to believe the predictions made by adherents of the long wave theory, it is a useful counterbalance to the 'short termism' inherent in so much business activity.

'Short termism' is what most trading in the stock market is all about, since many investors want to make money quickly. We will now look at the well-known, though controversial, method known as 'technical analysis', which promises a way to beat the market in the short term.

TECHNICAL ANALYSIS

Technical analysts, some of whom are called 'chartists', try to predict future stock trends by analysing past movements. The purists don't ever look at any other information, such as political events or industrial data; they concentrate on studying the changes in stock values alone, believing that it is unnecessary to know why the changes have occurred.

Technical analysis makes three main assumptions:

1. That patterns identified in charts of stock movements recur.
2. That stock price changes move in trends, and are predictable.
3. That all the factors that influence stock prices are immediately reflected in the price, and so do not need to be considered separately.

Patterns in charts

Figure 7.2 shows an example of one of the best-known patterns used by technical analysts, called the 'head and shoulders reversal pattern'. Points 'A' and 'E' are called the 'left and right shoulders', respectively, points 'B' and 'D' the 'neckline', and point 'C' is called the 'head'. The idea is that if you see a head and shoulders pattern forming, prices have reached a ' top' and will start declining.

Figure 7.3 shows a 'flag'; this is supposed to be a reliable sign that an upward price trend will continue.

There are many other patterns recognised by technical analysts, and each analyst seems to have his own particular favourites. Many technical analysts believe that it is the psychology of investors *en masse* that are the cause of these patterns.

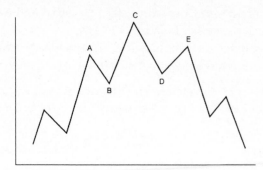

Figure 7.2 The 'head and shoulders reversal pattern'

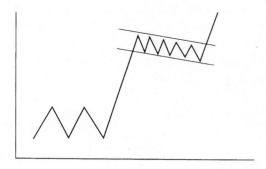

Figure 7.3 A 'flag'

The Dow Theory

Charles Dow published the first stock market average in 1884 and was the father of technical analysis. His theory is based on the following principles:

1. There are three kinds of trends in the market, primary, secondary and minor. To explain them, Dow used the simile of the movements of the sea: a primary trend is like the tide, a secondary trend is like the waves in the tide; and a minor trend is like the ripples on the waves.

2. There are three phases to major trends. Dow said that there is an 'accumulation phase', when the smart money spots the right moment to buy, a second phase when the technical analysts jump on the bandwagon and a final 'distributive' phase when the public starts buying as the news gets out, and the smart money starts selling, or 'distributing'.

3. All the averages – in Dow's time, the Industrial and Rail averages – must confirm each other for a trend to exist.

4. A trend continues until signals (the patterns that technical analysts think are important) appear in the charts that it has reversed.

There are lots of other versions and theories of technical analysis. These days, the 'Elliot Wave' is more often used than the Dow Theory.

The Elliot Wave

The Elliot Wave theory was invented by an American accountant named Ralph Elliot who, like all good technical analysts, believed that you could spot recurring patterns in the stock market. Figure 7.4 shows a simplified Elliot Wave.

The idea is that the stock market has a 'supercycle', as depicted in Figure 7.4, which is rather like the Kondratiev Wave. There are two and a half cycles on the way up, followed by one and a half on the way down. The same pattern is supposed to exist in smaller portions of time, such as annually, monthly and even daily.

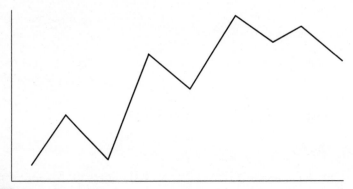

Figure 7.4   The Elliot Wave

Should private investors avoid technical analysis?

Private investors must use brokers to buy and sell, and brokers take a commission for each transaction. Technical analysis encourages trading – you are supposed to respond to the 'buy' and 'sell' signals indicated in the charts in order to make your money. This means that your brokerage charges are going to be far higher than those of a long-term investor who holds on to stocks for years, so the system must do better than simply holding what you have bought in order to cover the trading costs. A private investor would do well to reflect on the fact that it is in a broker's interest to have clients trade frequently, and that a client who believes in technical analysis is going to make the broker more money in commissions than one who rarely buys and sells.

> ....Technical analysis encourages trading – you are supposed to respond to the 'buy' and 'sell' signals indicated in the charts in order to make your money. ....

When brokers themselves persuade clients to switch investments unnecessarily in order to earn fees, it is known as 'churning' – and is certainly not confined to followers of technical analysis.

Does technical analysis work?

Batteries of mathematical tests on a century of stock prices in London and New York seem to have shown that such correlations as exist between past and future prices are too small to beat trading costs. Essentially, there is no evidence to support the idea that trends in stock movements are other than random, except for an overall trend of growth across the entire market. Randomly selecting stocks and holding them produce results which are just as good, if not better. Flipping a coin many times will produce long runs of just heads or just tails, and when plotted on a chart will produce patterns of the kind that technical analysts like. However, we know from probability theory that each flip of the coin is independent of the previous flips, and that long runs are simply chance, not trends.

> .... When brokers themselves persuade clients to switch investments unnecessarily in order to earn fees, it is known as 'churning' .....

Nevertheless, large banks and other financial institutions continue to pay large salaries to technical analysts, some of whom presumably do make good predictions. The point about this phenomenon is that, from a mathematical point of view, success does not in itself prove anything. A Cambridge mathematics professor says, 'There are traders who may be successful due to intuition and specialised knowledge who honestly ascribe their success to a baseless technique'. In other words, it is very human to try to explain good results, but the explanation may simply be wrong.

Alternatively, it may be that if there are enough technical analysts engaged in advisory positions, they somehow unintentionally combine together to produce a self-fulfilling prophecy. Things can't be quite as simple as this, however. There is another group of analysts, the 'counter-cyclical analysts' who believe that the best strategy is to do exactly the opposite of what technical analysts and others are recommending. This view is called 'contrarian'.

So, if we don't believe in technical analysis, is there any other way to make money from the market in the short term? The theory of fundamental analysis says that there is.

FUNDAMENTAL ANALYSIS

Fundamental analysts attempt to predict future prices by finding out what a stock is really worth – its intrinsic value – which may have little to do with its current quoted price. First, the prospects for the industry as a whole are examined, and then the records, plans and management of individual companies within the industry are subjected to a thorough scrutiny. An estimate of the company's future earnings is then made, incorporating estimates of future sales, overheads, accounting policies and a host of other factors that might affect profit. Broadly speaking, stock market professionals tend to have a lot more faith in fundamental analysis than technical analysis, because it is dealing with the nuts and bolts of real companies. Professional fundamental analysts, so the argument goes, will achieve better returns than the small investor because they are better informed.

> Broadly speaking, stock market professionals tend to have a lot more faith in fundamental analysis

Price/earnings ratios

Having estimated what a particular company will earn in the future, the analyst then looks at its current share price and calculates the ratio of price to earnings. In fact, if you look at the stock market pages of the *Financial Times*, you will find that the p/e (price/earnings) ratio is listed for you. If the p/e is 6, it means that the price of the share is six times the share's proportion of the annual profit stated in the most recently published accounts of the company. Thus:

p/e ratio = price per share ÷ earnings per share

so if the earnings per share is 9p and the share price is 180, the p/e ratio is

$$p/e \text{ ratio} = 180 \div 9 = 20$$

Notice that this is equivalent to the earnings being 5 per cent of the share price.

A big, well-established company may have a fairly low p/e ratio, say 10, because it is thought that its prospects for growth are low, while a small company in a high technology industry may have a very high p/e, say 40 or more, because it is thought likely that its earnings will sky-rocket in a few years' time. P/e ratios are also affected by factors such as recessions, when they tend to go up in anticipation that a recovery will increase future earnings.

What the fundamental analysts do is to decide whether the current p/e ratio is right, based on their own detailed examinations of the company. They are comparing the p/e ratio with their own estimate of what the p/e ratio should be.

Interest rates

When interest rates are high, an investor can make a high return by keeping money in safe, stable bonds and other interest-bearing instruments outside the market. Fundamentalists, therefore, compare interest rates with returns from stocks. Low interest rates are seen to make the market more attractive because of their potential for higher returns, so when interest rates are low, the 'intrinsic value' of stocks is thought to be higher.

Does fundamental analysis work?

Fundamentalists believe that past earnings can be a good indicator of future growth; if the management of a company is very good, so the thinking goes, then it will continue to be good in the future. Five years is a long time in the stock market, and most fundamental analysts hope to make good predictions for shorter periods than this.

Many studies have shown, however, that the analysts' predictions show massive errors and are, if anything, worse for short-term predictions than for five-yearly ones. Two reasons why this may be so are randomness and the variety of different accounting methods in use. The effects of random events in the real world, such as natural disasters and political events, can throw out the most sound estimates of a company's future earnings for obvious reasons; as yet there is no way of predicting them. Accounting methods (particularly the so-called 'creative' accounting methods) can distort profits hugely – the special accounting methods for depreciation, land, leasing, insurance and conglomerates, to name but a few, can confuse even the most sharp-eyed analyst.

So, if the theories used by market professionals don't hold water, how does the market really work? In the 1960s, academics developed the idea that there was absolutely no way to beat the market other than by getting information more quickly than anyone else. Since all the highly competitive analysts were getting information at the same time, the market must be 'efficient'.

THE EFFICIENT MARKET THEORY

Whenever there is news affecting a stock, fundamental analysts will react immediately, and the stock price will adjust very fast as they trade. The efficient market theory says that it is precisely because fundamentalists are good at their job that their predictions don't work – the prices of stocks and shares are immediately adjusted as the professionals buy what they think is undervalued and sell what they think is overvalued, leaving the smaller investor as well off by selecting a portfolio by throwing darts at the financial pages as by following the advice of the professionals.

In essence, what the efficient market theory says is that *fundamental analysis is no more helpful at improving investors' returns than if they simply bought shares and held them for a long time.*

But if examining companies in detail in order to value shares has become too efficient for investors to beat the market, is there no other way to value them? Efficient marketeers think that there is, by looking at shares in terms of their risk.

RISK

It has been argued that risk is the only characteristic of a stock that is worth measuring. The idea is that 'blue chip' stocks – the shares of certain vast and stable corporations – are safer, or less volatile, than other stocks, and that it is therefore worth paying more for them. In other words, the price/earnings ratios of blue chip stocks should be higher. Investors endeavour to spread their risk by investing in a number of shares (a portfolio), hoping that while some of the shares may go down, others will go up.

Figure 7.5 shows the relative performance of a representative sample of American mutual funds (called unit trusts in the UK) measured against the Standard and Poor Index of 500 US stocks during a recent 20-year period. Mutual funds invest in a large number of shares in order to spread the risk. In Figure 7.5, the growth funds are those that invest in shares expected to produce above average returns, while the balanced funds look for a safe and steady return by balancing their portfolios between bonds, which give a guaranteed return, and stocks, which do not. The triangle marks the Standard and Poor 500 Index, which is the average of the performance of a sample of 500 shares, and is taken to represent the average of the market overall.

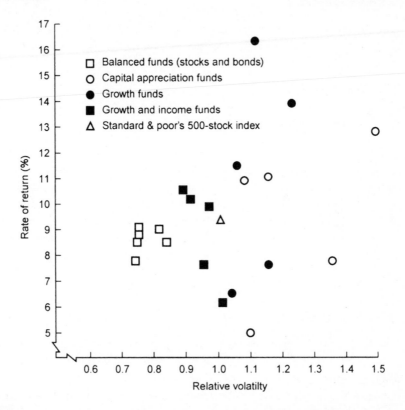

Figure 7.5 **Relative performance of mutual funds over a recent 20-year period**
(Reproduced with permission from *A Random Walk Down Wall Street* by Burton G. Malkiel)

As you can see from the chart, the balanced funds are all grouped together and did slightly worse than the market average. The growth funds, on the other hand, are widely spread – some did very well and some did very badly. This shows that there is something in the idea of risk; an investor who wants to do better than the market average may well be able to do so by investing in riskier shares, but is taking the chance that the shares may do worse than, for example, a balanced fund.

> An investor who is prepared to buy and hold stocks for several decades is likely to do better than one who holds bonds for the same length of time.

There is a vast amount of literature on the performance of unit trusts. From it, one might be led to believe that a particular unit trust has 'got it right', and will perform as well as it has done in the past. Statistical studies tell us that this is not the case, since there is no evidence that the past performance of a unit trust is a guide to the future. So how can you measure risk? One way is to measure the swings of a stock price over a year against the changes in the market overall. A blue chip company does not swing much. If the market goes down by 15 per cent, it may only go down by 7 per cent, and if the market shoots up, it will lag behind.

Risk over the long term

Figure 7.6 shows the results of an American study comparing the performance of stocks with other forms of investment. From the distribution column, we can see that the dispersion of returns for common stocks and small company stocks is far wider than for bonds and US Treasury bills, indicating that stocks are more volatile, or risky. The average annual rate of return has been far higher, however, as we can see from the first column, and has far outpaced inflation, represented by the consumer price index.

Risk and expected return

The evidence in Figure 7.6 tends to confirm the idea that you 'get what you pay for' in terms of risk. Stocks are more risky than bonds but produce a higher rate of return over the long term. An investor who is prepared to buy and hold stocks for several decades is likely to do better than one who holds bonds for the same length of time.

MODERN PORTFOLIO THEORY

Modern portfolio theory, (MPT), assumes that investors want the least possible risk for a given return, and offers a way of investing in a portfolio of shares that is less risky than investing in any of the particular stocks within it.

Selected perf ormance statistics, 1926 – 88

Series	Annual (Geometric mean rate of return)	Number of years returns are positive	Number of years returns are negative	Highest annual return (and year)	Lowest annual return (and year)	Standard deviation of annual returns	Distribution
Common stocks	10.0%	44	19	54.0% (1933)	−43.3% (1931)	20.9	
Small company stocks	12.3	43	20	142.9 (1933)	−49.8 (1931)	35.6	
Long-term corporate bonds	5.0	48	15	43.8 (1982)	−8.1 (1969)	8.4	
US Treasury bills	3.5	62	1	14.7 (1981)	−0.0 (1940)	3.3	
Consumer price index	3.1	53	10	18.2 (1946)	−10.3 (1932)	4.8	

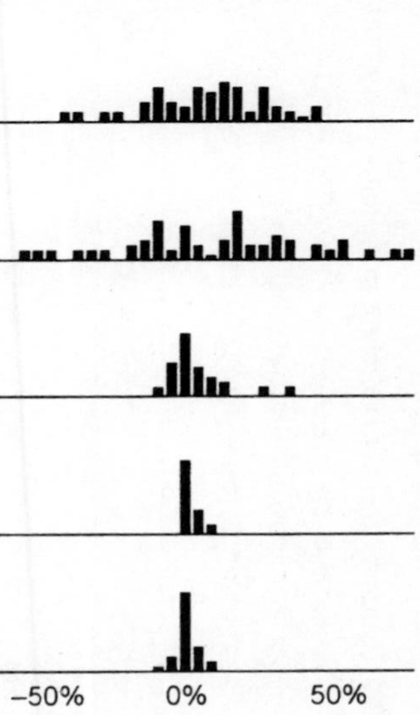

−50%   0%   50%

Figure 7.6   US investment performance comparison 1926–1988

(Reproduced with permission from *A Random Walk Down Wall Street* by Burton G. Malkiel)

Imagine you are investing in a tiny country that has only two industries and two seasons. It has an alpine resort and a beach club.
When the weather is good, the beach club does well, and when the weather is
bad, the alpine resort booms. The returns for the two resorts are:

	Alpine resort	Beach club
Good weather	–30%	60%
Bad weather	60%	–30%

If the probability of a particular season having good or bad weather is one in
two, investing in the alpine resort would produce returns of 60 per cent half the
time, and –30 per cent half the time, giving an average, or expected return, of
15 per cent; the same is true for investing in the beach club. It would be risky,
though, to invest in only one of the resorts because there might be many seasons one after the other with the same weather, just as you might get a long row
of heads when flipping a coin.

If you invested £100 in each of the resorts, your results over five seasons
might be as follows:

Season	Alpine resort	Beach club	
Good	–30	60	
Bad	60	–30	
Bad	60	–30	
Bad	60	–30	
Bad	60	–30	
Total:	210	–60	= 150

You have lost £60 on the beach club, but made £210 on the alpine
resort, giving you an overall return on your £200 investment of £150.

If you had invested all of your £200 in the alpine resort, you would have made
£420. If you had invested the whole £200 in the beach club you would have lost
£120 of your capital, leaving you with only £80 to re-invest – it would take time
to get your money back to its original level, and if you attempted to do so by
investing again in only one of the two resorts, you might well make a further
substantial loss. Thus, the argument for spreading the risk is very strong.

The two resorts have negative covariance. Here is the formula for calculating covariance:

Let A_g and A_B be the actual return from the alpine resort in good and bad weather respectively, and A be the expected return (average), $\overline{B}_g$ and B_B be the actual returns from the beach club and B the expected return:

The covariance between A and B =

COV_{AB} = Probability of good weather $(\overline{A}_g - \overline{A})(B_g - \overline{B})$ + probability of bad weather $(A_B - \overline{A})(B_B - \overline{B})$

In our example, the probability of good or bad weather are both 0.5, so:

$$COV_{AB} = [0.5(-30 - 15)(60 - 15)] + [0.5(60 - 15)(-30 - 15)]$$

$$= 0.5(-45 \times 45) + 0.5(45 \times -45)$$

$$= -0.10125 + -0.10125$$

$$= -0.2025$$

In real life, however, stocks tend to move up and down together, so it is rare to find a perfect opportunity to eliminate risk. It is possible, though, to reduce risk by investing in shares with a low covariance or, better still, a negative covariance. This is called diversification, and can be achieved by investing across a wide number of industries and countries.

THE CAPITAL-ASSET PRICING MODEL (CAPM)

The variability of the stock market as a whole, known as market risk, is different from the variability of individual stocks. Fundamental analysis may discover influences on a particular company that cause it to rise or fall, such as labour problems or a new patent, but all stocks tend to rise and fall with the market overall. The market risk prevents investors from being able to eliminate completely their risk of making a loss by diversifying in companies with negative covariance. In our example of the tiny country, we

> It is possible, though, to reduce risk by investing in shares with a low covariance or, better still, a negative covariance.

could think of the market risk as being the possibility of, say, fewer tourists coming to the country because of economic or political problems elsewhere. Fewer tourists would reduce the profit potential for both resorts, whatever the season.

To compare the movements of a particular share against the market overall, we say that the 'beta' (the Greek letter β) of the market risk is 1. A share with a beta of 3 will swing three times as much as the market does in either direction, and a share with a beta of 1.5 will swing only one and a half times as far. Thus, the higher the beta of a portfolio or individual share, the more risky it is.

Because, as we have seen, diversifying cannot reduce the investor's exposure to market risk, what it can do, however, is bring the risk of a portfolio down to a beta of 1, the same as the market risk beta. This is a refinement of fundamental analysis (see page 124), which can be extended to value stocks in terms of the total risk. CAPM says that it is only the overall market risk that is relevant for valuation of a stock, since the part of the risk that is peculiar to an individual stock, the 'unsystematic risk', can be eliminated by diversification, just as we did in our hypothetical country. As a rule of thumb, CAPM says that a portfolio of as few as twenty diversified stocks should be enough to eliminate almost all of the unsystematic risk.

Giving the overall market risk a beta value of 1, and a 'risk-free' investment, such as a bank deposit, a beta value of 0, CAPM uses the following formula to work out the expected return on a diversified portfolio:

Expected return on a share = 'Risk-free' interest rate + [Beta of the share x (Expected return on the market – 'Risk-free' interest rate)]

The reason for calculating the expected return is that CAPM states that if, in the long term, you want to get a higher rate of return than the market average, all you have to do is to increase the beta value of your portfolio.

✳ EXAMPLE You have £100,000 to invest and you decide to work out the expected return from four choices:

1. A 'risk-free' investment in a bank deposit.
2. An investment of half your money in the stock market and the other half 'risk-free'.
3. Investing the whole sum in a portfolio with a beta in line with that of the market average.
4. Investing in a high risk portfolio.

You find that you can get 5 per cent interest from the bank deposit, and that the market average return is 8 per cent.

Choice 1 – Your expected return is the interest rate the bank gives you, i.e. 5 per cent, or £5,000. Remember that no investment is completely 'risk-free'; in the UK, for example, only 75 per cent of a deposit at a major bank is protected if the bank collapses. Short of a major crisis, however, it is argued that it is reasonable to describe such an investment as 'risk-free', although inflation will eat into the capital and the interest.

Choice 2 – You decide to put £50,000 in a portfolio with a beta of 1, and the rest in a bank. Using the expected return formula, the expected rate of return = 5% + 0.5(8% − 5%) = 6.5%. Note that although the portfolio has a beta of 1, you have only invested 50 per cent of your money, so you must halve the beta value.

Choice 3 – You invest all the money in a portfolio with a beta of 1; your expected rate of return will therefore be in line with the market average, 8 per cent.

Choice 4 – You invest in a portfolio with a beta of 2.5, which should generate higher returns; expected rate of return = 5% + 2.5(8% − 5%) = 12.5%.

Beta is an officially approved way of measuring risk, and you can obtain estimates of the beta of a stock from brokers and investment advisers.

Criticisms of CAPM

A portfolio with a beta of 0 should, according to CAPM, produce the same return as a risk-free investment outside the market which also, by definition, has a beta of 0. Studies have shown, however, that over the long term stock portfolios with a beta of 0 have done better than risk-free investments, contradicting the theory. In addition, in the 1980s mutual funds in the United States produced returns that had no correlation to their beta values. There have been objections to the way that beta values are measured, and it has been shown that betas for individual shares fluctuate significantly over time.

Perhaps the most serious criticism of CAPM, though, is the argument that none of the market indices are a perfect reflection of the overall market risk. In fact, calculating beta using different indices has produced widely differing beta values for stocks. It has been said that you cannot measure the overall market risk accurately; if this is so, then CAPM is untestable, and therefore useless. Many traders do continue to use CAPM, and claim that they have good results and are refining their techniques.

Arbitrage Pricing Theory (APT)

Like CAPM, APT says that it is the overall market risk element of the total risk of a stock that should be measured. To do this, a number of risk factors have been identified to be used in addition to beta. These include inflation rates, interest rates, company size and price/earnings ratios.

...GARCH may work but not all the time. ....

CAPM and APT are perhaps the nearest thing to a mathematically sound analytical approach to the stock market. We should look briefly at two more theories that have been applied recently, and upon which the jury is still out: the GARCH and chaos theories.

THE GARCH THEORY

GARCH, or Generalised Auto-Regressive Conditional Heteroskedasticity (you can see why people prefer to call it GARCH!), predicts that there are trends in volatility – if a stock price has had a large swing on one day, then it will have a large swing on the next. Trends were identified by squaring the returns, which produced an apparent correlation over time. The investment strategy suggested is to purchase options to buy and to sell, thus betting that the stock price would move one way or the other. You would only lose if the stock price remained the same. Other studies, however, have contradicted the GARCH theory – the trends only seem to appear when the market is not very volatile. Thus, GARCH may work but not all the time.

CHAOS THEORY

The chaos theory has been devised to explain the discovery that some apparently complex and random patterns have simple underlying causes, and can be predicted in the short term even though prediction accuracy decreases over time. The spread of disease epidemics and growth patterns of micro-organisms, for example, have been successfully modelled using chaos theory.

Attempts to apply chaos mathematics to the stock market have so far met with only limited success. The idea is to identify periods when the 'Lyapunov time horizon' (the point in the future when a predictable trend disappears) is high, allowing predictions to be made for longer periods than normal. The techniques employ staggeringly large amounts of trading data on computer, and the companies using them are secretive. So far the consensus is that there may be 'pockets of predictability' that chaos theory can predict, but that the market undergoes frequent changes which disrupt the predictions generated by chaos theory.

NEURAL NETWORKS

Computer programs that are able to spot patterns in the data are increasingly being used in market forecasting. These programmes, known as 'neural networks', are a tool in the never-ending trawl of market data in search of relationships and trends. Their popularity has made them affordable – you can now buy neural network software that will run on a personal computer at home.

> The paradox is that the market seems to be protected against the monopoly of one method in the long term by its own nature

Neural networks are simply tools. You still need to use judgement to know when and if to exploit the patterns they throw up. For example, they tend to 'overfit', which means that they often identify patterns that are purely coincidental. It is then up to the operator to weed out such spurious patterns. As computer technology improves, so will the usefulness of neural networks, but the complexity of their operation may keep them in the hands of the biggest traders.

CONCLUSION

Many brokers will tell you that new techniques for predicting the market may work for some time, but as more and more people catch on to them they will become less effective. Most of the theories that we have looked at in this chapter have probably been effective at one time or another in the history of the stock market. The paradox is that the market seems to be protected against the monopoly of one method in the long term by its own nature – if it works, everyone will start doing it, and it will stop working.

Stay out of commodities: the same goes for financial futures unless you are hedging. …
Regularly buying traded options is an expensive gamble – you'll probably end up losing money.

8

Commodities, futures and options – for gamblers only?

In this chapter we will examine 'derivatives' (futures and options), which are financial instruments that are related to the prices of 'real' things such as shares and bonds, and commodities, which are basic standardised products such as oil, tin and wheat. Apart from traded options (examined below), they are no place for the smaller investor, but it is important to have an understanding of how they work since they have a bearing on other financial markets and the world economy generally. Essentially, these markets are systems for the reduction of risk in trade between large companies and institutions, overlaid with a large number of speculators who hope to make profits from price fluctuations. They have a reputation for being highly volatile and dangerous, but this is true only for the speculators. The underlying business is an essential part of the world's economy.

The topics covered in this chapter are:

- Commodities – what they are and how they work.
- Futures – how they developed. The difference between hedgers and speculators.
- Financial futures – how money is treated as a commodity.
- The London International Financial Futures and Options Exchange (LIFFE).
- Chicago and other US futures markets.
- Tokyo futures.
- Far East futures markets.
- The smaller futures markets.
- Options and traded options – what they are and why you should avoid them. Calls, puts, hedging and option writing.

COMMODITIES

Commodities are the basic raw materials that the world needs in order to function – they are the fruits of the earth. They include wheat, coffee, oil, sugar, livestock and precious metals such as gold and platinum. People who are in the business of producing or processing these commodities are performing a vital function for which we should all be grateful. Many of these businesses trade in their commodities on a cash basis; prices fluctuate according to supply and demand, often in seasonal cycles. For instance, the cash price for wheat is lowest at harvest time, when there is plenty of it about. Precious metals have seasonal cycles too – prices usually increase in the autumn as jewellers begin to prepare their products for sale at Christmas and need more raw materials.

....**Commodity prices are unpredictable – all kinds of events can affect prices**....

Commodity prices are unpredictable – all kinds of events can affect prices, including wars, political unrest, strikes, extremes of weather, changes in consumer buying patterns, plagues of insects, plant and animal diseases, and the activities of financial interests who wish to influence the market. This has been the case for hundreds, if not thousands, of years. It makes life difficult for producers and users alike, since it is very hard to run a business if you don't know how much you can buy and sell your goods for. For this reason, a market has grown up in 'commodity futures'.

FUTURES

Buyers and sellers of commodities can make a contract to deliver a product at some time in the future at an agreed price, thus taking the uncertainty out of their operations. They can agree on the amounts, quality and date of delivery, and both parties will put down deposits to protect each other from one side defaulting on the deal. This is known as a 'futures contract'. Futures are a kind of insurance policy, or 'hedge', against the risks of price volatility – businesses can simultaneously trade in futures and in the cash market. In fact, most futures contracts are cancelled before the delivery period.

This is where the speculators come in. It is argued that speculators are a vital part of the futures market, because they provide it with greatly improved liquidity. Speculators aren't interested in using the commodities themselves; they are gambling on the difference between the price of a futures contract and the actual delivery price. Thus the commodities businesses, or 'hedgers', and the speculators behave differently in the market. The hedgers are able to offset, roughly, gains or losses in the cash market by an opposite effect in the futures market, and are thus able to run their businesses more steadily. The speculators have to watch the fluctuations of futures contracts every day, and get out on top when they can.

Commodity swaps

Suppose you are an aluminium company who agrees to protect a customer against a rise in price over a fixed amount. In return, the customer agrees to compensate the company if the price falls below a certain level. This is known as a 'swap', though it is related to options (see page 150). Swaps generally last for two or three years, though some can be for as long as fifteen. Oil is the most actively swapped commodity, and there are even bonds available with redemption values stated in terms of an amount of oil, thus tying themselves to future oil prices.

Buying on margin

Hedgers have never liked to pay the full price for their purchases long before the goods are delivered. Traditionally, when you purchase a futures contract, you only pay a small percentage of its value as a deposit. This is the main attraction for speculators, since it means that you trade futures 'on margin'

✳ EXAMPLE If you buy £200,000's worth of a futures contract, you only have to pay, say, £20,000 as an up-front deposit. If the gamble pays off and the value of the contract goes up to £280,000, you can sell, making a profit of £80,000 on a deposit of £20,000, an increase of 400 per cent rather than the 40 per cent increase you would have made if you had paid out £200,000.

It is the fact that you buy on margin that makes futures risky for the speculators, since the margin means that prices are around ten times more volatile for speculators than they are for the hedgers, who actually trade in commodities themselves and do not use the margin to buy more than they otherwise would. The futures markets have grown massively as more and more speculators have become involved, and this has increased short-term volatility.

FINANCIAL FUTURES

Shares, bonds and currencies can be treated as commodities and futures contracts can be made on them. There is a wide range of financial futures and new ones are being invented all the time. Most futures are tied to important currencies or widely followed indices, such as the FTSE 100, the Standard and Poor's 500, sterling, yen, US Treasury issues, Eurodollars, and so on. They are also tied to interest rates and bonds. Margins on financial futures can be considerably less than the 10 per cent or so required as a deposit on commodity futures, and this increases the risk unless you are using financial futures to hedge against changes to large liquid investments you have elsewhere, in which case you are behaving in the same way that a hedger in the commodities business does.

Suppose you are dealing in futures based on 'long gilts' (e.g. long-term gilts). In this case, the contract size is £50,000. Suppose that **EXAMPLE ✳** the price when you buy is 100–28 (this means 100 28/32). Gilts move in 32nds of 1 per cent; each 32nd is called a 'tick'. The margin you must deposit is £500. If you are certain that gilts are going to go up and you want to buy gilts at a future date when money becomes available, you might buy the futures contract now to hedge against the expected higher cost of the gilts when you have the cash to buy them. If you are wrong, all is not lost, because the lower cost of gilts will roughly balance the loss you make on the futures contract. You can close out a futures contract either by delivering the gilts on the due date or by selling an identical contract. Most people do the latter.

If you are speculating, however, the situation is rather different.

> **✳ EXAMPLE** Suppose the underlying value of your gilts contract dropped by 50 per cent; you would not have lost £250, but £25,000, all on your £500 initial deposit. The rules of the system say that investors' contracts have to be checked daily for losses and profits; if you are losing, you will get a 'margin call' for more money to cover the losses, and you can close out the contract to stop any further losses.

Players in financial futures

Owners of very large share portfolios, such as brokers, unit and investment trust fund managers, pension funds and other institutions, trade in financial futures to hedge against the chance that share prices will fall. Anyone can speculate by taking a buy or sell position on a futures contract, betting that shares will either rise or fall. Futures are either traded on exchanges using the 'open outcry' system, where traders shout at each other over the din of the 'pit' where they trade, communicating using a system of hand signals, or using linked computers. Futures prices generally keep in step with cash prices, but are adjusted to account for interest rate differences. Occasionally futures prices can become much more expensive due to activity in the market; then the arbitrageurs step in to profit from the difference, pulling futures prices back to normality in the process.

> **Futures prices generally keep in step with cash prices, but are adjusted to account for interest rate differences.**

Trading in futures for guerrillas

The majority of players in commodity futures are speculators. Each year, they leave billions of pounds' worth of commissions with the brokers. It's a casino with the odds firmly rigged against the smaller investor. It may seem exciting, but it's not a good investment – almost everyone gets wiped out within a few years. To win as a speculator, you have to possess an enormous amount of knowledge and huge amounts of cash to get any kind of an edge. The only people who really know what is going on are the commodities businesses themselves – so don't expect your broker to have any special expertise. Stay out of commodities. The same goes for financial futures, unless you are hedging.

THE LONDON INTERNATIONAL FINANCIAL FUTURES AND OPTIONS EXCHANGE (LIFFE)

LIFFE (pronounced 'life') is a public limited company owned by its members. Set up in 1982, it provides the facilities for the financial futures and options market in London. There are about 200 members, the great majority of which are from the UK, the United States, Japan and Europe. LIFFE is regulated by the Securities and Investment Board, and almost all its members are supervised by the Securities and Futures Authority. Private investors can receive compensation for loss from the Investors' Compensation Scheme for sums up to £48,000. Like other exchanges, LIFFE runs inexpensive seminars to explain to investors how the system works.

Most of the trading is done using the 'open-outcry' method in 'pits' on the floor of the exchange, but after hours the trading goes on for a certain time through a computerised system called Automated Pit Trading (APT). All the traders in the pits are employees of member companies and wear colour-coded jackets to show who they are:

- Yellow jackets are worn by administrative workers employed by members. Generally, they are learning to become traders themselves.
- Red jackets (or many-coloured jackets) are worn by the traders.
- Blue jackets are worn by LIFFE staff, who do not trade.

Among the blue jackets on the floor are the Pit Observers, who make sure that no rules are broken, and watch the movement of prices, which they report through microphones to computer staff. The prices are typed into the LIFFE's computers and instantaneously appear on screens and boards at the Exchange, as well as in international news systems.

The hand signals

In the mayhem of the pit, traders use hand signals as well as their voices to communicate. Figure 8.1 shows a few of these signals. The signs for prices refer to the digit on the extreme right of the price, which is usually four digits in all. The full prices are shown on computerised boards hanging near the pits so traders are able to check the price that the hand signal refers to easily. The price signals shown in Figure 8.1 are bid signals – the trader who is offering (selling) turns the palm of the hand away from the body, but uses the same finger signs. The price and amount signals are the most used, since traders have a convention that the nearest month of the futures

Buy – palm in hand pushed towards body

Sell – palm out, hand pushed away from body

Prices

1   5   6   9   Fist, palm towards
                                              body 10 & 0

Palm towards body to indicate bid, away to indicate offer figures refer to extreme right hand digit of total price

Amounts
The same signs as for price but on the chin for numbers 1 – 9

and on the forehead for tens

1   7   10   70

Months

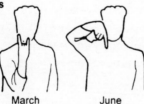

March   June   Sept   Dec

Deal agreed

Figure 8.1   Some LIFFE trader's signals

cycle is referred to unless otherwise indicated. When a trader wants to make a deal for a different month, the signals indicated in Figure 8.1 are used. Once both sides have agreed a price, the traders waggle their hands from side to side, signalling the agreed price. Thus, what appears to the casual observer to be a rabble of screaming, gesticulating lunatics is actually an effective system for making a large number of trades very quickly.

The link to the client

If you want to make a deal on the LIFFE, you telephone your broker, who must be a LIFFE member. The broker telephones a booth on the floor of the Exchange and a trader is given your order, either by a note or by signalling. The trader then signals and shouts to other traders until he makes a deal. Both sides fill in forms which are then cleared through LIFFE's system and the broker calls you to tell you that your deal has been done.

> .... **What appears to the casual observer to be a rabble of screaming, gesticulating lunatics is actually an effective system for making a large number of trades very quickly.** ....

Some LIFFE futures contracts

LIFFE financial futures are usually traded in three-month cycles for delivery in March, June, September and December. Below is a brief look at the details of the financial futures contracts available on LIFFE. The 'tick size' means the minimum value of a change in the value of the contract and the 'contract size' means the amount of money to be delivered:

	Contract size	Tick
3 month sterling interest rates	L500,000	12.50
3 month Eurodollar interest rates	$1,000,000	$25
3 month Euromark interest rates	DM1,000,000	DM25
3 month Euroswiss interest rates	SFr1,000,000	SFr25
3 month Eurolira interest rates	ITL1 billion	ITL25,000
Long gilts	50,000	15.625
German Government bonds	DM250,000 with 6% coupon (notional)	DM25
Italian Government bonds	ITL 200 milion	ITL20,000
Japanese Government bonds	Y100 million 6% coupon (notional)	Y10,000
Medium-term German Government bonds	DM250,000	DM25
FTSE 100 Index	25 per index point	12.50
FTSE Mid 250 Index	10 per index point	5.00

■ US FUTURES

The world's largest and most important centre for futures is Chicago.

Chicago Board of Trade (CBOT)

Established in 1848, the Chicago Board of Trade developed through the latter half of the nineteenth century as methods of grain storage improved, allowing producers and traders to keep grain for longer periods and take advantage of price fluctuations. In this century, a wide variety of agricultural futures were introduced and, after the abolition of exchange controls in 1971, the volatility of bonds and other financial instruments gave the Chicago Board of Trade the opportunity to introduce futures trading in Ginnie Maes and other financial futures. The market is connected with the two other Chicago markets listed below as well as with other US exchanges.

Chicago Mercantile Exchange (CME)

The CME started in 1874. Until World War 2 it traded principally in futures on onions, potatoes, cheese, eggs and butter. More foods were added in the post-war period and in 1961 the market greatly expanded with the introduction of pork belly futures (pork bellies are frozen lumps of uncured bacon). In the mid-1960s, futures contracts began to be written on live animals, such as cattle and hogs (pigs). When exchange controls came to an end in 1971, the CME began trading in foreign currencies through the International Monetary Market (IMM). The IMM has become the world's most active market in financial futures. An Index and Option Market (IOM) began in 1982.

The CME requires its members to deposit money to cover the gross margins, rather than the net as in most other markets.

Chicago Board Options Exchange (CBOE)

The Chicago Board Options Exchange began in 1973, creating the world's largest options exchange. Almost all US index options are traded on the CBOE, in the Standard and Poor's 100 and in the Standard and Poor's 500. Since 1989, it has been possible to trade in options on the interest rates of US Treasury bills, notes and bonds. More recently, trading in conventional shares, warrants and bonds has been introduced.

JAPANESE FUTURES

Japanese futures trading began in rice. There are now some 16 exchanges trading commodity futures and two exchanges trading financial futures. Precious metals futures account for more than 25 per cent of the total trading volume. Markets have poor liquidity and high commissions. Since 1990, foreign brokers have been allowed to become members. Although attempts are being made to streamline the multiplicity of regulations, liquidity problems are likely to continue. It is possible to trade in financial futures tied to the Nikkei Index on the Tokyo and Osaka stock exchanges.

Tokyo Commodity Exchange for Industry (Tocom)

Tocom trades futures in platinum, silver and gold using a screen system, and wool, cotton and rubber on open outcry. More futures are expected to be introduced.

Tokyo International Financial Futures Exchange (TIFFE)

TIFFE is rather new and it is so far unclear whether there will be enough business to keep it going. The main futures traded are in yen/dollar exchange rates, Eurodollar interest rates, and short-term Euroyen interest rates.

FUTURES IN THE MAIN COMMODITY-PRODUCING COUNTRIES

New Zealand, Australia, South Africa and Canada are highly developed industrial countries which are nevertheless reliant on commodity exports. Their futures markets are dominated by mining companies and agricultural producers. The principal futures markets are:

- New Zealand Futures and Options Exchange (NZFOE).
- Sydney Futures Exchange.
- South Africa Futures Exchange (Safex).
- Winnipeg Commodities Exchange.

■ CONTINENTAL EUROPE

While London accounts for more than 90 per cent of the share trading in Western Europe, the next biggest markets are in Germany and France. Futures and options are traded in the following markets:

- Marché à Terme des Instruments Financiers (MATIF). With ambitions to outstrip London in futures trading, MATIF offers bond futures, futures on the Paris share index CAC–40, short-term interest rates, Eurodeutsch-marks and ECU bonds, among others.

- Deutsche Terminborse (DTB) is screen-based and is the most important options market in continental Europe, with many foreign participants, also trading German government bond futures and share futures tied to the German DAX index.

- Frankfurt Corn and Produce Exchange.

- Berne Grain and Produce Exchange.

- Vienna Commodity Exchange.

- Options Markand (OM) in Sweden has exchanges in London and Stockholm with links between the two for trading.

- European Options Exchange-Optiebeurs (EOE) in Amsterdam.

- Marché des Options Négotiables de Paris (Monep).

- Copenhagen Stock Exchange and Guarantee Fund for Danish Options and Futures (Futop) in Denmark.

- Irish Futures and Options Exchange (IFOX) in Eire.

- Belgian Futures and Options Exchange (Belfox) in Belgium.

- Ostereichische Termin und Optionenborse (OTOB) in Austria.

- Swiss Options and Futures Exchange (Soffex) in Switzerland.

- Mercado de Opciones Financerio Espanol in Spain.

- Mercado de Futoros Financerios (MEFF) in Spain.

- Futures markets in Padua and Bologna, Italy.

■ OTHER FAR EASTERN MARKETS

These markets can be expected to become increasingly important as the Far East becomes an ever-stronger economic region:

- Singapore International Monetary Exchange (SIMEX). With a special link with the CME in Chicago, SIMEX is an important and active international market in currency futures for the yen, deutschmarks and sterling pounds, futures in Eurodollar interest rates and some commodities.

- Hong Kong Futures Exchange Ltd. Futures traded include the Hang Seng Index, sugar, soyabeans and gold.

- The Kuala Lumpur Commodity Exchange (KLCE) trades futures in cocoa, tin, palm oil and rubber.

- There are other small commodity exchanges in India, Thailand, the Philippines and Indonesia.

SMALLER FUTURES MARKETS

Russia and Eastern Europe

Forget it, unless you have a commando background and are prepared to go and live there! The Hungarians and Czechs are probably the best of the bunch, but the whole region is in the direst political uncertainty, and anything could happen. Pity them, but stay away!

China

Unlike the ex-USSR, the People's Republic of China is still in one piece, and is rapidly developing pseudo-capitalist markets with the help of American expertise. Wait and see.

Other markets

From Turkey to the Gulf states, to India and Pakistan, eastern governments are all trying to open up their economies to the delights of capitalism and financial markets. It may be fine for big western financial institutions to be involved, but for the small investor they are hopeless. Africa is worse. Latin America does have some well-established futures markets, in Brazil in particular:

- Bolsa de Mercadorias de Sao Paulo (BMSP).
- Bolsa Mercantil e de Futuros (BM&F).

The smaller futures markets for guerrillas

Guerrilla investors should do their best to be well-informed about what goes on in the smaller foreign markets since it will help to keep your macro-economic views up to date and may sometimes throw up clues you might otherwise have missed. Investing in these markets may be dangerous, though; not long ago, for example, the Winnipeg Commodities Exchange was the subject of a criminal investigation into alleged trading abuses. You should be aware that sharks are attracted to small markets where their nefarious activities are less likely to be stamped out. If you do decide to invest, check the charges and taxes carefully, as they vary widely – sometimes they are lower than in the UK.

OPTIONS

Share options give you the right to buy or sell a share at a certain price within a fixed time period. You pay for the option but you don't have to exercise it. You can also buy options on futures contracts, interest rates and currencies in the same way. The price you pay for the option is called the 'premium', and the price at which it is agreed that you may buy or sell the shares or futures contract is called the 'strike price' in the United States and the 'exercise price' in the UK.

> Guerrilla investors should do their best to be well-informed about what goes on in the smaller foreign markets

The price that you pay for an option depends upon the period of time allowed until the option expires (the longer it is, the more expensive the option), and also upon the difference between the strike price and the current market price of the share or futures contract.

Options give you leverage. All you have to pay is the price of the premium to make a bet that the exercise price will be better than the market price at some point before the option runs out (in the case of traded options) or at the point that the option runs out (in the case of 'European style' options). You don't have to come up with any more money unless you already know you have won your bet.

> Options give you leverage.

There are two kinds of options, 'puts' and 'calls'. A call option gives you the right to buy, and a put option gives you the right to sell. Traded options enable you to buy or sell your option if you win the bet, instead of buying the shares or other securities themselves.

As we have seen, unlike paying the margin when you buy a futures contract, all you can lose on an option is the premium, while the possible gain can be as high as you could get in futures. Options on shares can usually be bought for between 8 and 15 per cent of the share's market price. Except for 'traded options', you cannot buy or sell an option after the initial purchase.

Call options

Suppose you think that shares in Company X are going to go up in the next three months. You can buy a three-month call option **EXAMPLE ✳** on 1,000 shares at, say, 184p; the premium will be 18p per share, so you will pay £180 plus dealing costs for 1,000 shares. If the share price is at 187p after three months, you could exercise the option to buy in the hope that the share price will continue to rise; you will have spent 180 + 1,840 = £2,020, so, not counting dealing costs, the shares will have to rise above 202p for you to make a profit.

Put options

Suppose that you think Company X's shares are going to go down in the next three months. You can buy a put option for 18p per **EXAMPLE ✳** share for 1,000 shares at 184p. If the shares go down to, say, 150p, you can exercise your option by 'putting' it on to an option dealer, forcing him to buy your shares for £1,840, which you now exercise your right to buy for £1,500, and pass them on to him. The cost to you, not including dealing charges, is 1,500 + 180 = £1,680, so your profit is 1,840 – 1,680 = £160. Since your broker can conduct both transactions quickly, you won't have to come up with all the money to buy the shares. (This applies to exercising call options as well.)

Double options

Double options are combined put and call options, with a premium which is nearly double a normal premium. You are betting that the share price will move out of the range represented by the premium cost.

Hedging

Suppose you own some shares which you don't want to sell, but you expect them to fall in the short term. You can buy a put option in the shares to protect them against a fall in value. In general, this kind of hedging is costly and unnecessary for the smaller investor.

Writing options

It is possible to 'write' options on shares that you own through your broker, who will try to find an option buyer. You get the premiums, less dealing charges, and you buy the shares when puts are exercised or sell your shares if a call is exercised. It is also possible to be a 'naked writer', which means writing options on shares you don't own – an absurdly dangerous activity.

Traded options

Traded options exist only in certain shares and their form is fixed by the options market. You can buy puts and calls at certain prices fixed around the share's market price for periods of three, six or nine months. As the share price moves, the option prices move with it. The big difference between traded options and ordinary ones is that you can buy and sell a traded option as often as you like during its life. As well as the market in shares, you can also buy traded options based on the FTSE 100 share index.

> It is also possible to be a 'naked writer', – an absurdly dangerous activity.

✻ EXAMPLE Suppose you want buy an option in Company X's shares, currently trading at 330p; put and call options may be available at 300p, 320p, 340p and 360p. The 300p and 320p prices are called 'in the money' if you are buying a call, because they are lower than the share's market price, and the 340p and 360p prices are called 'out of the money' because they are higher. Conversely, if you are buying a put, the 340p and 360p prices are 'in the money' and the 300p and 320p prices are 'out of the money'. If you bought a call at 300p, the premium might be 50p, so if you sold it immediately you would make a loss of 20p per share, even though the option is 'in the money', since you would buy the shares for 300 + 50 = 350p and only be able to sell them for 330p.

The way that the price of the option is calculated is complicated. Essentially, it is split up into two parts, the 'time value' and the 'intrinsic value'. The time value is set according to the time that an option has left to run – the longer the time left, the higher the time value – and at the moment that the option expires there will be no time value left. Time values are worked out on computer and are based on an estimate of the chances of an investor being able to exercise an option. Factors that influence time values are the time left, how near the option is to being in the money, and the volatility of the underlying share or commodity.

Intrinsic values are simply the amount by which an option is in the money, so if you had bought a call at 300p in shares selling at 330p, your option is in the money by 30p, which is its intrinsic value. The sale value of the option will vary throughout its lifetime. With a nine-month option the time value reduces fairly slowly for about six months before dropping at an increasingly rapid rate. In the money options tend to move in parallel with the share price, while out of the money options are less responsive.

As with shares, options have a 'spread' – you pay the higher price when you buy and get the lower price when you sell – and you pay dealer's charges on top of this.

How to trade in options

First, find a broker who will take you on. As with investing in shares, options brokers will offer different levels of service, such as execution only or advisory and discretionary services, which carry different levels of commission. Your broker will want you to deposit money with him, from which he will take the premiums as you deal. When you contact your broker with instructions to deal, the broker will try to get the price you ask for; if he can't, you can ask him to have the order put on the Public Limit Order Board (PLOB) for a fee. LIFFE staff will then do the deal for you later that day if prices make it possible to do so.

Why private investors buy traded options

The rationale for private investors' interest in traded options is essentially the attraction of leverage combined with the limited risk of loss. If you buy an out of the money call and the share price rises, you make around ten times what you would have made if you had simply bought the shares, and the most you can lose is the premium, part of which you may be able to get back by re-selling the option before the expiry date. The

> .... **The longer the option, the more expensive it is because there is more chance of you making a profit.** ....

longer the option, the more expensive it is because there is more chance of you making a profit. In the money options give you lower profits, but a bigger chance of making one, so they are a safer bet. Investors tend to buy puts less often than calls, perhaps because it is easier to imagine that a share is going to go up than it is to believe that it is going to go down.

For guerrillas: who really benefits from options?

The dealers certainly do. They make a profit on the transactions irrespective of whether the purchaser wins or loses. There may occasionally be moments when you are sure that a price is moving in a certain direction and can buy options at a price that will give a profit, but regularly buying traded options is an expensive gamble – you'll probably end up losing money.

A reader of the first edition of this book, Peter Hicks, has a slightly different view of the benefits of traded options; he writes that:

'I have found writing naked puts to be most rewarding: a way of making money without actually holding stocks and using up the annual tax-free capital gains allowance of around 12,000 pounds for a married couple whilst leaving one's capital safely on deposit ... In the traded options market, buyers far outweigh sellers. Many interested institutions are forbidden to be sellers by the terms of their constitutions. Loosely, there are too many 'punters' (buyers) and too few 'bookies' (sellers). Hence traded options tend to be a sellers' market, and prices favour sellers, I believe – particularly put sellers.'

Mr Hicks, an experienced private investor, keeps funds outside the market in order to back up his speculation, which, strictly speaking, does not count as 'naked writing'. He makes the following points:

- *Buyers* – no margin is required. The potential loss is restricted to the size of your initial cheque, just like placing a bet with a bookie!

- *Writers and sellers* – you are the bookie! Margin is required, but the amount depends to a large extent on the relationship between you and your broker. If you have a significant portfolio of shares lodged in a nominee account with your longstanding, friendly broker, he might not require any further margin.

- *Taxation* – option gains are subject to CGT, so you should restrict your potential gains to the annual tax-free allowance. For buyers, the tax point is the date when the gain occurs – when you sell your option for a price above that which you paid. For sellers the tax point is the expiry date of the option. This can result in a worthwhile tax holiday. In July, it is possible to sell options with an expiry date in the following April (the next tax year). The CGT 'will not have to be paid until the following year – a two-year tax holiday'.

It doesn't occur to most people to invest outside their own countries because they have a feeling that it is risky. In fact, the reverse may be true.

9

Foreign exchange

The world has recently undergone a revolution – currencies can now be exchanged with one another more freely than ever before. This offers a great deal of scope to the guerrilla investor who wishes to take advantage of investment opportunities in currencies other than his or her own. In this chapter we will look at the origins and mechanisms of foreign exchange. The areas covered are:

- The Bretton Woods system – why it was set up after World War 2, how it worked and why it has ended.
- The floating rate system – how it emerged and why it is good news for private investors.
- The Euromarkets.
- The Foreign Exchange market. How currencies are traded.
- Exchange rates – how to calculate them, and how to hedge in currencies. Arbitrage and speculation, and how to predict exchange rates.
- The special drawing right (SDR).
- The European Monetary System (EMS).
- Why the yen will probably replace the dollar as the world's most important currency.

THE BRETTON WOODS SYSTEM

As World War 2 drew to a close, the Allied nations and their supporters met in the United States at Bretton Woods in New Hampshire to plan an international monetary system for the post-war era. They created the International Monetary Fund (IMF) and the World Bank, and set up a system which was intended to provide stability to exchange rates. Since the United States had become by far the most powerful country in the world, the system was tied to the US dollar at $33 to an ounce of gold. All other currencies were defined in terms of dollars. If a country wanted to change its rate of exchange against the dollar, it had to make a formal announcement that it was revaluing, or devaluing, its currency. In 1949, 28 countries devalued their currencies.

Bretton Woods set the stage for the rise of socialism. Countries were able to pay for the huge cost of creating welfare states by issuing bonds, which in turn encouraged inflation. As world trade mushroomed and the economic balance between countries began to change, vast funds grew up which were highly mobile and could be switched from one country to another without the permission of governments. The demand for gold was high, and the official price of $33 to an ounce was undermined by the creation of secondary markets, where gold was traded at much higher prices. As its economic strength diminished, the United States decided unilaterally to abandon the Bretton Woods system when, in 1971, it suspended the right to convert dollars for gold at $33 to the ounce, and devalued the dollar.

THE FLOATING EXCHANGE RATE SYSTEM

Bretton Woods was supplanted by the floating exchange rate system, where no currency is formally linked to any other, or to gold. The rate at which you can exchange one currency for another is simply the best rate that someone will give you, so exchange rates are highly volatile (this is why they are called 'floating'). During the oil crises of 1973 and 1979, when OPEC dramatically increased the price of oil, the floating system helped to minimise the chaos, as the strain was taken by an adjustment in exchange rates (the OPEC countries' currencies suddenly became much more valuable), rather than by curtailing real economic activity, as would have happened if the Bretton Woods system had still been operating. The floating system does have disadvantages. The principal ones are that it encourages countries to act 'selfishly' rather than cooperatively and that it greatly exaggerates the extremes in the cycle of exchange rates. Countries are tempted to manipulate their exchange rates for short-term advantage. For instance, Japan managed to keep the yen artificially low for some years in order to encourage exports, as did Britain, with less success. This kind of manipulation can only work for a few years before it becomes impossible to sustain.

> **Countries are tempted to manipulate their exchange rates for short-term advantage.**

The United States, too, tries to use the floating system for its own advantage. Its massive trade deficit will eventually have to be paid for with higher taxes, more unemployment and lower living standards, but the US government has staved off the evil day for some time by allowing the dollar to depreciate against other currencies. State banks throughout the world have attempted to counteract this by buying dollars to raise its rate.

THE BALANCE OF PAYMENTS AND THE BLACK HOLE

Countries are like companies in that they have accounts; money flows in and out of them, and one can take a 'snapshot' of a country's accounts which purports to show its debts and assets, just as a balance sheet does for a company. Balance of payments accounts are produced each year, identifying the state's net earnings from abroad (the 'current account'), its savings or debts (the 'capital account'), and the borrowings the government may have to make to balance the books.

When a government has to borrow in order to balance its accounts, it usually goes to banks or other governments for a short-term loan. If all else fails, it must go to an international organisation such as the International Monetary Fund (IMF) which will insist on rigid economic controls. For this reason, governments tend to regard this last course of action as highly undesirable.

If a country's current account is negative, meaning that it has spent more than it has earned when trading abroad, it usually means that the country's currency is weakening. Conversely, if the current account is in surplus year after year, it usually means that the currency is getting stronger.

Much is made of balance of payments by politicians, economists and commentators. However, they are unreliable, just as the accounts of many companies are. If you reconcile the annual balance of payments figures for every country in the world, they should all add up. They don't – there is a 'black hole' of many tens of billions that cannot be accounted for. This black hole makes it impossible to know the true picture, and thus there can be no description of the world's economy that is entirely accurate.

> ....There is a 'black hole' of many tens of billions that cannot be accounted for. ....

THE EUROMARKETS

The Euromarkets are a banking system which is truly international and operates beyond the control of governments. It handles huge amounts of cash belonging to companies, institutional funds, countries and wealthy individuals. The amount of money in the Euromarkets is so large that it can significantly affect exchange rates, the money supply and inflation as it moves around the world. The ease with which money can be borrowed through the Euromarkets makes them attractive as sources of finance for large projects. Because of its international character, there is no central organisation controlling it, and no complete figures on its size or movements. The City of London has benefited from the growth of Euromarkets because its physical location, halfway between Tokyo and New York, has enabled it to exploit its 'middle position' in the time zones.

THE FOREIGN EXCHANGE MARKET

The important difference between doing business with a company in your own country and doing business with one abroad is that the two currencies of the respective countries will usually be involved. A German importer will usually pay a Japanese exporter in yen, a French exporter in francs, an American exporter in dollars and so on. The importer will have to buy the required currency on the foreign exchange market.

The foreign exchange market is international and consists of banks, brokers and others buying and selling currencies from most of the countries in the world. Rates change very fast, so they communicate by fax, computer, telephone and telex continuously.

The main centres for foreign exchange trading are New York, London, Tokyo, Zürich and Frankfurt, which turn over hundreds of billions of dollars a day. The US dollar is by far the most frequently traded, and is called a 'vehicle currency'. This means that commodities such as coffee, gold and oil are normally priced in dollars. It is often cheaper for, say, a Japanese dealer who wants to buy Italian lire to buy dollars first and then use the dollars to buy lire, rather than buying them directly with yen.

The central banks in each country often try to influence the exchange rate of their currency by buying and selling in large amounts. For example, when there is an agreed target exchange rate, the central banks have to buy and sell their own currencies according to the fluctuation in supply and demand, to try to drive their currencies towards the desired rate.

The merchant banks, or commercial banks, trade in currencies for themselves, and also on the behalf of clients such as companies and large investors who want foreign currency. They trade with other banks, and also use brokers.

The brokers are used by banks because they can get the best price quicker and more cheaply than the bank itself. There are just a few authorised brokers in each financial centre.

What is an exchange rate?

An exchange rate is simply the ratio at which one currency can be exchanged for another at a given time. It can be given in two ways, either as the amount of currency A that will buy one unit of currency B, or the amount of currency B that will buy currency A. It doesn't matter which way round the ratio is expressed, as long as it is made clear which currency is being taken as one unit, though there is usually a convention for any given pair of currencies.

If the rate for marks per dollar has changed from DM2:$1 to DM2.01:$1, you will have to pay more in marks for a dollar, so the mark has 'depreciated' and the dollar has 'appreciated'. If the dollars per mark rate has changed from $0.50:DM1 to $0.51:DM1, you will have to pay more in dollars for a mark, so marks have appreciated and dollars have depreciated. This is why it can be confusing if someone says that the exchange rate has risen – which way round do they mean?

The nominal exchange rate

The nominal exchange rate is the prevailing rate of exchange between two currencies on a given day. In other words, it is simply the price of buying one currency with another. It is sometimes given as an index relative to some base time.

If the base dollar/deutschmark rate is, say, $0.50:DM1, and some time later the rate is $0.55:DM1, the nominal index of the mark **EXAMPLE ✳** will then be 110 – the mark has appreciated against the dollar by 10 per cent.

The nominal rate doesn't tell you anything about price levels in the respective countries, however, so a formula is used to convert it into the 'real exchange rate' which does.

The real exchange rate

The real exchange rate takes the price levels of the two countries into account. The formula for calculating it is:

$$E_r = (E \times P) \div P^*$$

(where E_r is the real exchange rate, E is the nominal exchange rate given as the amount of foreign currency for one unit of domestic currency, P is the local price index and P^* is the foreign price index).

Some indices include the prices of fast food, which are hardly a good guide to value.

Suppose that the nominal exchange rate of dollars to marks is $0.50:DM1. If both the German and the US price indexes are 100, then the real exchange rate is

$$E_r = (0.50 \times 100) \div 100 = 0.50$$

which is the same as the nominal rate. Now suppose that at a later date the nominal exchange rate is still the same, but the US price index has risen to 110. The real exchange rate is now

$$E_r = (0.50 \times 100) \div 110 = 0.4545$$

The real exchange rate is telling you what the nominal exchange rate doesn't, namely that the mark will buy less goods in America than it could have previously. One problem though, is what price index is used; for instance, some indices include the prices of fast food, which are hardly a good guide to value.

The effective exchange rate

Have you ever heard a news report about your local currency going up or down against 'a basket of currencies'? What is happening is that the local, or domestic, currency is being compared with the currencies of several countries with which your country trades. The result is called the 'effective exchange rate'.

To understand the principle, let's take an example.

✳ EXAMPLE Suppose Japan does 60 per cent of its foreign business with the United States and 40 per cent with Germany. The exchange rate index is weighted by 0.6 times the exchange rate with the dollar and 0.4 times the exchange rate with the mark.

At the base period, the indices are all set to 100 and will look like this:

Nominal index	Nominal index	Effective index
DM:Y1	$:Y1	Y
100	100	100

If the yen subsequently appreciated against the mark by 20 per cent and depreciated against the dollar by 20 per cent the indices would look like this:

Nominal index	Nominal index	Effective index
DM:Y1	$:Y1	Y
80	120	104

The effective exchange rate index has been calculated by multiplying the nominal indices by their respective weights, thus:

$$80 \times 0.4 = 32$$

$$120 \times 0.6 = 72$$

Adding them together we get 32 + 72 = 104, which is the effective rate index given above.

Spot rates

The 'spot rate' is the rate between two currencies for delivery at once. Once a deal has been done, it usually take two days before the currencies are actually exchanged because of the paperwork involved – it is a 'paper transaction' where bank notes are not physically exchanged.

The forward exchange market

If you know you want to buy yen in 90 days' time to settle a bill, but you want to be sure of exactly how much it is going to cost you, you can buy currency at the forward exchange rate, which will be different from the spot rate.

Suppose you are a German company who owes $100,000 to an American company, due on 31 June. You may decide to buy $100,000 on 1 April at the three-month forward rate, and the money will be delivered to you on the day you must pay the American company.

EXAMPLE ✲

To see why companies do this, let's look at the participants in the foreign exchange market.

Hedging

The German company doesn't want the uncertainty of not knowing how much its American debt will cost in three month's time on 31 June. Perhaps it suspects that the dollar will cost more in deutschmarks at that time than it does now. Suppose the spot exchange rate on 1 April is $0.50:DM1 and the three-month forward exchange rate is $0.52:DM1. If it buys at the spot rate, $100,000 will cost DM200,000, and if it buys at the three-month forward rate it will cost DM192,307 now. Suppose that when three months have elapsed, the spot rate has changed to $0.53:DM1. The company could have kept its money in deutschmarks until the last moment and paid DM188,679 for its dollars instead of DM192,307, saving DM3,628. The company is more interested in being sure what its liability will be in three months' time than in speculating, so no sleep is lost over the gamble. It has protected itself against nasty surprises by making a 'forward contract'. This is known as 'hedging'.

EXAMPLE ✲

> **Companies often don't want to spend the cash in advance – the money is needed for other things.**

You may wonder why companies don't simply buy the necessary currency at the spot rate far in advance of the time that they need it. This is because companies often don't want to spend the cash in advance – the money is needed for other things.

Arbitrage

'Arbitrage' means being able to buy something and then selling it immediately at a higher price, thus guaranteeing a profit. The communications in the foreign exchange market are so good that arbitrage opportunites only occur very briefly and require rapid trading if they are to be taken advantage of.

There are two kinds of basic arbitrage:

- *Financial centre arbitrage* has the effect of keeping the exchange rates in different financial centres the same. If you can get $0.50 for DM1 in Tokyo, but $0.52 for DM1 in Frankfurt, you would frantically buy as many dollars as you could in Frankfurt and sell them immediately in Tokyo, making a no-risk 4 per cent profit. Every time a chance like this comes up, people take advantage of it, which brings the rates in different places back into line.

- *Cross-rate arbitrage* works in the same way to keep exchange rates in different currencies compatible with each other. If you are in France wanting to buy deutschmarks and you see that the rate for yen to the mark is Y100:DM1, the rate for yen to the franc is Y40:FF1 and that the rate for francs to the mark is FF3:DM1, you could buy DM100 for FF300, or you could buy Y12,000 for FF300, and then buy DM120 with the yen for a no-risk profit. As with financial centre arbitrage, the constant exploitation of such opportunities keeps bringing the rates into line with each other.

'Arbitrageurs' are people who engage in arbitrage, the process of looking for opportunities to make profits without risk by buying and selling currencies. They are usually banks. Another kind of arbitrage opportunity they can sometimes exploit is in the difference between interest rates in different countries combined with the difference between forward and spot rates. It is also possible to find arbitrage opportunities in mispriced futures contracts.

So, why isn't everyone an arbitrageur? The reasons are that they need very sophisticated equipment, and also that the more arbitrageurs there are, the less opportunities there are for arbitrage.

Forward discounts and premiums

If the spot rate is less than the forward rate for a currency (in other words, if you get more of the foreign currency for your money by buying at the forward rate), the currency is at a 'forward premium', as it was for our German company on 1 April. If the forward rate is less than the spot rate, the currency is at a 'forward discount'.

> **The more arbitrageurs there are, the less opportunities there are for arbitrage.**

The discount or premium of the forward rate is most often given as a percentage of the spot rate. The formula is:

$$\text{Forward premium/discount} = (F - S) \div S \times 100$$

(where F is the forward rate and S is the spot rate). Thus, if the forward rate is $0.52:DM1 and the spot rate is $0.50:DM1, the premium is:

Forward premium $= (0.52 - 0.50) \div 0.50 \times 100$

$= (0.02 \div 0.50) \times 100$

$= 4$ per cent

Speculation

Speculators are different from arbitrageurs because they are taking a risk. They try to make money on the basis of predictions about the way the markets are moving, rather than looking for momentary mismatches between exchange rates as arbitrageurs do. Speculators who think a currency is going to cost more in the future than it does now are called 'bullish' (optimistic) about the currency, and ones who think it will cost less are called 'bearish' (pessimistic).

EXAMPLE ✳

Suppose a speculator in, say Hong Kong (it could be anywhere), bought $100,000 in deutschmarks at the forward rate of $0.52:DM1 on 1 April, at the same time as the German company in our example, hoping to sell the dollars back into deutschmarks at the end of June for a quick profit. This is called 'going long' on the dollar. At the end of June the spot rate is $0.53:DM1. The speculator agreed to pay DM192,307 for the dollars. Changing the dollars back into marks would produce DM188,679, so the speculator has lost DM3,628 if the dollars are exchanged.

To make the principles of foreign exchange easier to understand, we haven't taken the dealing costs into account. These are small, however (fractions of 1 per cent of a unit of currency), so they do not prevent banks and large investors from making a profit. All this is a very different business from the 'tourist rates', where paper money actually has to be moved around physically.

The frenetic activity in foreign exchange is possible due to most of the world's countries allowing free trade in currency. This has not always been the case in the past, and if free trade in currency were to be slowed by governments at some time in the future, the markets would slow down with it.

PREDICTING EXCHANGE RATES

As we saw on page 160, it is the trading profits or losses of countries which are the main force affecting exchange rates in the long term. However, when trying to predict exchange rates, many other factors are considered:

- *Inflation*. Countries with high inflation relative to other countries find that the prices of the goods and services that they export rise also. This leads to fewer customers for their goods, a higher amount of imports, consequent trading losses and a weakening currency.

- *Monthly and quarterly trade figures*. These tend to be far less reliable than the annual balance of payment accounts, which, as we have seen, are not very reliable themselves. Nevertheless, the foreign exchange market grasps eagerly for such interim figures as they are published, in the hope of finding clues about the future.

- *Flows of capital*. If, for example, a country is trading at a loss but is enjoying a large amount of investment from abroad, its currency may not weaken as it otherwise would.

- *Interest rates*. A country which offers a higher rate of interest than others do will often attract money from abroad in the short term. However, if investors believe that the currency is likely to become worth less, they will switch their money to a safer currency.

- *Investment abroad*. Countries whose companies are purchasing or setting up businesses overseas are generally thought to have currencies which will get stronger for a decade or more, since it will take that length of time for the companies to make their profits.

- *Money flowing into a country's stock markets* is usually a sign that the currency will be strong, at least for three years or so.
- *Productivity*. A country with a high rate of productivity and economic growth is often thought to have a strengthening currency.
- *Savings*. Populations who spend everything they earn make their currencies weaker by increasing trading losses. It is notable that economically strong countries, such as Japan and Germany, have a high rate of saving per head of population.
- *Bank intervention*. A country's central bank may buy its own currency to make it stronger, or sell it to make it weaker.
- *Confidence in policies*. Investors from outside a country will look at its political situation to assess the risks of investing there. Not many people will buy bonds, for example, from a government which looks as if it is collapsing.
- *Bull and bear markets*. As with shares, if investors think that a currency is increasing or decreasing, they will invest accordingly, creating a self-fulfilling prophecy in the short term.
- *Singular events*. Wars, commodity price hikes and other one-off occurrences will have short-term effects on exchange rates.

THE EFFECTS OF EXCHANGE RATES ON SHARES

It doesn't occur to most people to invest outside their own countries because they have a feeling that it is risky. In fact, the reverse may be true. If you invest in the well-regulated stock markets of nations with strong currencies, you are helping to reduce the risk by spreading it across several currencies. This is of great importance to British investors, since the natural tendency to keep their money at home will almost certainly produce lower returns, as Britain lumbers towards a future of lowered international status and industrial uncertainty. Holding high-quality shares in several countries does complicate matters, certainly, but not necessarily to such a degree that it is not worth a private investor's while to do so. The main factor affecting an international portfolio is that exchange rates will affect real profits and losses.

✳ EXAMPLE If you are British and make, say, a 50 per cent profit investing in a Japanese company, the profits that you will actually receive if you sell and convert the money into sterling will depend on what has happened to the sterling/yen rate in the interim.

To make the sums easy, suppose that when you invested, the yen/sterling rate was 1:1, and that in the meantime the yen has depreciated by 50 per cent against the pound. If you had invested £10,000 (e.g. Y10,000), you would now have Y15,000, but since the sterling/yen rate is now 1:2, you would only get £7,500 back. However, since the future for yen is bright, it is more likely that the yen would actually appreciate against the pound. If the sterling/yen rate were now 1:0.5, you would receive £30,000 for your Y15,000. Thus, the ability to assess correctly currency trends over periods of more than five years can add value to your returns.

This kind of bet is nowhere near as risky as the short-term gambling on quarterly or annual exchange rates that the professionals go in for. If you take a global view of investment, you should be able to develop a framework for yourself by identifying the industries in different countries which are likely to prosper, the currencies which are likely to become stronger and the political outlook in those regions. Once you have done this, you can then select individual stocks in the normal way, by assessing their p/e ratios and fundamentals.

THE EFFECTS OF EXCHANGE RATES ON BONDS

> If you take a global view of investment, you should be able to develop a framework for yourself

When the interest rates of a country falls, the value of its bonds usually goes up. As rates are currently low throughout the world, bond markets are active. When investing in bonds from other countries, care should be taken to check credit ratings and to assess the country's record on previous defaults. It is also possible to invest in foreign bonds through managed funds. Bonds in strong currencies usually offer lower interest rates than ones in weaker currencies. By convention, 2.5 per cent is the lowest acceptable 'real' rate of interest. When the average yield of interest of international bonds is higher than this figure, bonds are thought of as being good value.

Interest rates on British gilts have been high on average over the past few decades due to the weakness of the pound and high inflation. When investing in bonds internationally, you must try to choose countries where the long-term exchange rates and inflation figures are improving and buy bonds there before yield rates have adjusted to the new conditions.

THE EFFECTS OF EXCHANGE RATES ON CASH

When stock markets around the world are falling, many investors sell shares and increase their bond and cash holdings. Since World War 2, the value of sterling has dropped dramatically against other currencies. If you had overcome exchange controls and had invested in a spread of currencies during this period, as some have been able to do, you would have done far better than if you had stayed in sterling exclusively.

There are now a number of managed currency funds which change the proportions of the various currencies they hold according to movements in exchange rates. Ideally, such a fund should pro-

> **Look for a fund that is not committed to basing itself around one particular currency**

duce a greater return than holding the strongest currency throughout a particular period. Look for a fund that is not committed to basing itself around one particular currency, such as that of its home country, since this may result in a poor result if the fund does not respond to a weakening trend. Usually, though, a fund will produce its final accounts in one currency, but this does not necessarily indicate a bias. Whether you are investing in a fund or on your own, you should stick to major countries or currencies which are closely tied to them.

THE SPECIAL DRAWING RIGHT (SDR) OF THE IMF

The International Monetary Fund's role during the Bretton Woods era was to be the lender of last resort to its member countries, which numbered about 150. Each member pays an annual subscription to the IMF which is a fixed proportion of its GDP, and this money is used to assist countries in difficulty. The amount a country pays determines the amount it can borrow, and affects its voting rights. A country can borrow foreign currency for between three and five years from the IMF up to its subscription quota. Switzerland is not a member of the IMF, but does participate in the 'Paris Club' or 'Group of Ten' countries which provide further monies for countries in trouble.

The special drawing right (SDR) was invented as a way of accounting between the IMF and central state banks. It is tied to a 'basket' of several strong currencies, and the proportions of each in the basket is fixed for five years. Member countries of the IMF can pay each other in SDRs, but they are not directly convertible into any currency, and countries may only hold limited SDR reserves. It is now possible to buy bonds denominated in SDRs. As a kind of benchmark of the strong currencies, the SDR is probably the fairest of those available.

THE EUROPEAN MONETARY SYSTEM (EMS)

The aim of the European Community (EC) is to create a truly united federation of Europe. This is an immensely difficult task and may well not succeed, owing to the natural rivalry between its member countries. Thus we have an EC divided into competing factions, with strong currency countries such as Germany, France, Holland and Luxembourg desiring low inflation and conservative economies, and weaker currency countries such as Ireland, Spain, Italy and Denmark seeking relaxed rules. The European Monetary System (EMS) is a compromise designed to stabilise exchange rates between its members' currencies as a step towards the EC's ideal of a single common currency for Europe. It has already created a currency unit called the ECU, which is a basket of various proportions of EC members' currencies, similar in principle to the SDR. As yet, the ECU is not very widely used. It is possible to buy bonds denominated in ECUs, and to borrow ECUs from some banks and state organisations.

THE FUTURE OF THE US DOLLAR

As Japan and Germany rebuilt their economies after World War 2, so the US dollar has weakened. After decades of being the world's 'reserve' currency, functioning as the benchmark for all others, the dollar is losing importance. Consumerism, reduced exports, the costs of wars and high living standards are all playing their part in increasing the United States' debt burden and putting its economy into decline in the long term. It seems likely that the yen will replace the dollar as the world's most important currency in the next century.

THE FUTURE OF THE YEN

Japan now has the world's second biggest stock market, the world's highest per capita savings rate, the world's highest average life-span, a history of low inflation, a sound economy and rapidly growing assets abroad. Its banks are supplanting American ones as the leaders of the industry and the yen's strength improves as more and more foreigners invest in it. As mentioned above, the yen may well become the world's premier currency within a decade. This doesn't mean, however, that Japan will become a superpower on the American

> It seems likely that the yen will replace the dollar as the world's most important currency in the next century.

model. As a mercantilist island power with a relatively small population, Japanese dominance is likely to have more in common with the British imperial era, which was based on international trade. Like the British Empire, it will always be out-numbered militarily by other developed powers, so it remains to be seen how much political power it will attain. However, this is a controversial view. Some people say that the Tigers and Dragons will actually support the dollar in the long run.

CONCLUSION

Whatever the merits and demerits of the floating rate system may be for nations, private investors can certainly benefit from the freedom and opportunities that it offers. Take advantage of it while you can – like all previous systems, it is unlikely to last forever. What will replace it is moot. There have been proposals for a world monetary system which would allow currencies, or linked currency blocs, to move against one another within fixed ranges. Such a system might reintroduce sweeping currency controls. One thing to appreciate is that the up and coming Far Eastern nations don't really subscribe to the floating rate system – watch for changes as the West reacts in horror against their increasing economic might.

> Being a Name is not really an investment ... but if you are under 40, with wealthy relatives who will support you if disaster occurs, and you are knowledgeable about risk management, it may be worthwhile

10

Lloyd's of London

Lloyd's of London has an almost legendary status as a very special investment opportunity for the very rich. In this chapter we will look at the procedures and mechanisms of Lloyd's market and its problems, and discuss its current merits as an investment. The topics are:

- The origins of Lloyd's.
- Lloyd's structure – the agents, Names and its governing body.
- The syndicates – how they work.
- The underwriters and brokers – how Lloyd's chooses what to insure.
- How to become a Name – deposits and premium limits.
- The down side – open years, excess of loss and the LMX spiral.
- The problems of asbestos, pollution and catastrophe claims.
- The Names' rebellion.
- Is it still worth becoming a Name?

INTRODUCTION

Lloyd's of London has been much in the news in recent years following a series of financial losses and the subsequent outcry from its investors, or 'Names'. It is a unique institution. Completely unrelated to its namesake, Lloyds Bank, Lloyd's of London was, until recently, entirely financed by private individuals, who gave the guarantees necessary for it to operate the world's most flexible and innovative insurance marketplace. Until about 1950, membership of Lloyd's was virtually exclusive to the highest echelon of male society in Britain, but since then the club has expanded to include Names of both sexes, mainly from the UK, Europe, the United States, the Commonwealth and many Islamic countries. Most Names could be described as upper middle class, with a generous sprinkling of celebrities, politicians and aristocrats. Since membership of Lloyd's has a minimum wealth requirement (see page 182), it is not for everyone, but it is nevertheless likely to be a topic of interest to guerrilla investors who aspire to the attainment of wealth, as well as to those readers who already fulfil the membership criteria.

ORIGINS

Lloyd's started in the 1600s in a London coffee house run by a man called Edward Lloyd. The discoveries in the New World had introduced coffee to Europe and in the seventeenth century coffee houses became the meeting places of the fashionable and prosperous classes. Here, political issues were discussed, news and gossip exchanged and business transacted. At Edward Lloyd's coffee house the shipping industry congregated. Gradually, a system of maritime insurance grew up whose basic principles have remained unchanged. Until the 1880s maritime insurance was virtually the only kind of insurance available, and even today it forms a major part of Lloyd's business. The idea was simple. The owner of a ship and its cargo could be wiped out if the vessel was lost through shipwreck, piracy or being seized by a foreign power, so he insured himself against total loss by paying a sum of money (a 'premium') to a large number of wealthy people who would each guarantee to pay ('underwrite') a proportion of the cost if the ship was lost. The underwriters hoped to make a profit from the premiums, the income of which would cover the occasional loss of vessels and cargoes.

The underwriters would sit in Edward Lloyd's coffee house and wait for people to come to them to ask if they would underwrite a particular risk. If they agreed to do so, they wrote their name on a 'slip' of paper, showing what percentage of the total risk they were willing to take in return for the same percentage of the total premium paid by the person seeking insurance. Thus, a 'Name' wrote a 'line' of insurance on a 'slip' of paper, terms which are still used at Lloyd's today. Naturally, the person being insured wanted to be certain that the Names would be good for the money in the event of a claim, so Names had to prove that they had enough assets to cover possible claims, and had to agree to sell all their assets if necessary in order to meet a claim. Since several Names were underwriting each risk, they realised that they were effectively in a syndicate together.

> Names had to prove that they had enough assets to cover possible claims, and had to agree to sell all their assets if necessary in order to meet a claim.

After the fiasco of the South Sea Bubble in the early 1700s, laws were passed to prevent all companies except two – London Assurance and the Royal Exchange Assurance – from offering marine insurance. The laws, however, did not prevent individuals from doing the same thing, so Lloyd's grew.

As business expanded, it became impractical for Names and customers to attend the coffee house regularly, so agents were appointed to handle the business of a number of Names, while brokers sought cover from them on behalf of their clients. By 1871 there were 18,000 Names; in this year Lloyd's was incorporated as a society of private underwriters by an Act of Parliament, but continued to operate on much the same lines as it had since the seventeenth century. It still does so today, with a peculiar mixture of tradition, mystique and flair for inventiveness; whether you want to insure a space station or your beard, Lloyd's is the place to seek cover.

LLOYD'S' STRUCTURE

The rules of Lloyd's are made by the Council, with an elected Committee which handles details and a Chairman who is elected once a year. Self-regulation by its members has always been a cardinal principle and it was with reluctance that, following a financial scandal in 1978, a 1982 Act of Parliament gave the Council greater powers to regulate Lloyd's. The Act allowed the Governor of the Bank of England to appoint four people to the Council from outside Lloyd's, as well as a chief executive. The Act also outlawed joint ownership of insurance brokers and underwriting agencies, the intention being to prevent conflicts of interest where brokers and managing agents might be tempted not to give customers – or Names – the best deal. Thus, unlike most investment services in the UK, Lloyd's is not regulated by the Financial Services Act.

The Lloyd's Council

From 1982 until 1992, the Council consisted of twelve working practioners at Lloyds, eight individuals nominated by other institutions (including the four appointed by the Governor of the Bank of England) and eight individuals elected by the non-working, or 'external' Names.

The Council chooses a chairman and two deputies from the twelve practitioners and another member of the Council is nominated as the chief executive and third deputy.

The Committee

The Committee consists of twelve practitioners, or working members, who manage Lloyd's on a day-to-day basis. Several sub-committees, working parties and other bodies are answerable to the main Committee.

Lloyd's syndicates

Syndicates are groups of Names on whose behalf an underwriter does business. They tend to specialise in one of four areas: marine insurance, aviation, motor and non-marine. This last category is a catch-all for all kinds of risks, from fire and theft to war risks.

Every syndicate keeps its yearly accounts 'open' for three years, awaiting the majority of claims, then 'closes' the year and shares out the profits on premiums to its Names. When the year is closed, the syndicate then re-insures the policies of the year into the following year's three-year accounting period, paying a premium to the syndicate for that year, which may have changed its composition of Names. This premium is based on an assessment of the future risk of claims relating to the closed year's policies. Thus, the 1990 year's accounts were not closed until the end of 1992.

As we will see later in this chapter, the three-year accounting system is the reason why Names do not know about losses until some time after they have occurred. The practice of re-insuring to close a year means that new Names can find themselves liable for claims against their syndicate dating back as far as the 1940s.

Member's agents

Names are introduced to Lloyd's by a member's agent. After a complicated admissions procedure (see page 182), the Name must then decide which syndicates to join. The member's agent advises on this, and charges a management fee and a commission (approximately 7.5 per cent) on the Name's net profits. The idea is that the member's agent steers the Name away from trouble, spreading the risk across several syndicates and seeking out the most profitable situations. It is possible, but unusual, for a Name to have several member's agents, in which case there must be a coordinating agent who takes an extra management fee for coordinating the Name's activities. A member's agent can be linked with a managing agent or with a Lloyd's broker, or can be entirely independent.

Managing agents

Managing agents run the syndicates, appointing the underwriters who choose which risks to insure and paying their salaries. Part of their job is to decide the proportion of 'long tail' and 'short tail' business. Short tail business is insurance on which any claims will come in quickly, and long tail business is where claims could arise many years later. Managing agents settle claims, put part of the premiums in reserve against future claims, and pay over the rest to the member's agents, who distribute it to the Names. Managing agents receive around 0.75 per cent of the premiums and approximately 15 per cent of the profits each Name on the syndicate makes, and are not allowed to own, or be owned by, a Lloyd's broker.

Underwriters

Underwriters, who can be managing agents themselves, deal with the day-to-day business of deciding whether or not to agree to insure risks brought to them by Lloyd's brokers. They are the hot-shots of Lloyd's, sitting in teams at long desks, called 'boxes', waiting for brokers to petition them for cover. Underwriters specialise in different kinds of insurance, such as shipping or aviation. A broker comes to an underwriter's box, sits on a stool at one end of it, and is pumped for information about the client, the broker's firm, and the activities of other underwriters.

A typical day at a box might consist of twenty or more brokers coming one after the other to the underwriter, seeking all kinds of insurance and re-insurance for new and old clients from all over the world. The underwriter is often highly knowledgeable about the clients and their industries and will either make a quick decision to reject or accept requests for cover, or ask for more detailed information which must be supplied later. Lines of insurance and the claims record of customers are recorded on computer as each deal is done.

> .... **A broker will seek cover from insurance companies as well as Lloyd's** ....

Rejections are on various grounds. For instance, US courts tend to award very high sums to claimants, so underwriters tend to be wary of insuring risks where claims may arise in the United States. This is no reflection on the client, only on the prevailing conditions in the United States. Clients who are financially weak may be rejected on the grounds that they may go into liquidation soon and fail to pay the premiums. Clients with poor claims records, or whose industries are considered too risky, are also likely to be rejected.

The brokers

Brokers must be accredited by Lloyd's in order to approach the underwriters. A broker will seek cover from insurance companies as well as Lloyd's – the bigger the risk, the more it will be spread across the whole insurance market, including Lloyd's. Brokers go to the Lloyd's building and enter the 'Room' (actually several floors) where they may have regular meetings with certain underwriters, and have made specific appointments with other ones. The underwriters are at their boxes between mid-morning and mid-afternoon. Frequently, there is a queue of brokers waiting to see them. The broker explains the kind of cover he is looking for and gives information about the client. If the underwriter agrees to a line of insurance, the slip (actually a large paper sheet folded several times) is stamped and signed by the underwriter.

The slip describes the client, the cover and the premium on its left-hand side. Below it are more details of the cover and any special conditions, together with information about the client, such as its number of employees. Below this are blank folded sections where the underwriters put their stamps and signatures. Next to their stamps, underwriters write the percentage of the total risk that they are willing to cover. The first underwriter on the slip is called the 'lead underwriter'.

The broker goes from one underwriter to another until 100 per cent of the risk is covered. The slip then forms a binding agreement. When all the broking has been done, the broker returns to the office to contact clients and complete the day's business.

The Lloyd's building

Lloyd's is housed in an ultra-modern building on Lime Street in the heart of the City of London. The old underwriting 'Room' now takes up four huge floors. Above them are housed the offices of the administration, including the famous Adam Room, an eighteenth-century wood-panelled room designed by Robert Adam. On the ground floor, the Lutine bell, recovered in 1859 from a sunken frigate insured by Lloyd's, is traditionally rung once for good news and twice for bad. Near to it sits a man dressed in red who calls out messages for people in the underwriting Room, and close by is an open casualty book in which the day's disasters are written with a quill pen. The Room is filled with brokers and underwriters plying their trade.

HOW TO BECOME A NAME

In the 1980s, you had to show evidence of personal assets worth at least £100,000 to become a Name (except for 'mini-Names' and 'working Names', whom we will look at later). In 1991, this requirement was raised to £250,000. The rules about what assets are eligible vary, but essentially they are:

- At least 60 per cent of the assets must be in stocks and shares or in gold bullion and coins (but not more than 30 per cent in either of these categories), or cash at a building society or bank, or premium bonds, life assurance policies, interests in trust funds, national savings certificates or guarantees from banks, insurance companies or building societies.

- In the case of gold, the valuation for the means test is 70 per cent of its current market value.

- Your principal residence, antiques, jewels, livestock, private company shares, cars, boats, pictures and house contents are not accepted unless supported by a letter of credit or bank guarantee.

- The remaining 40 per cent of the assets can be in the equity of freehold property, or leasehold property having more than 50 years left in the lease and where the length of the lease and the age of the Name totals more than 100 years.

- Names from other countries are required to show means in a country from which it is legal to remove assets or to provide bank guarantees or letters of credit. US citizens residing in certain States must comply with further conditions to safeguard Lloyd's against local laws.

> ..... **No one can truthfully say later that they did not know that they had agreed to unlimited liability.** ......

You can probably see that these rules are designed for a single purpose; to ensure that Lloyd's can convert the Name's assets to cash at the accepted value as quickly as possible should it become necessary to do so.

The application process

Prospective Names have to apply for membership by the end of August of the year preceding the one in which they begin underwriting, and Names resigning must do so by the same date. The paperwork must be completed by the end of November in order to start underwriting by the following January.

Prospective Names must have two sponsors who are members of Lloyd's, one who vouches for the person's character and the other who is a partner or director of the member's agency which the new Name is joining. Members' agents are allowed to pay Lloyd's members to sponsor new Names.

Once you are over these hurdles, you are then summoned to a 'Rota Committee' in the Adam Room where all the risks of being a Name are explained in grave terms. No one can truthfully say later that they did not know that they had agreed to unlimited liability.

Deposits and premium limits

Once new Names are accepted, they must undertake to keep the value of their assets above the level set by Lloyd's. If the value of the assets goes down, the Name must declare the fact and either produce evidence of more assets to reach the required £250,000 minimum or withdraw from Lloyd's. The Council can check on the value of a Name's assets at any time.

The Name decides how much insurance to underwrite each year – this is called the 'premium limit'. In 1992, for example, the minimum value of premiums a Name could underwrite for was £50,000 and the maximum was £2,000,000. Having agreed a premium limit, the Name must deposit 20 per cent of the value of the limit in a 'failsafe' deposit held in trust by Lloyd's. Another 10 per cent or so must be deposited either in a reserve controlled by the member's agent or in a reserve run jointly by the member's agent and Lloyd's.

The failsafe deposit can be in the form of cash, letters of credit, shares, life policies and other liquid instruments. The interest in the deposit is either paid to the Name or deposited in the Name's personal reserves. Lloyd's rules make it difficult for the Name to withdraw capital gains on such deposits.

On 31 December every year, Lloyd's makes a solvency test on every Name, consisting of a check on the true value of the Name's reserves held at Lloyd's and by the member's agents. Often changes in the value of shares and foreign currencies bring the value of a Name's reserves below the required limit. If this happens, the Name's premium limit is reduced for the following year.

When agreeing their premium limits, Names fall into several categories:

- *Category 1* members have assets of more than £250,000 and have deposited a minimum of £25,000. Their premium limits can increase by £25,000 each year to a maximum of £2,000,000, in which case they must have deposited reserves of £600,000.

- *Category 2* members have assets between £100,000 and £250,000. This can occur when a Name's assets have decreased in value due to factors such as share fluctuations. Category 2 members can also be individuals working at Lloyd's (in other words, a perk for Lloyd's workers is a reduction in the net wealth requirement). They must deposit at least £25,000 into the failsafe and reserves, and the deposits must be at least 40 per cent of their premium limit. The allowable premium limit is between £50,000 and £600,000.

- *Category 3* members are Names whose assets have fallen below £100,000 or Lloyd's workers with assets below this figure who are allowed to become Names as a perk. Failsafes and reserves must total 50 per cent of the premium limit and the premium limit cannot be more than £190,000.

- *Category 4* members are Lloyd's workers who are not required to show any wealth at all. They must deposit at least 50 per cent of their premium limit and the limit cannot be more than £100,000.

Names who are working in the market are known as 'working Names' and those who do not have to show assets of £250,000 are called 'mini-Names'. Names who are not otherwise connected with Lloyd's are called 'external Names' or 'non-working Names'.

These rules may seem very wise and cautious, but two things are obvious. First, that external Names can, contrary to what is often said, use their principal home as 60 per cent of the wealth requirement by providing a bank guarantee or letter of credit, and they can use the equity in a holiday home for the remaining 40 per cent. In the UK property boom of the 1980s you didn't have to be very wealthy at all to have the value of two houses meeting the means test. Secondly, the perks for working Names could be said to be provided to the detriment of external Names.

> **Names on an open year cannot resign**

OPEN YEARS

As we have seen, syndicates usually 'close' their accounts for a particular year after three years inclusive (e.g. 1992 is closed at the end of 1994), the rationale being that most claims will have been made by then. The year is re-insured to close, and any other claims that subsequently arise will be met by the re-insurers, who are the syndicate members for the following year. If, however, a large number of claims have been made and are in dispute, the year cannot be re-insured to close and must remain open indefinitely. Names on an open year cannot resign – they remain liable for all valid claims that may arise against the year. In such cases, it is often impossible to estimate what the total liability may be, so Names must just wait and hope, while, in the meantime, they are called upon to come up with cash sums to replenish their reserves.

EXCESS OF LOSS (XOL)

In the last two decades, Lloyd's has been up against increasingly strong competition from other insurance companies, and has been losing its market share. This led a number of underwriters, particularly newer ones, to seek profit in the field of 'excess of loss insurance', or XOL. To understand XOL, think what happens when you insure a car. You will probably find that if you agree to pay an 'excess' of, say, £100 of the cost of car repairs in case of an accident, the insurer reduces your premium; you have agreed to pay the first £100 of the claim and the insurer has agreed to pay anything above that. XOL works the same way, except that it is a deal between two insurers. The first insurer agrees with the second, the 're-insurer', to pay for, say, the first £1 million of any claim and the re-insurer agrees to pay for the rest. The re-insurer may then re-insure again with a third insurer in a similar way. This process can continue with yet more insurers.

THE LMX SPIRAL

The market in London (not just at Lloyd's) for excess of loss cover is called London Market Excess, or LMX. In the 1980s, the LMX boomed as some Lloyd's underwriters dived into it, re-insuring and re-insuring again, taking a cut of the premium and earning commissions each time. This became known as the 'LMX spiral'; it seemed good business at the time, but when a number of natural catastrophes occurred (see page 189) and re-insurers became liable, the complexity of unravelling which re-insurer would be liable for what was so great that each syndicate involved had to assume the worst and call on its Names to boost their reserves with more cash. The result of this is that, overall, Names have had to deposit much more money than necessary in their reserves while they wait for the unravelling process to finish.

LLOYD'S IN TROUBLE

Despite Lloyd's hitherto grand reputation and aura of effortless success, there have been many scandals and losses during its 300 years of existence – being a Name has never really been 'money for old rope'. Lloyd's present troubles, which may be life-threatening, have a number of causes, which we will examine here.

The sins of the fathers

As the world reaches the millenium, it is undergoing a 'paradigm shift', a profound change in its understanding of the effects of industrialisation. Gone is the boundless faith in progress, science and the inevitability of economic growth. It is now plain that many industrial practices have caused the world enormous harm, and that they cannot be allowed to continue unchecked. The insurance business is sensitive to this change; as the claims pour in, insurance companies wake up to the trends behind them.

Asbestos

Asbestos is a general name for a number of naturally occurring mineral fibres which are highly resistant to heat. Between about 1870 and 1960 it was used in an enormous variety of products, more than 3,000 of them, such as building materials, fire-resistant fabrics, electrical equipment, motor parts, and insulation materials. In World War 2 thousands of workers laboured in an atmosphere filled with asbestos dust fitting out warships.

Like many other minerals, asbestos has a nasty characteristic; quite a brief exposure to it can cause fatal lung diseases which may not manifest themselves for 50 years or more. It is often said that the dangers of asbestos were not known – not known by whom? They were certainly known, at least in part, in Britain in 1931, when the Asbestos Industry Regulations set out rules for asbestos dust extraction in the workplace. They were known by the US Navy in 1943, when it issued a pamphlet laying down minimum safety standards for working with asbestos. Nevertheless, the world went on using asbestos, and in the first half of this century companies were able to obtain general liability insurance which covered possible claims against industrial disease.

Although insurance companies have long ago given up offering general liability cover, many of the old policies are still valid. By the late 1970s, a huge series of asbestosis claims began in the United States, and courts were making vast awards to sufferers. Lloyd's was hit badly.

Underwriters at Lloyd's had re-insured excess of loss cover against general liability policies dating back decades. As the US courts made awards against employers, they in turn sought to claim on their policies. Since so many Lloyd's underwriters had re-insured their excess of loss cover with the small number of syndicates who had been willing to take the business, the huge burden of liabilities fell mainly on them. Richard Outhwaite, an underwriter who had re-insured only 32 contracts covering asbestos risk in 1982, on behalf of a syndicate numbered 317/661, had to announce in 1985 that the 1982 year could not be closed due to the large number of asbestos claims coming in.

The syndicate's 1982 year was still open in 1992, with more claims arriving, resulting in frequent calls for more funds from its Names, each Name paying amounts proportionate to the premium limit for the 1982 year. Many of the Names were celebrities; among them were former British Prime Minister Ted Heath, golfer Tony Jacklin and tycoons John Ritblat and Robert Maxwell. Nine hundred and eighty-seven of the Names went to court, eventually receiving a settlement in 1992. Another 627 Names on the syndicate, who didn't go to court and were now time-barred from doing so, got nothing. Claims are expected to continue for another decade or so – the average potential loss per Name has been estimated at £625,000.

Pollution

Some say that the worst is over for asbestos claims, but a new monster is on the insurance horizon. Governments want to do something about industrial pollution and most have adopted the view that the polluter should pay. Once again, the movement started in the United States, where the Carter administration introduced the Comprehensive Response Compensation and Liability Act (CERCLA), in 1980. Under CERCLA, a 'Superfund' was formed, consisting of a levy on industries, principally chemicals and oil, which is administered by the Environmental Protection Agency (EPA). The Superfund brief is to clean up polluted sites, ruthlessly pursuing any company that has been involved for the cost. Lloyd's syndicates that have re-insured old general liability policies are in the firing line, and with estimates of the cost of the clean-up running as high as $750 billion, they have become enmeshed in a web of complex litigation.

> The average potential loss per Name has been estimated at £625,000.

Insurers have sought to establish in the US courts that they are not liable; if they win, they can walk away from the problem, leaving the companies to slug it out with the EPA alone. The problem has become a 'lawyer's party' – the EPA has spent most of its budget so far on litigation. Every US State court can take its own view on whether insurers are liable, and what for. With up to $750 billion at stake, it is worth everybody's while to spend hugely on legal costs – the overall results will not be known for several years as the cases creep their way up towards Supreme Court appeals.

While Lloyd's insurers fight to escape liability in the United States, they have also been calling on their Names to produce cash so that reserves can be built up in case they lose. Sharpened by their experience in fighting asbestos claims, Lloyd's seems to be in with a chance of surviving the assaults of the Superfund, but in the meantime Names are forced to increase their reserves.

Where the United States leads, others follow. GATT, the World Bank and the EU are all making moves to go 'green'. The political ramifications are enormous and many governments would rather chase corporations for the clean-up costs than introduce green taxes. The insurance industry is in for a hard time and many Names are bound to suffer.

Catastrophes

Since 1987 there have been a series of natural disasters and accidents that have wreaked havoc at Lloyd's. The first hurricane to strike Britain in 200 years devastated the south of England, costing Lloyd's hundreds of millions of pounds. Added to this, the so-called 'Black Monday' of October 1987, when stock markets around the world crashed, greatly reduced the value of many Names' assets, compounding their difficulties.

There were 19 other serious accidents and natural disasters in 1988, costing the whole London insurance market around £1 billion. The Piper Alpha accident, where an oil rig exploded, costing 167 lives, accounted for more than half of this figure. The complexity of the LMX spiral forced Lloyd's syndicates to build reserves to £12 billion until the true liability, around £370 million, could be allocated. Piper Alpha settlements were

> ....**Those who are trapped on open years may never be free of them.** ....

delayed by the shock experienced by survivors of the disaster. Also in 1988, a Pan-Am jet exploded over Lockerbie in Scotland, resulting in claims totalling £100 million.

In September 1989, Hurricane Hugo caused enormous damage across the Caribbean and Carolinas. The next month, there was an earthquake in San Francisco. In December there was another one in Australia. In the spring, 95 people died in the Hillsborough football stadium; in August, 51 people were killed at a party on the river Thames when the Marchioness was rammed by a barge; while in March an oil tanker, the Exxon Valdez, polluted the coast of Alaska.

It was no better in 1990. Another hurricane hit England, followed by another in Continental Europe. The total cost is estimated at £8 billion. When Iraq invaded Kuwait, Lloyd's had to pay a large part of the $300 million claim for lost Kuwaiti planes.

In the wake of these losses, thousands of Names have been resigning from Lloyd's, while only hundreds have been signing up. They are the lucky ones; those who are trapped on open years may never be free of them.

The Names' rebellion

The number of Names at Lloyd's has fallen dramatically since 1988, when there were about 32,000 of them. Over 15,000 Names, a majority of the remaining members, are stuck on one or more open years. They are drawn from all walks of life, including some 50 British Members of Parliament, former Prime Ministers and Cabinet Ministers, celebrities, foreign businesspeople, bankers, farmers, professionals and entrepreneurs. Lloyd's is a pillar of the establishment and being a Name has high social status.

As the non-working Names began to receive calls for tens, in some cases hundreds, of thousands of pounds to cover losses and build reserves, they began to ask questions. A huge proportion of the losses were centred on a few syndicates, which were made up of mainly external Names, many of whom were new. The older syndicates at Lloyd's had been harder to get onto, since they were generally already fully subscribed. In the boom of the 1980s, Names were confident of profits, but when the losses began, many of them found themselves unable to meet their cash calls from Lloyd's. Many turned to the law, issuing writs against their member's agents and managing agents, alleging negligence.

Others turned to the Hardship Committee, set up by Lloyd's to help Names raise the necessary money. The Committee requires Names to agree to keep the details of their help secret, and not to sue Lloyd's. The Committee does not pay Names' debts for them, but requires that applicants fill out a highly detailed questionnaire about their, and their spouses', financial circumstances, after which it may arrange attachments to Names' salaries, charges on their houses and so on as ways of meeting cash calls. The deal is generally that the Name must pay 25 per cent of the debt upfront and make an agreement to pay the rest over a long period – in some cases, a lifetime. Most of the hardship cases are older people, with low premium limits and few means. The Committee agrees not to dispossess these individuals from their only home, especially if it is modest and they have no other assets.

Despite it being 'bad form', many external Names ignored official appeals for cooperation and decided to fight it out. Committees of external Names banded together to sue the 'insiders' of Lloyd's, alleging that they had been misled and badly advised by their agents. In the United States and Canada, many Names were able to avoid their obligations on legal technicalities, and bit back – Lloyd's found itself under investigation by the FBI over alleged violations of the notorious RICO anti-racketeering laws, while Names struggled to freeze Lloyd's Names' deposits held in North America to prevent them being drawn on by Lloyd's.

External Names complained of the lack of information given them by Lloyd's, the activities of touts who earned commissions from the recruitment of new Names, and that some agents had advised Names not to resign, resulting in further losses. There is a feeling that many underwriters and agents were neither bright, efficient, nor honest, and that there was a general attitude among insiders that external Names are punters who can be taken advantage of. Following the Outhwaite settlement, Lloyd's has become a little more cooperative towards external Names and a process of reform of its systems is underway. Whether or not Lloyd's will survive in the long term remains to be seen. As government policies and the insurance markets change, conditions may well improve. For the hundreds of ruined Names, though, this is small consolation.

IS IT WORTH BEING A NAME?

Given Lloyd's problems, becoming a Name may not seem to be a wise committment; however, it still may be. Membership of Lloyd's is certainly not for widows and orphans, people whose dependents will be destitute if all is lost, nor for the elderly. One view is that if you can meet the means test before you are forty, it can be worth being a Name for 20 years or so. If everything goes wrong, younger people have more of a chance of building up their wealth again by their own sweat.

Being a Name is not really an investment. Short of becoming a fugitive, a Name stands to lose everything, not just the deposit – if you invested in, say, shares, all you can lose is what you paid for the shares. If your assets far exceed the £250,000 minimum, or if your close relatives are exceedingly wealthy and will support you if things go wrong, you are in less danger of ending up on the street.

> **Being a Name has had quite a social cachet.**

Being a Name has had quite a social cachet. Clearly, it is extremely unwise to enter into any financial commitment for reasons of vanity. However, some ambitious people may genuinely benefit from the social opportunities of Lloyd's membership – a Name does have the chance to 'hob-nob' with the peers and politicians who are fellow Names.

If you are exceedingly wealthy, with relatively liquid assets of more than, say, £10 million, Lloyd's membership would seem to be unwise, since the benefit to you of the income is unlikely to outweigh the risk of unlimited liability.

If you are under 40, with wealthy relatives who will support you if a disaster occurs, and are knowledgeable about risk management, it may still be worth becoming a Name. The payments which you receive from Lloyd's should not really be regarded as income which you can spend, since there is a possibility of loss in future years. A large proportion of such income should be used to build up your own reserves against potential losses.

The careful selection of syndicates, managing agents and member's agents, the willingness to monitor the business actively, a knowledge of the law and the physical and mental endurance to battle it out if things go wrong would seem to be essential qualities for a Name who intends to survive.

➡ update for 1997

Lloyds has been reorganising itself, and hopes to end most of the litigation with disgruntled Names soon with a large settlement. It has also set up Equitas, a 'second Lloyds', as a vehicle for new insurance business. Lloyd's has changed its rules to allow businesses to become Names with limited liability, and a large number of insurance companies have joined.

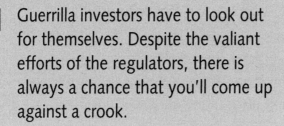

Guerrilla investors have to look out
for themselves. Despite the valiant
efforts of the regulators, there is
always a chance that you'll come up
against a crook.

11

Fraud and the regulatory bodies

In this chapter we examine:

- The Securities and Investments Board (SIB).
- The Self-Regulatory Organisations (SROs) – IMRO, LAUTRO, FIMBRA and SFA.
- The Department of Trade and Industry.
- The Securities and Exchange Commission (SEC) in the United States.
- Two perennial scams: The hard sell and Conning the law breakers.
- Insider trading in the 1980s – Boesky, Milken and Levine.

INTRODUCTION

There is a big difference between blue-collar crime and white-collar crime. White-collar criminals are far less likely to be caught and, when they are, they don't usually go to jail for very long. This is true in most countries: the more capitalist a country is, the more it seems to be true. It is sometimes argued that financial fraudsters are an unavoidable evil in a free market, and that it is so difficult to catch them that the degree of supervision necessary would stifle business activity. While this may be true, it is also true that many professionals in the financial world spend their lives trying to work out ways of circumventing the rules, and for such people it becomes quite difficult to distinguish between theft and 'good business'. As private investors, we must face reality: the different financial centres of the world have different methods of trying to keep the market fair, and they enforce them with varying degrees of severity. Some markets are fairer than others, but none of them offer a 100 per cent guarantee that you won't be ripped off. If you buy something in a shop and it turns out to be faulty or shoddy, it is usually possible to get redress quite quickly, but once you have handed money over for investment, it can be an expensive process trying to get it back, and you cannot often be confident of success.

Guerrilla investors have to look out for themselves. Despite the valiant efforts of the regulators (discussed below), there is always a chance that you'll come up against a crook. While anyone may be unlucky enough to be cheated, however careful he or she is, thinking and doing the following seem to increase your chances of being ripped off:

- Believing in a scheme because it has been discussed positively on a radio programme for small investors (as the disastrous Barlow Clowes firm was).

- Trusting people just because they are 'posh'.

- Trusting people just because they are not 'posh'.

- Investing in schemes you haven't thoroughly checked out.

- Doing something illegal which involves trusting someone you don't know.

- Investing for ideological reasons.
- Investing for improved social status.
- Failing to study the deal in the context of world markets.
- Believing that the regulators will always protect you.
- Having faith in booms.
- Putting all your eggs in one basket.
- Being too eager to get rich quick.
- Being seduced by schemes that involve a lot of trading.
- Getting into schemes that you haven't first made sure you can get out of.

This may all sound rather negative but it isn't; the point is simply that self-defence is always vitally important.

THE REGULATORS

The regulatory system in the UK is undergoing changes, though the revolutionary Financial Services Act 1986 is only eight years old. New rules are expected for the 'retail' end of investment in particular, concentrating on the stricter regulation of the sale of life assurance products.

The Securities and Investments Board (SIB)

The SIB is an umbrella organisation with legal powers to oversee the financial markets and to implement the Financial Services Act. The main features of the Act are:

- All investment businesses have to be authorised by the SIB or one of the regulatory bodies that are answerable to it.
- Investment advisers have either to sell the products of one company only or to be completely independent and sell all the financial products available in the market.
- Investment advisers are supposed to give you the 'best advice' they can.
- There is an Investors Compensation Scheme which reimburses investors for all of the first £30,000 lost in a collapse and 90 per cent of the next £20,000.

One of the drawbacks of the system is that the SROs (Self-Regulating

Organisations) which answer to the SIB are 'self-regulating' – it has been suggested that this does not make them independent enough. The SROs are:

- FIMBRA (the Financial Intermediaries, Managers and Brokers Regulatory Organisation), which regulates independent financial advisers and insurance brokers.
- LAUTRO (the Life Assurance and Unit Trust Regulatory Organisation), which regulates the retail end of unit trusts and life assurance companies.
- IMRO (the Investment Management Regulatory Organisation), which regulates fund managers, including those of unit trusts and pension funds.
- PIA (the Personal Investment Authority) is taking over from FIMBRA and LAUTRO, and also includes some ex-members of IMRO.
- SFA (the Securities and Futures Authority) which regulates the operators in the futures and equities markets.

Some organisations are members of more than one SRO. In addition, most professional bodies on the periphery of finance are regulated by one of the nine Recognised Professional Bodies (RPBs) which in turn are answerable to the SIB.

The Securities and Exchange Commission (SEC)

The Securities and Exchange Commission in the United States is the equivalent of the SIB but with more teeth. It may be a matter of taste, but the SEC's rigorous and determined approach to catching and disgracing the rule-breakers contrasts strongly with the less direct approach of the British. The role of the SEC in cracking high-level insider dealing in the 1980s is discussed later in this chapter.

THE HARD SELL

The scope that commodities offered a fraudster was considerable in the past. Here's one way investors have regularly been fleeced over the years.

✳ **EXAMPLE** You are telephoned by a member of a telephone sales team working from a carefully written script. You are asked if you want to invest in the commodities market, and the benefits are explained to you. If you seem interested, you are asked how much you want to invest. The salesperson then tells you that he or she will call you back if a good investment opportunity comes up. An hour or two later you get another call – the firm's analysts have identified a 'positive buy signal' in some commodity. If you don't want to buy, the salesperson passes you over to a 'chief analyst' who explains everything to you, frequently in domineering or patronising tones. You are pressurised to come up with a cheque. If you resist, the salesperson lets you go.

On the same day, you get another call; sadly, the opportunity has gone – you would have made a fortune already if you'd invested on margin. Fortunately, there is another 'positive buy signal' in some other commodity and you are pressurised into coming up with some money, which may be collected by a motorcycle messenger. If you part with your money, you receive an agreement form to sign, containing clauses which protect the broker against your future ire.

Your money really does go into the commodity, minus some hefty commissions; if you make a paper profit you are encouraged to let the broker keep trading for you, and if you make a loss, the broker asks you for more money to keep the contract open. The fraud is in the fact that the broker is decidedly not making every effort to find you a good deal – he couldn't care less what happens to your investment, as long as he gets some commission. Proving such a fraud in court is extremely difficult indeed.

This hoary sales technique is well-known in all fields of business – it is called the 'hard sell'. It means bullying people into buying overpriced goods and it pops up anywhere that is under-regulated. The commodities market in the UK has been tightened up so the hard sell probably won't be tried again, but watch out for it in other areas. Anyone who promises miracles should be regarded with suspicion – if it sounds too good to be true, it probably is too good to be true. If someone is desperate to get you to invest in something, offer to lend them the money in return for cast-iron security of greater value to which you can get good title. Usually this is enough to make the promoter evaporate, but if it is not, you may end up with a bargain house or shareholding. This of course, is a sound method of banking!

> **Anyone who promises miracles should be regarded with suspicion.**

CONNING THE LAW BREAKERS

Here's another fraud that has been perpetrated on investors from continental Europe.

EXAMPLE ✳

Like many successful European businesspeople, you have a substantial sum of money that you have not declared to your tax authority. A compatriot approaches you, telling you of the wonderful investment opportunities in London-based options. If you agree to invest, your money is passed though a chain of companies and an account is opened for you in London. Every time a commodity is purchased for you, the price you pay is, say, more than double the price actually paid. After some time, the fraudsters disappear with the money. Many Europeans are unaware of the ease and cheapness with which companies can be formed in the UK, and tend to assume that limited companies are as well-regulated as they are in their own countries.

This is an example of how people who try to evade tax become vulnerable to fraud. Strangely, people like this never seem to check out the schemes they invest in very carefully.

INSIDER TRADING – MICHAEL MILKEN, IVAN BOESKY AND DENNIS LEVINE

Boom times are good times for fraudsters as well as for the rest of us, and a series of dramatic prosecutions on Wall Street in the late 1980s brought to light well-organised wrongdoing on a massive scale. In 1986, Dennis Levine, a merchant banker of limited ability and a director of Drexel Burnham Lambert Inc., a highly successful New York stock broking firm, was arrested on charges of insider trading.

Levine had indeed been trading on inside information, purchasing shares in companies just before a takeover bid sent their value rocketing. This was done through an account at the Swiss Bank Leu in the Bahamas, which the SEC was able to pressurise into revealing details of its client after an anonymous tip-off led them there. Levine was eventually sentenced to two years in prison, paying over nearly $12 million in illegal profits to the SEC, but not before he revealed the names of a group of individuals employed within different companies on Wall Street with whom he had swapped privileged information over several years. One of the names was startling – Ivan Boesky.

Ivan Boesky was an 'arbitrageur', a business which was originally to trade on the price differences of shares being sold on more than one stock market, but had become a high-risk, daring game of buying heavily into companies in the hope that they would be taken over. Boesky seemed to have a magic touch. He had accumulated net assets of over $130 million through the control of his arbitrage fund, through an apparently miraculous ability to anticipate takeover bids before they were announced. The truth was more prosaic; he had become deeply involved in illegal schemes with another powerful figure of the period, Michael Milken, the 'junk bond king'.

Michael Milken had become interested in 'junk bonds' while still at university. Junk bonds are corporate bonds that are considered too risky for a rating by the two main rating systems, Moody's and Standard and Poor's. When Milken started out in Wall Street in the 1970s, junk bonds were in bad odour, but through his high degree of technical ability he began to persuade investors that these bonds, which offered higher rates of interest than normal, would outperform the blue chips. By 1977 Milken was in control of nearly quarter of the junk bond market, enabling him to improve the bonds' liquidity by acting as a market maker. He promised his clients that he would buy back bonds when they wanted to sell them; these he was able to pass on to other investors at a wide profit margin. Milken worked for Drexel, a Wall Street firm, but was able to operate semi-independently by locating his offices in his native California. Drexel had an investment banking department and Milken soon saw the opportunity to earn huge advisory fees for the firm by helping client companies raise finance through the issuance of junk bonds, a market which he increasingly controlled.

> He began to persuade investors that these bonds, which offered higher rates of interest than normal, would outperform the blue chips.

Although Dennis Levine eventually got a job at Drexel, his connection with Milken was tenuous. While still very junior, Levine had decided to develop a network of contacts throughout Wall Street with whom he could exchange inside information. A spell in Paris alerted him to European private banking methods and on his return to the United States he was able to put his plan into action. Curiously, Levine never mastered the mathematical skills necessary for the mergers and acquisitions field in which he now worked. Dominating his associates, he began to trade on his own account through his secret bank account in the Bahamas, purchasing shares in US companies which he expected to shoot up. Occasionally, he was even able to persuade his cronies to let him into their offices after hours so he could search files for confidential information. Not content with his private profits, Levine also used the information at work, telling his bosses that they should offer their investment banking services to companies which he knew were soon to be the subject of takeover bids, and claiming that he had acquired these insights through careful financial analysis. Once at Drexel, Levine desperately tried to ingratiate himself with Boesky by feeding him inside information and asking for nothing in return. In fact Boesky, by this time deeply involved in illegal activities himself, reciprocated with useful information of his own.

When Ronald Reagan became president in 1980, the financial community received clear signals that there would be little government interference during Reagan's term of office. As the markets freed up, the takeover field boomed. In 1981 Boesky was able to double his firm's capital, perfectly legally, by buying shares in Conoco, an oil company, during a bidding war. He earned some $40 million on the deal by using borrowed money, or 'leverage'. In 1982 he attempted to repeat this coup by taking a huge position in Cities Services in similar circumstances. This time the deal collapsed and Boesky narrowly escaped insolvency through conducting a complicated exchange of options with a Wall Street associate. Two weeks later, another bid for the company caused the shares to rise again, and Boesky was able to cut his losses and get out.

This painful experience appears to have prompted Boesky to take his first serious steps into illegality. Determined that he would never again take such a risk, Boesky approached an investment banker, Martin Siegel, offering cash payments in return for advance information on takeover bids. An additional benefit to Siegel was that Boesky's arbitrage activity would help to 'soften up' target companies, which would help Siegel's clients launch their bids.

Boesky wanted to become more involved in leveraged buy-outs but he needed more capital. Gaining control of Vagabond, a company partly inherited by his wife which owned the Beverly Hills Hotel, Boesky renamed it Northview Corporation and raised $100 million by issuing junk bonds through Drexel. Drexel took massive fees and a large number of warrants to buy Northview shares. Other deals with Drexel followed.

In 1983 a corporate raider named Victor Posner, a client of Drexel, was in difficulties. He had signed an agreement not to increase his holding in the Fischbach Corporation, a building concern, which he had attempted to merge with one of his own companies. Milken asked Boesky to buy shares in Fischbach, guaranteeing him against any losses. When Boesky bought over 10 per cent of the company, he filed a statutory disclosure form with the SEC, the '13-D', giving false information. This action freed Posner from his obligations and allowed him to continue his attempts to takeover Fischbach. The '13-D' form is meant to protect stock market investors since it involves the public revelation of the buying of large stakes in a company, and the purchaser is supposed to disclose his or her intentions and associations with regard to takeovers.

Milken continued his contact with Boesky. Soon he asked him to buy into Diamond Shamrock on the understanding that they would secretly share any profits. Boesky did so, but took large losses which Milken had guaranteed. By 1985, however, Milken had paid back Boesky for all his losses. Both men were setting their sights higher than ever before. While Boesky was able to control his own staff by a 'divide and rule' policy, Milken ensured loyalty by paying his employees huge bonuses. 'I think greed is healthy,' Boesky told an audience of students at the University of Southern California's business school, a phrase which was much used by commentators to symbolise the mood of the 1980s. He even wrote a book, *Merger Mania*, a detailed exposition of the technical aspects of arbitrage which gave no hint of his cavalier attitudes to the law.

> Many companies which hoped to become 'raiders' had no hope of raising the requisite capital without Milken's junk bond skills.

Milken began to use his network of junk bond-buying clients, who by now included Savings and Loan and insurance companies, as a pool of finance with which to exploit the craze for leveraged buy-outs and mergers. Many companies which hoped to become 'raiders' had no hope of raising the requisite capital without Milken's junk bond skills. Every year Milken presided over a conference in Beverly Hills, dubbed 'the Predator's Ball', at which he waxed lyrical on the joys of junk bond financing to an audience of institutions, clients and illustrious financiers, such as Sir James Goldsmith and Rupert Murdoch. Since Milken now dominated the junk bond market, he was able to buy back bonds from clients of Drexel, who were not in a position to assess their true value, then sell them on to Ivan Boesky; Boesky would sell the bonds back to Drexel at a large profit, and Drexel was able to sell the bonds to other customers at still higher prices.

When the founder of CNN, Ted Turner, came to Milken for help in financing a takeover bid for MGM/United Artists, the film company, also a client of Drexel, Milken asked Boesky to buy MGM shares, creating the illusion that the company was already the subject of a bid, which helped to persuade junk bond purchasers that MGM bonds were worth buying.

Boesky made a profit of $3 million, sharing it with Milken, while Drexel earned some $66 million in financing fees from Turner. By this time Boesky and Milken had become dependent on one another, but Milken was gaining the upper hand, as it was he who supplied all the information. Boesky was becoming Milken's tool.

Milken helped Boesky to raise a vast amount of capital for an arbitrage fund, insisting that Boesky pay over large amounts of money now due from their illegal activities before the deal was closed. In his eagerness to get the fund off the ground, Boesky paid Milken $5.3 million that he was unable to explain to his accountants until Milken supplied an invoice after the fact. This was one of the slips that forced Boesky into a corner when he finally came under suspicion from the SEC.

When Levine was arrested in 1986, Boesky and Milken met to discuss how to avoid the attention of the SEC. Agreeing to tread carefully in the future, Boesky returned to New York to instruct his book-keeper to destroy records of illegal transactions. In August, Boesky was served with a subpoena by the SEC, demanding records and his testimony; he came clean with his own lawyers, describing the insider trading, tax frauds, manipulation of the market and false statements he had made in concert with Milken. Following negotiations, he signed a 'plea bargain' with the US Justice Department, agreeing to plead guilty on a single count of conspiracy to commit securities fraud, to pay the SEC $100 million, and to cooperate fully with the investigation. To safeguard the $100 million, and to avoid chaos in the markets, the SEC allowed Boesky to begin selling off his share portfolio. Boesky agreed to telephone other market players in an attempt to incriminate them, and had a secretly recorded meeting with Milken in which he engaged in a discussion on how to avoid detection. In November, Boesky was arrested and charged.

> **Although the crooks may have their wings clipped eventually, it can take a very long time for regulators to catch up with them.**

In 1987 Levine was sent to prison, paying $11.6 million to the SEC and a fine of $362,000. Released in 1988, he started a firm offering financial advice and still appears to be affluent. Following the 'Black Monday' October stock market crash, Milken fought tirelessly to keep the junk bond market alive, despite being under investigation, along with his employer, Drexel. Boesky was sentenced to three years in prison in December, but was released after two years. He still remains wealthy. Milken mounted a costly and spirited defence, but when other associates signed plea bargains he was abandoned by Drexel. In 1990 Drexel finally collapsed and Milken was brought to trial, eventually being sentenced to ten years in prison.

If there is a conclusion to draw from this tortuous story, it is surely that although the crooks may have their wings clipped eventually, it can take a very long time for regulators to catch up with them. Cheating in the markets is not a victimless crime – it is stealing from the millions of ordinary people who save through the institutions, and from the private investors struggling to understand the reasons for price movements.

► The reason why people take their money abroad is generally to protect it, rather than out of greed for more; having everything in one place makes it vulenerable, as history has proved over and over again.

12

Overseas investments

This chapter is not aimed at the British who simply want to own a second house in France or Spain and have a few shares in the Far East; it is for the guerrilla investor who has accumulated enough capital to have the increased choices, and increased responsibility, that go with wealth. If your net worth is less than £200,000, active overseas investment is probably not for you – yet. In fact, overseas investment becomes a necessity rather than an option as an individual's wealth increases, so in this chapter we will look at the following:

- Why you should invest overseas.
- The companies and individuals that do so.
- Tax havens, what they are and how they work.
- Offshore trusts and corporations.
- How to avoid the sharks.
- How to minimise risk.

INTRODUCTION

Once you are in possession of a large amount of capital, your thoughts inevitably turn to how to keep it safe from all the unrelenting forces that are continually trying to take bites out of it. The world looks different to the wealthy; they are much more interested in international political and economic patterns than most people, since these have a bearing on the future of their money. Obviously, it is vital to be as well-informed as possible, but before we look at the benefits of moving money around the world, we should consider the reservations that many people have about taking a step outside the conventions of their own country. People often think that there is something wrong with investing abroad, but there is nothing necessarily odd or improper about doing so – in fact, it is an essential part of the international economy.

Unlike continental Europe, where centuries of wars, revolutions and expropriations have made people wary of their own countries, in the UK and the United States the popular view is that one is better off keeping one's money at home. This perception is sustained by a variety of commercial and political lobbies in whose interests it is that the public continue to think this. Most countries want to keep their citizens' money where they can control it – inside their own borders. Sometimes laws are passed that prescribe dire penalties, even death, for individuals holding investments outside their own borders. When the situation is that bad, citizens are often not allowed to leave their own countries, except with the greatest difficulty; they must resort to drastic measures to remove themselves and their money to freer places, often running the risk of reprisals against their relatives and friends whom they leave behind. Less drastically, there are often situations like the one at present in Hong Kong, soon to become part of the People's Republic of China. Despite Chinese assurances to the contrary, many Hong Kong nationals think that life will get harder for them when this happens, and are seeking to emigrate. This is difficult because many desirable countries will only let a few Hong Kong nationals in, often basing their immigration policy on the amount of money the immigrant has. Latin America, Asia and the Middle East abound in regimes that limit the amount of money their nationals can take abroad, while the wealthy rack their brains to find ways of getting money out. Even clean, civilised Sweden is the enemy of the rich, with its draconian tax laws, and many wealthy Swedes have found it necessary to leave permanently.

Most people, perhaps, would like to keep their money at home, all things being equal. The reason why people take their money abroad is generally to protect it, rather than out of greed for more; having everything in one place makes it vulnerable, as history has proved over and over again.

TAX HAVENS

A tax haven is simply a country or territory which has low taxes. Some countries have made being a tax haven their main business, going out of their way to attract companies and private investors from other countries by developing sophisticated financial services combined with taxes that are deliberately set at rates well below those in the investors' countries of origin. Many of the world's largest companies and banks use tax havens as a matter of course, often basing their headquarters in them. As well as saving tax, this can also give the advantage of having part, or all, of the business outside the jurisdiction of bigger, more tax-hungry governments.

> ...Most people, perhaps, would like to keep their money at home, all things being equal.............

The important thing to remember about tax havens is that they are vulnerable to change. Simply putting your money in a tax haven and forgetting about it is unwise; you have to keep on top of developments that may affect your investments. Each tax haven has different laws and different prospects, and all are vulnerable to pressure from foreign governments. To make a tax haven work for you, you generally have to be resident there, or to form a company based there. This doesn't mean that you have to live there all the time – you can usually qualify by simply renting a property on a long lease. Holding an investment portfolio through a bank or trustee in a tax haven, and keeping the physical securities in another country, gives you the benefit of low or no taxes, freedom from any future currency controls and protects you from the dangers of expropriation. Thus, since your deal-making and income-earning abilities are likely to be confined to a higher tax country, the best time to make the move is when you can afford to live off your investment income indefinitely – hence the large numbers of retired people in tax havens. Tax havens offer some opportunities to people who are still trying to accumulate capital, but it is expensive and can be difficult legally, especially if you find that you have to return home permanently at some point.

> ....**Tax havens offer some opportunities to people who are still trying to accumulate capital, but it is expensive and can be difficult legally** ....

If you are intrigued by tax havens and want to investigate them further, it is worth visiting them in person. Detailed information is easier and cheaper to get on the spot rather than going to consultants in other countries, and many schemes and wrinkles cannot be advertised in the countries where they are of most interest. Remember that many countries, including the UK, don't tax money held abroad unless it is 'repatriated', so if you spend income from your overseas assets abroad you may not need to move to a tax haven.

The tax havens of Europe

You may wonder why it is that the EU countries allow such a variety of tax havens, almost like pirate strongholds, to exist on their doorsteps. When I put this question to an eminent international tax lawyer, he replied that, 'the politicians and big businessmen of Europe are corrupt; they have to have somewhere to put their money'. While this may be so, it would seem wiser for anyone resident in Europe to take their money farther afield to the havens of the Americas, well away from any possible EC legislation in the future, and to regard the European tax havens as halfway houses for specific operations. In the same way, North American investors may be wiser to keep their money in the European tax havens rather than in the Caribbean.

The UK

Curiously, the UK is technically a tax haven – but not if you're British. Because of the arcane distinctions between 'residence' and 'domicile' (see page 242), someone who was born in another country, or whose father was domiciled in another country at the time of birth, can live in the UK for many years without having to pay tax on investments held outside the UK, as long as the income is not brought into the country. The rules allow such a person to hold property and businesses in the UK via a company incorporated abroad, so Capital Gains Tax and Inheritance Tax can also be legally avoided. Why does the government allow this? Simply because it wishes to attract wealthy foreigners into Britain. The UK has an advantage over many tax havens in that it is relatively large and offers a wide range of business and professional opportunities.

Switzerland

Switzerland is a small country with good natural borders. For centuries it has survived by playing complex economic games with its more powerful neighbours and since World War 2 has acquired a worldwide reputation as a haven for capital. An ultra-conservative society with a world-class financial sector, Switzerland does not, in fact, let people settle within its borders easily. If you are a millionaire you can probably get citizenship, at a cost of £200,000 or so, as long as no objections about your morality or other civil virtues are made, although cheaper schemes appear occasionally. The main attraction is the famous 'secret' banking system which hitherto has enabled third-world dictators and other notorious types to hide their money. Since the collapse of the USSR, Switzerland is allying itself more closely with the rest of Europe and has applied for EU membership. While it is true that a lot of money is hidden in Switzerland, it is by no means completely safe since Swiss banks with branches in other countries have been known to succumb to pressure from foreign governments, particularly from that of the United States. Taxes are relatively high, so while Switzerland may still be a haven for capital, it is not really a tax haven.

Monaco

Monaco is a tiny principality on the Côte D'Azur, surrounded by France but very close to Italy. The French do their best to tax assets in Monaco. It's relatively easy to acquire residence there, but it is probably wise to keep your assets elsewhere. Monaco is an eyesore of skyscrapers – its *fin de siècle* romance is long gone – and even the casinos are just for tourists.

The Channel Islands

By an accident of history, these islands are subject to the British Crown but have their own governments; in theory, the British government cannot tell them what to do. The larger islands, such as Jersey and Guernsey, are awash with millionaire lawyers and accountants. Income tax is set at 20 per cent on money brought into the country, there is no Capital Gains Tax or VAT, and the cost of living is delightfully low. For wealthy Britons, making a permanent move to the Channel Islands gives immediate benefits, and is close enough to the UK for it to be easy to make short trips home, but it costs. You have to be a multi-millionaire to settle in Jersey and on Guernsey you must buy a house for at least £200,000. The tiny island of Sark allows you to become domiciled there if you rent a property for more than a year, which is a cheaper option. Jersey and Guernsey have highly sophisticated banking and financial facilities. Running a Channel Islands-based company costs about £2,000 a year, which is on the high side.

Other Euro tax havens

Territories such as Andorra and Gibraltar offer similar advantages to the Channel Islands: cheap living, expensive property and low taxes. Gibraltar is popular as a base for offshore companies, but its close ties to the UK make it undesirable for British nationals. Luxembourg and Liechtenstein are not really tax havens, but they are excellent places to keep money and to trade from, probably better than Switzerland in most cases.

Tax havens in the Americas

These are mostly in or near the Carribean – the Cayman Islands, the Bahamas, Bermuda, the Dutch Antilles and Panama are the best known. The big international banks all have a presence there, as do thousands of corporations. They are more vulnerable politically than European tax havens but you can often obtain residency cheaply, and Europeans are generally more welcome than Americans, owing to the pressures applied by the US bureaucracy.

Free trade zones

These turn up from time to time and often don't last for very long. They have something of the atmosphere of the frontier bar full of piratical aliens in the movie 'Star Wars' – one is never quite sure what is going to happen next. The United Arab Emirates (UAE) has recently set up the Jebel Ali free zone which offers a financial playground with minimal controls and very low taxes to all-comers. The Gulf Arabs have been good at money for millenia – although they haven't always had much of it – so there is no reason to regard this haven as more doubtful than the others, but its advantages are really for highly sophisticated investors with plenty of wealth who can get out quickly if the balloon ever does go up.

Languages

People who don't speak another language are shooting themselves in the foot. The best opportunities are for the multi-lingual investor, so take the trouble to learn a language or two and don't be afraid to go to countries where they don't speak your native tongue.

OFFSHORE TRUSTS AND COMPANIES – ARE THEY WORTH IT?

I believe that the short answer to this question is generally 'No'. There are hordes of parasitical professionals who are only too keen to set you up with any number of paper organisations which have a curious tendency to be expensive to run. Usually you must appoint company officials and trustees who are resident in the tax haven concerned, and while you can make every effort to ensure that such individuals are bona fide, they may be vulnerable to outside pressure in a crisis. If your objective is principally to protect your capital and you are prepared to live a fairly mobile life, it is generally cheaper and safer to keep control of your assets as far as possible by gaining domicile in a tax haven, understanding the tax regimes of the countries where you spend your time, and carefully diversifying your portfolio, trading through banks and brokers situated in tax havens other than your own. Trusts are examined in detail in Chapter 14; if you are committed to remaining in your own country there is a case for having a trust in a tax haven in favour of dependents in order to avoid inheritance tax.

> if a shark steals their money, the tax evaders can do nothing about it without inviting the attentions of their tax authorities.

Avoiding the sharks

People who are trying illegally to evade tax in their own countries are the prime targets of sharks. The reason is simple; if a shark steals their money, the tax evaders can do nothing about it without inviting the attentions of their tax authorities. Some people are always trying to be too clever and are 'suckers' for complicated schemes that they don't really understand. Changing your domicile is a far cheaper, safer and, above all, legal move than setting up over-complex schemes that may not be accepted by the tax collectors.

Dual nationality for guerrillas

While governments and passport officers don't particularly like dual nationality, having two passports gives the private investor enormous scope for 'arbitrage', in the sense that it is possible to exploit differences in the regulations between different countries. The United States is one of the few countries where it is usually illegal to hold dual nationality – my view is that this is a disgraceful attack on civil liberties.

There are many ways to obtain a second passport. The cheapest methods are through marriage, ancestry and religion. Specialist immigration lawyers can advise on your particular needs and opportunities. Clearly, some passports are worth more than others – try travelling around the world on an Israeli, Lebanese or Syrian passport, or on one from an African country, if you want to experience how the less-advantaged half of the world lives! Many people are eager to get US nationality but, while it may be better than being, say, from Paraguay, my view is that most other First World passports are an infinitely better bet. Most countries are hypocritical enough to give passports to people who are able to pay for them, often by 'investing' in the country concerned, and this may be worthwhile as a last resort.

The collectibles would make the stock market look like a convent.

13

Other investments

In this chapter we will examine some of the investment opportunities outside the stock market. They come in two kinds:

1. Businesses, where you must take an active role and take risks in the hope of reaping substantial rewards.
2. Financial products, which offer a high degree of 'security' but are expensive and can reduce your ability to respond to changing economic conditions.

The areas covered in this chapter are:

- Property – its advantages, how to profit from its unique qualities, and the varieties of property.

- Collectibles – why most people fail to make money in 'things', what you must do to have a fighting chance and the dangers of the collectibles markets.

- The Enterprise Investment Scheme (EIS) – the successor to BES (the Business Enterprise Scheme), this is a new tax incentive programme in the UK designed to attract higher-rate taxpayers to invest in new companies. Its advantages are, as yet, doubtful.

- Cash – where to keep it and how safe it is.

- Annuities – why they are bad news for retired people.

- Pensions – why you don't have to have a pension.

- Life insurance – the varieties on offer, and how to profit from the trade in second-hand policies.

PROPERTY

Property, or 'real estate', has to be a good investment for most people. You can see it, smell it and touch it. It's part of life – even if you are not a natural handyman, there is an enormous amount you can do yourself to improve its value, simply through physical work. You'll improve your health in the process. As a property owner you are well protected in most stable, capitalist countries and can participate in a market in which the powerful of the land have an important stake themselves. In addition, the property market is an imperfect economic system in which good deals appear all the time for those who seek them out.

As in all businesses, to succeed you must avoid the consumer mentality. Many home buyers are unsophisticated; they are willing to pay the market price for a property even when the income they could get if they let it would be far lower than the cost of the mortgage. They will tell you that gains in the equity of a property are 'cancelled out' because you must always pay an equivalent price for any house that you move to. This is plainly false. As an illustration of the consumer mentality in property, consider the UK property crash of 1989. In the preceding years, almost everyone saw huge gains in the value of their property, far outstripping inflation. Thousands of people in their twenties felt that they would never be able to buy a home if they didn't buy immediately. It seemed as if prices would continue to rise forever, and the industry professionals, including estate agents, solicitors and money lenders, did everything that they could to encourage this belief. It was easy to get a mortgage and one could borrow larger sums than normal. Controls were lax and borrowers were able to exaggerate their incomes to mortgagors in order to increase the amounts they could borrow.

> As in all businesses, to succeed you must avoid the consumer mentality.

When interest rates rose and the crash came, the effects were disastrous for home-owners at the bottom of the ladder. People had paid upwards of £60,000 for revamped slum dwellings in the grimmest parts of London in 1988; in 1994, these properties are going for around £25,000 at auction. I possess a detailed 1988 price guide to London properties – six years on, its prices still seem ludicrously inflated. Mortgagors repossessed thousands of homes and sold them for prices lower than the outstanding mortgage; many of the people who had lost their homes found that they still owed the balance of what they had borrowed. Some were prosecuted for fraud for exaggerating their incomes on the mortgage applications. Predictably, the government and institutions worked to mitigate these effects and, at the time of writing, the UK market seems to be settling down. In my view, the sufferings of the worst hit could have been avoided if they had been more cautious about their borrowing levels and more sceptical about the trend in prices and interest rates. First-time buyers who have bought subsequent to the crash have benefited from low interest rates and low prices.

Property prices move in cycles. During a slump, or stagnation, owners must simply sit it out until things improve. There are other disadvantages to owning property; the principal ones are poor liquidity, high trading costs, the dangers of legislation and the possibility of expropriation. Before looking at the different types of property, we should examine these problems in more detail.

Expropriation

Property owners are vulnerable to expropriation during wars and revolutions. Property is conspicuous and immovable; it is very easy for an undemocratic government to take it away, either directly or through taxation. Unless you see this coming early, there is little you can do. Sometimes there is a 'window of opportunity' when you can borrow money against the property and move it abroad. The good news, though, is that you can probably see such disasters coming in good time if you are alert and objective. If the worst comes to the worst, cut your losses and leave before the government takes your liberty and your life as well as your assets.

> **Property owners are vulnerable to expropriation during wars and revolutions.**

Legislation against property owners

Western societies seem to be in two minds about property. On the one hand, they want everyone to benefit from ownership and on the other they want to limit profits, particularly those of landlords and developers. Most Western countries have some kind of 'rent control' legislation, ostensibly to protect tenants from their landlords. These laws produce all kinds of absurdities. In the UK, as in many other countries, some tenants are able to rent properties permanently for tiny sums, while others must pay well over the odds with virtually no security of tenure. If rent controls become too draconian, invest in a country with better laws. Despite the difficulties, a working knowledge of the law and the careful selection of rental property still enable landlords to profit from their investments in many places. In California, for example, mortgages are tied to the property that they are lent on, and a house owner is not liable to repay any shortfall if the property must be sold at a price lower than the mortgage. This is a significant benefit to an investor.

As we will see below, renting out commercial property, such as shops and offices, is generally regarded as a better investment than renting out residential property, on the grounds that it is easier to evict a business than a private person. My own view is that the degree to which you specialise is more important than the category of property in which you invest.

> .... **If rent controls become too draconian, invest in a country with better laws.** ....

The tax rules are always changing. In the UK at the present, you pay no Capital Gains Tax (CGT) on your own home. This means that you can accumulate a large amount of tax-free capital by moving up through a series of increasingly more valuable houses (not necessarily increasingly large houses) by means of leverage (see page 6). It is not impossible to accumulate £1 million in this manner over a period of years, provided that you are always able to service your debt and are not sentimental about moving. There are various quirks to this CGT relief which can benefit owners of more than one property. Anyone who intends to make money in property must read widely on how it is taxed and use a good accountant.

If you invest in a foreign country, you should study the rules, and their history, carefully. It is not unknown for a government to offer attractive concessions to foreign property investors, only to impose swingeing taxes once enough people have been beguiled into purchasing. This happened recently in Spain when property-related taxes in Marbella and elsewhere rose by 2,000 per cent in one year.

The costs of buying and selling.

These vary enormously from country to country but are considerably larger than the cost of trading in shares or bonds. In the UK, industry professionals do not give value for money, but put up a barrage of propaganda about how necessary their services are. A little research and the willingness to do it yourself can reduce costs significantly. For example, it is not obligatory to use an estate agent or a solicitor when conveying a property in England and Wales, and there are many instances where their services can be dispensed with altogether. For more information about this, read *The Conveyancing Fraud* by Michael Joseph (see Bibliography for details). Similarly, it pays to shop around when getting a mortgage since some lenders have cunning ways of increasing the costs.

Liquidity

Property cannot be sold as quickly or as easily as high-quality financial securities. Owners can get squeezed when taxes and interest rates increase. For this reason, it is important to diversify by keeping a proportion of your assets in other, more liquid, forms.

Types of property

Legislation and the degree of commitment necessary vary according to the kind of property you invest in. Here are the main categories.

Raw land

'Raw' land is land that has not been developed in any way. Several studies have shown that it generally keeps its value in real terms. It is a passive investment; you buy a field, walk about on it all your life, and can be confident of reselling it without loss – it effortlessly keeps pace with inflation. Raw land is illiquid and produces little or no income, but it cannot burn down or be burgled so you can sleep easily at night. You can improve its value by getting permission to develop it. With such a long-term investment, the occasional opportunity to do this should arise as local planning policies change. People have made their fortunes by simply waiting for a town to grow out as far as their property.

Most of the increase in the value of a piece of land occurs before any construction begins; the big money is in getting permission for change of use. If you buy in your own area, you will be at an advantage because you will be well-informed about local affairs. Buying in decaying areas is dangerous, and you should always buy at a low or moderate price. Make sure you have the soil properly surveyed, checking drainage and stability.

Residential property

We all need to live somewhere; owning your own home will save you rent and usually give you a capital gain into the bargain. Mortgages are effectively subsidised by the government, as there is income tax relief on interest payments. Avoid new houses if you can – most of them will rot away long before the old ones do and they are usually over-priced. Improve your house and insulate it, but don't spend a lot on trendy alterations that will be out of fashion in ten years' time. In old countries like Britain there are many houses whose foundations are hundreds of years old – they've been altered again and again over the generations and always require careful maintenance, but most of them will still be standing long after you're dead.

Buying a house or flat to rent out takes more knowledge, but a home-owner has, perforce, acquired many of the requisite skills. When buying, a rough rule of thumb is not to pay more than 80 times the monthly rent you can get. This may seem impossible until you become aware of the bargains available through repossessions, deaths, divorces and so on. Seek out a bargain in a good area that you know well, maintain it yourself and you should be able to cover the mortgage, tax and maintenance costs with the rental income. Wait for a capital gain as inflation pushes up prices and reduces your debt.

> ....Wait for a capital gain as inflation pushes up prices and reduces your debt. ......

Being a landlord is a business, requiring effort on your part. However, it will not take up all your time unless you own a large number of properties. Your main headache will be the management of tenants. In the UK at present one can offer tenants an Assured Shorthold Tenancy for a minimum of six months; the rules allow for relatively easy eviction in case of rent default or, in any case, at the end of the lease, but the rules are strict and you must make sure that you follow them to the letter. Failing to serve notices at the proper time, for example, can result in tenants acquiring the right to stay indefinitely, which will greatly reduce the value of the property. There are unscrupulous local authorities and charitable agencies that encourage tenants to exercise their rights in this regard, so get it right. Choose your tenants carefully. Specialising in a certain kind of tenant, such as Japanese business families, military personnel or some other group who are motivated to behave well, can be mutually rewarding. As a landlord you will be faced with the reality of society's inequities, not with its myths.

There are other types of residential tenancy. Letting to limited companies was popular before the introduction of Assured Shorthold Tenancies because you could get the tenant out, but be careful to check that the company is genuine, or the tenant may be able to get security of tenure. Licences are appropriate for flat sharers, but you should get expert advice. Fully protected tenancies should be avoided at all costs, except where you are acquiring an occupied property and are certain that you can buy the tenant out.

Commercial property

As mentioned earlier, the law regarding the letting of business premises is less weighted against the landlord. However, if you are considering shops and offices, you should be aware that it is extremely hard for a small business to stay solvent in the current regulatory environment; the vast majority of new businesses fail within two years. This means that you are likely to have problems with tenants defaulting, and you must factor in the costs of dealing with this when budgeting. The treatment of bankrupts has become so mild in the UK that you cannot count on personal guarantees, although you should always attempt to get them. These problems will be exacerbated if you lock tenants into long leases at high rents at the peak of a boom, or persuade a tenant to rent a shop in a poor position. Give them a chance to make a living and they will be far more reliable. As always in property, the location is of prime importance, so take great care when purchasing.

Time sharing and property bonds

Purchasing a time share gives you the right to a fixed period of time in a property in perpetuity. They may sometimes result in a profit, but they are essentially a scheme for consumers, not investors. Property bonds are insurance-based schemes offering holiday accommodation on a points system. Again, they are for the unsophisticated investor and would appear to be of doubtful value.

Investing through the stock market

You can buy shares in publicly quoted property companies, subject to the same risks as any kind of equity investment.

Developing property

The tycoon Jacob Astor used to say 'neffer develop'. It's a rough and risky business even for the professionals, but some people find they have a talent for it. Very small developments, such as converting a house into flats, are realistic projects for the amateur, but it is hard to control costs and stay on the right side of all the red tape.

Ground rents and freeholds

In England and Wales there is an interesting trade in the freeholds of buildings which have been sold off, usually as flats, on leases of 99 years or so. The leaseholders pay you an annual 'ground rent', which can be raised every few years, and when the lease expires your building becomes yours again, so you can resell the lease. It is possible to buy parcels of such freeholds at auction at prices which may allow a profit on the ground rent income. The value of any improvements carried out by the tenants become yours at the end of the lease, and can be taken into account when selling a new lease. If the building has become dilapidated, most leases require tenants to restore the building to its original condition, which can be a substantial benefit to the freeholder. A leaseholder may generally renew the lease by agreement before the term is up, and will usually pay a large premium for doing so. The Leasehold Reform, Housing and Urban Development Act 1993 has introduced new rights enabling many long leaseholders to compel landlords to sell them the freehold. Contact the Leasehold Enfranchisement Advisory Service (see page 255 for the address) for more information.

> ..... **It is possible to buy parcels of such freeholds at auction at prices which may allow a profit on the ground rent income.** .....

COLLECTIBLES

Collectibles are works of arts, antiques, memorabilia and similar objects. Unless you are highly knowledgeable they are not a good investment. Here are the principal reasons why.

Illiquidity, no income and doubtful increase in value

Being objects, they do not produce a cash income. You hope to make money on resale alone. Changes in fashion make speculation, even in the highest quality art, very uncertain. For example, the works of many of the most fêted Victorian artists sell for less now, in real terms, than they did in their own lifetimes. You may find that you cannot sell an object at any price if it is not in vogue.

High maintenance costs

Valuable objects must be maintained, stored and insured at high cost. They are easily stolen or damaged. There is nothing more burdensome than having to be suspicious of tradespeople and strangers who are in your home. Their admiring glances at your beautiful possessions can become a strain.

Careful selection doesn't work

Only professionals and experts can really succeed consistently in spotting winners.

It is hard to find bargains

We have all heard the stories of the person who recognised a hugely valuable antique at a low price in a provincial shop, or the discovery of a famous signature on an apparently worthless painting. It does happen, but you must invest a lot of effort and time in the search, so it's more like prospecting for gold than investing. If you really enjoy this kind of thing, consider it as a hobby or as a full-time business.

The traders are against you

The collectibles world makes the stock market look like a convent. There is very little regulation and a lot of dishonesty. Unless you are knowledgeable, you are a punter who, in the eyes of many professionals, deserves to be fleeced.

Forgery

Forgery is a very real problem, especially with high-value objects. Many forgers are brilliant artists in their own right who cannot get the recognition they deserve. Anything can be forged – the museums and galleries of the world are full of forgeries.

Successful strategies

If you still want to dabble in collectibles, here are some strategies which are said to work.

Fashions can be cyclical

If you really do have taste, and are fascinated by, say, mediaeval Indian miniatures, you can buy when they are completely out of fashion, wait fifty years or so and make a killing. Of course, it may be your children who make the killing – but they'll have had to avoid inheritance taxes on your collection to do so.

Things can 'become' art

American folk art, Buddhist temple paintings and African sculptures were all considered curios rather than art at one time. Now they have great value. If there is a category of attractive objects that you really like, and can buy for less than it would cost to have made at the present time, then they may increase in value dramatically one day.

Wine

Suppose you spend £10,000 on fine wine in a vintage year and store it. A few years later, it is ready to drink, and you can sell part of your purchase to recover your £10,000, and drink the rest for free. That's the theory, and in recent years it has worked for buyers of fine French clarets and vintage ports. No other wines are thought to be safe bets – even champagne, which the uninitiated might think of as an investment, isn't really safe, because it is past its best after about twenty years. The investment market in wine is basically limited to the products of about 30 chateaux in Bordeaux

Joining in with the hype

The great game of the professionals is to collude in the collection of objects when they are cheap and then to hype them in as rigorous and expensive a manner as it takes to launch a consumer product onto a mass market. This is the world of glamour, publicity, high-profile exhibitions and auctions. It's not for the amateur, but a full-time career in collectibles may be very rewarding.

THE ENTERPRISE INVESTMENT SCHEME (EIS)

Known as 'Son of BES', the EIS was introduced in 1994 as the successor to the Business Enterprise Scheme (BES). Both schemes are supposed to give investors a chance to 'get in at the ground floor' on new and expanding businesses – you get a tax break, the new company gets its capital cheaply, and, hopefully, everyone profits hugely after the five-year lock-in period. It's a mug's game. Britain is a country which is so inimical to business start-ups that it is a surprise that any succeed; the extreme over-regulation, the absurd employment laws, the ubiquitous monopolies, the high costs of professional advice, the lack of fast, inexpensive legal remedies for businesses and the simple fact that the country is not booming, kill most new businesses. Little wonder, therefore, that BES promoters looked for ways to offer greater security.

> .... Little wonder, therefore, that BES promoters looked for ways to offer greater security. ....

They found them in a variety of property schemes where the profit came from sales after the five-year lock-in period and offered a reasonably secure investment. This provoked howls of public protest – the BES was supposed to help businesses which would create employment and bring about other social benefits, not to provide an opportunity to make money on one-off deals. Hence the EIS was introduced, with rules (examined below) that are supposed to limit investment under the scheme to 'genuine' trading companies.

Up to the time of writing (summer 1994), there has been little take up; very few companies have tried to raise capital in this way. Why? Because it is very, very risky to start up a 'genuine' trading business in a socialist state, and no one has worked out how to get around the EIS rules yet. All this human comedy is typical of the political difficulties which surround any attempt to encourage entrepreneurial activity in the UK – anyone who succeeds is vilified for exploiting others. If you really want to invest in a new trading company that is going to grow, look for it in the Far East, not in Britain.

Since some attractive EIS schemes may emerge in the future, here is a summary of the rules.

Qualifying companies

Qualifying companies can raise up to £1 million per tax year from investors. To qualify, the company must be:

- Unquoted on any stock exchange and its shares must not be dealt in on the Unlisted Securities Market.

- The business of the company must be trade, rather than investment. Exclusions include trading in property, financial instruments and providing financial service. The company must carry on the qualifying trade for at least three years after it has raised the money through EIS.

- New companies must begin a qualifying trade within two years of raising the money, and tax relief is only available to investors from four months after the trading begins.

- Companies do not have to be resident in the UK but their activities must take place mainly in the UK.

- An EIS company can own other companies but it must not be owned itself by another company.

- Not more than half of the company's net assets can be in land and buildings.

- The scheme allows EIS funds to be set up where investors can spread their money across several companies.

The investors

- If you are associated with an EIS company, then you are not allowed to invest in it. Thus close relatives of the directors, business partners, employees and trustees are all excluded.

- You can invest a maximum of £100,000 a year and a minimum of £500. You can invest in more than one EIS company but the total must not exceed the annual limit.

- You may only invest in new, fully paid up ordinary shares.

- You must not own more than 30 per cent of the company.

- If you and a relative, except for a spouse, invest in the same scheme, your investments may be treated as one investment.

- You must hold the investment for at least five years to qualify for tax relief.

- You must be a UK taxpayer to claim the relief.

- Losses can be carried forward against capital gains in other years.

- An investor who has had no previous connection with the company is allowed to become a paid director after investing.

The tax reliefs work broadly as follows: you get 20 per cent relief on the amount you invest into the scheme, any capital gains you make after five years are tax free, and if you make a loss, you get relief at your current tax rate.

✳ EXAMPLE Suppose you are a higher-rate taxpayer, paying 40 per cent income tax, and you invest £2,000 in a EIS scheme which results in total loss. You would claim the reliefs thus:

Investment	£2,000
Relief at 20%	£400
Cost to you	£1,600
Total loss of net investment	£1,600
Relief at 40%	£640
Net loss	£960

Thus you would have only lost £960 by investing £2,000 which was totally lost by the enterprise. If the company broke even, you would make a profit:

Investment	£2,000
Relief at 20%	£400
Cost to you	£1,600
Net investment	£1,600
Sale of shares	£2,000
Tax-free profit	£400

All this assumes that you will be able to sell your shares. The company cannot, at the outset, promise to buy back the shares at the end of five years.

The managing director of one EIS company recently told me: 'One in ten EIS companies will do well, so you should put £1,000 into 20 different EIS companies. If the share prices in the two good companies go from 50p to £2 in five years, you have more than covered any losses that you might have made in the other companies'. Frankly, I can think of better investment propositions than this blarney. If the £2,000 that you have invested

> ....If you make a loss, you get relief at your current tax rate. ....

in the two best-performing companies quadruple their value, you have made £6,000 with which to cover any other losses, which, presumably, could be as high as £18,000. In any case, the EIS scheme has not been going long enough for anyone to be able to make a truthful statement about the proportion of the companies that will succeed. Perhaps he was extrapolating from BES figures: 'It's high risk', he enthused, as if that justified the mediocrity of his business and its management. Knowing his particular company and its background well, and being determined not to invest in such a poor prospect, I was surprised to see hundreds of small investors, many of them lower-rate taxpayers, buy shares in the company. Apparently it is the triumph of the gambling instinct over the evidence. It is, perhaps, an example of the utter falsity of the reasoning that many people use regarding money – that because everyone else is doing something, it must be okay.

CASH

Saving cash is often thought of as being the safest kind of investment. However, it is not 100 per cent safe, since even banks can go bust, and inflation can eat into its real value. Nevertheless, we all need easy access to cash to pay for unexpected costs, so you should try to keep a minimum of 5 per cent of your assets in this form.

Bank and building society accounts

Your first £20,000 in a UK account is guaranteed by the government – 90 per cent of it in the case of building societies and 75 per cent of it in the case of banks. Interest rates are comparatively low and are paid net unless you register as a non-tax payer. If you keep more than you need in these accounts, you can be sure of one thing only; the real capital value will depreciate over the long term because of inflation.

National Savings Bank accounts

These are essentially in competition with banks and building societies, and are less convenient for most people. Most of the other National Savings products, such as premium bonds and capital bonds, offer worse terms than can be had elsewhere. The National Savings Yearly Plan, offering a tax-free fixed rate of return after five years, may be of interest to higher-rate taxpayers.

TESSAs

Tax-Exempt Special Savings Accounts, or TESSAs, are five-year savings accounts tax free to British taxpayers. You can withdraw the interest without affecting the scheme but if you close the account before the end of the five years you lose the tax exemption. This tax break allows the money to grow faster through the power of compound interest and is particularly attractive to higher-rate taxpayers. The disadvantages are that it is not directly index linked, and that you lock up your money for five years. You can save up to £9,000 in a TESSA, with a maximum of £3,000 in the first year and up to £1,800 in each subsequent year, as long as the total does not exceed £9,000.

Annuities

This is where you pay an insurance company a lump sum in return for a regular income for either a fixed number of years or for the rest of your life. The fixed term variety can be useful if you are planning to pay for school fees or to fund some other savings plan. The payments are partly from the capital, which is tax free, and partly as interest, which is taxed as income. Most annuities give no protection against inflation, so the real value of the payments reduce over the years, and you are locked in forever – there is no way to change your mind and get your money back. Having watched an elderly relative being slowly reduced to penury by buying an annuity because she 'didn't want the bother' of looking after her investments actively, I have a horror of them as a retirement plan.

PENSIONS

Pensions are intended to provide money for you after you have retired; they are very tax effective but are not necessarily the best way to provide for your old age. If, for instance, you build up a large fund through PEPs, you might well find yourself in possession of a capital sum which would provide you with a much higher retirement income than a pension could. The developed countries of the world have ageing populations; within a few decades, there will be fewer people of working age to support a much larger population of pensioners, and it seems likely that scandals, rule changes and collapses will occur. National Insurance, for instance, is not really insurance at all. It is simply a tax whereby the working population pays for the existing pensioners – there is no solid guarantee that a state pension will be paid to you when you are old. Private pensions are better, but the rules lock your money in until you retire and most of the capital is turned into an annuity on your retirement, depriving you of control. If you work for a large, benevolent company which offers you an ultra-generous pension, then it is probably worthwhile, but Robert Maxwell was not the only tycoon to misuse his companies' pension funds so check out the operation of the scheme very carefully indeed.

Pension funds are largely invested in the stock market, so, in effect, you are using a middleman to do something you could do yourself. Something is rotten in the pension industry – my opinion is that guerrilla investors should provide for their old age in other ways.

INVESTMENTS LINKED TO INSURANCE

There are a number of investment products that are dressed up in insurance policy clothing; generally they are unitised, in the same way as unit and investment trusts are, but they receive different tax treatment. You can contribute to these schemes either by paying regular premiums or by investing a lump sum. They can be unit-linked, where the money goes into an investment fund and the policy will vary in value according to the value of the units, or they can be 'with profits', which means that they are guaranteed not to reduce in value and you may also get annual and terminal bonuses.

Single-premium bonds

These are where you invest a lump sum. Usually, you receive life cover, guaranteeing the return of the capital, or a larger amount, if you die. The initial charges can be as much as 6 per cent, with a 1 per cent annual management fee, which are higher that unit and investment trusts. Unlike unit and investment trusts, the insurance company's fund is subject to Capital Gains Tax and they are all subject to Income Tax. In addition, investors who make withdrawals from a single-premium bond of over 5 per cent may be subject to Income Tax on these. They can be attractive to higher-rate taxpayers, who can 'roll up' the gains until they retire when they may be taxed at a lower rate. A variation of this kind of bond is the 'broker bond', where the fund is managed by a professional in return for additional fees; the advantage of these is doubtful, to say the least.

Qualifying life policies

Most policies where you pay regular premiums are Qualifying Life Policies, which means that they are tax free when they mature or when you surrender or assign them. The premiums must be payable for at least ten years and the policy gives a degree of death cover. Not many people realise that it takes more than five years for a life policy investment to beat saving in a building society and that more than a third of the people who buy life policies end them within three years, and lose money in doing so.

One variety, the endowment policy, is frequently used to repay a mortgage, but it is often not the best way to do so. More than 70 per cent of endowment policies are surrendered early and the insurance companies offer low surrender values.

Second-hand life insurance policies

An interesting, and relatively unknown, investment is to buy someone else's life assurance policy. This works because the surrender values offered by the insurance companies are low to discourage early encashment. It is worth buying them at a higher price than the surrender value and taking over the annual payments since you will receive the full maturity value and all the bonuses due. It is also possible to re-sell the policy before maturity. The capital growth is subject to Capital Gains Tax but you can use your annual CGT allowance and organise losses to offset the rest of the gain. Essentially, you are profiting from someone else's inability to keep up the payments. Specialist companies dealing in these policies – sometimes they are auctioned – advertise in magazines such as the *Investor's Chronicle*.

> ......Essentially, you are profiting from someone else's inability to keep up the payments. ....

Friendly Society Bonds

These are like qualifying life policies but are completely tax-free both within the funds, so they will grow faster, and to the investor on withdrawal. The maximum premiums are very low and the penalty for withdrawing before ten years is high. Some funds have done remarkably well. These schemes are good for this purpose, which is to encourage the poor to start saving.

OTHER FINANCIAL PACKAGES

Schemes combining several financial products, such as back-to-back policies, capital conversion plans and school fees plans are usually heavily sold and rotten value. You should be able to achieve better results by arranging the underlying deals yourself.

A person does nothing wrong by arranging his or her tax affairs to take advantage of the rules, so long as they are not broken.

14

Tax

Tax is a burden on everyone in society, from the richest to the poorest, and the rules are Byzantine in their twisted incomprehensibility. Use an accountant, even if you don't have much money; a good one – often these are provincial and charge very reasonable fees – will stop you getting into a mess and should be able to save you substantial amounts of money. Some people think that you can 'monkey' with the Inland Revenue in the way that you can with some other government organisations. Don't – you won't have a prayer. When it comes to collecting its revenue, the state apparatus loses its kindly, socialist face and gets very tough indeed. Nevertheless, there is scope for considerable tax saving if you are prepared to study the rules. This chapter can only scratch the surface of the subject, but it should give you some food for thought. Remember, though, that the rules are always changing so always take professional advice. In this chapter we will look at:

- Tax avoidance and tax evasion – why avoidance is legal and desirable.
- Residence, ordinary residence and domicile – how these different categories affect your tax status.
- Income Tax – the current allowances and reliefs in the UK.
- Capital Gains Tax (CGT) – how to reduce your liability.
- Inheritance Tax – why it is never too early to make a will, and some ideas on how to plan for passing on your estate.
- Trusts – the varieties of trust and their uses.
- Tax avoidance through starting a limited company.
- Working abroad.

TAX AVOIDANCE AND TAX EVASION

Tax avoidance is when you make efforts to reduce or avoid paying tax legally by exploiting the complexity of the rules. Tax evasion is the same thing, except that you break the law. The right to avoid tax is well established and, to paraphrase Lord Clyde's comments in a famous tax case of 1929, a person does nothing wrong by arranging his or her affairs to take advantage of the rules, so long as they are not broken. The extraordinary complexity and unfairness of tax legislation mean that, in practice, there are many circumstances in which a layperson could not possibly tell the difference between avoidance and evasion. Nevertheless you should make sure you use the very best adviser you can find and do all that you can to stay within the law.

> **In practice, there are many circumstances in which a layperson could not possibly tell the difference between avoidance and evasion.**

RESIDENCE OUTSIDE THE UK

If you are legally resident outside the UK, you only have to pay UK tax on income arising in Britain. Tax havens charge their residents little or no tax, and wealthy people have often found it necessary to move to a tax haven for this reason. Residence has nothing to do with nationality or passports. There are several tests that the Inland Revenue use to decide whether or not you are resident in the UK:

- If you are in the UK for more than 183 days in any tax year, you are considered to have been resident in the UK for that year.

- If you come to the UK for an average of three months a year for a series of four or more years, you will be considered resident from the end of the fourth year. If, when you first arrive, the Inland Revenue think you are going to be doing this, they will tax you from the beginning.

- If you have 'accomodation available for your use' in the UK, you will be subject to UK tax in any year that you visit the UK, for however short a time.

If you are away for a year, you may still be liable for tax if the Inland Revenue think that this was 'occasional residence' in another country. This can be awkward if the other country decides you were resident there too – you could be taxed twice.

Ordinary residence

'Ordinary residence' is a strange notion, quite distinct from residence. As it is the main criterion for Capital Gains Tax (CGT), it is important to get the Inland Revenue to agree that you are 'not ordinarily resident' before you make a capital gain, if you want to avoid the tax. You can be resident in more than one country at the same time but 'ordinarily resident' in only one country at a time. It's relatively easy to work through this nonsense if you are leaving for ever, but it can cause serious problems if you return to the UK within three years, since the Inland Revenue may decide that you were ordinarily resident in the UK for the whole time you were away and ask for the CGT on any capital gains you made during that time.

Domicile

Domicile is another strange notion, quite distinct from 'residence' or 'ordinary residence'. If you are not domiciled in the UK, you are not liable for tax except on the money that you bring into the country. There are two kinds of domicile: domicile of origin and domicile of choice. Your domicile of origin is usually the country where your father was domiciled when you were born. If you have a domicile of origin outside the UK, you can live in the UK for a long time without ever having to pay UK tax. Domicile of choice is more tricky; you have to be resident in a country and have 'the intention of permanent or indefinite residence' there. If you want to change from a UK domicile, you must intend never to return for anything more than brief, infrequent visits, or the Inland Revenue will say that you haven't changed your domicile.

Unlike many other people, the British have a curious fear of emigrating. It really is not as bad as it sounds – life in many other countries can be better than in the UK, especially if you are affluent and capable of adapting. Nor will you lose out on culture or modern conveniences; in fact, you may find more of them in other countries than there are in Britain.

INCOME TAX

The Income Tax rates often change: currently they are 20 per cent on taxable earnings of £3,000 or less; 25 per cent, (known as the basic rate), on earnings between £3,001 and £23,700, and 40 per cent, (the higher rate), on earnings above £23,700. People who are employed are taxed at source through the PAYE (Pay As You Earn) system.

The allowances are:

- *Personal allowance.* Everyone, including children, has an annual personal allowance, currently £3,765, which is free of tax.
- *Married couple's allowance.* A married man can claim an extra annual allowance of £1,790 or transfer it to his wife.
- *Age allowance.* If you are aged between 65 and 74 and earn less than £15,200, you get a personal allowance of £4,910, and if you are aged 75 or over, you get a personal allowance of £5,090. If one spouse is aged over 65, the married couples' allowance is increased to £3,155.
- Single parents get an extra allowance of £1,790.
- There are other allowances for the blind and for a widow in the first year after her husband's death.

As well as the allowances, there are also 'reliefs' on the following:

- The interest you pay on the first £30,000 of a mortgage on your main home is eligible for tax relief.
- The interest on a mortgage to purchase rental property can receive relief but check the rules with your accountant.
- The interest on a loan to be used for a business.
- If you sign a covenant to give money annually for more than three years to a charity, you can deduct tax at your rate and the charity can reclaim the deducted tax.
- A one-off gift to charity of over £250 is treated in the same way.
- If you are over 60, you may be able to get tax relief on private medical insurance; check the rules with your accountant.
- Within certain limits, pension contributions get tax relief.
- If you are self-employed, you can claim a wide range of business expenses against tax. If you are employed, it may be possible to do this, but it is much more difficult in practice.

Tax relief on investment income

Interest, which is taxable if you are a taxpayer, is paid gross on the following:

- Bank deposits and building society deposits, if you register as a non-tax payer.
- Gilts purchased through the National Saving Stock Register.
- National Savings Bank investment accounts.
- National Savings Bank Capital Bonds.
- National Savings Bank Income Bonds.
- Some offshore accounts.

Interest is paid net of tax on the following:

- Bank deposits and building society deposits if you do not register as a non-taxpayer.
- Shares and bonds.
- Unit trusts and investment trusts.
- The income portion of annuities.

You get tax free income from the following:

- TESSAs.
- PEPs.
- SAYE and National Savings Certificates growth.

Here's a checklist for the essentials of income tax saving:

- Check your assessments carefully and claim all your entitlements. Even low earners can benefit by using an accountant.
- Keep up to date with the tax-free investments available and make an annual review when you consider how much you should be investing in them.
- Higher taxpayers should consider using trusts (see page 250).
- Use mortgage relief if possible.
- If you are self-employed, make sure you claim all your business expenses.
- Take advice on how to use your company car.
- Take advantage of benefits in kind offered by your employer.

CAPITAL GAINS TAX (CGT)

Capital Gains Tax is tax on the profits you make on an asset, charged at different rates according to your income. Almost all assets will be chargeable to either Income Tax or to CGT. However, it is possible through tax planning to influence how money is treated, to take advantage of the different reliefs which apply to the two taxes. Gambling winnings and damages awarded for defamation are tax free. Cars are also exempt from CGT, since most cars are sold at a loss. If you invest in classic cars, and can convince the Inland Revenue that you are not trading in them, you can keep your profits from their sale tax free.

> **Gambling winnings and damages awarded for defamation are tax free.**

Everyone has an annual exemption from CGT of £6,300, but this only applies to a particular year and cannot be carried forward. Thus, if you make no profits for four years and then make a profit of £25,000 in the fifth year, you will have to pay CGT, whereas if you had made £5,000 profit a year for five years you would have avoided CGT altogether.

If you are going to realise a gain that is subject to CGT, you can take advantage of timing. Disposing of an asset just after 5 April (the end of the tax year) will give you a whole year before you have to pay over the CGT, so you can benefit from the use of the money, and the interest it can earn, during that time. The 'date of disposal' of an asset is a thorny subject; the Inland Revenue say that it is the date of the contract, not the date on which you received payment, so if, for example, you signed a contract to sell a company where you received payment over a period of years, you would be liable for CGT on the whole amount in the first year. One way around this is to arrange for 'cross options' between you and a purchaser, where you sell an option to buy the asset and the purchaser sells you an option to insist on the sale – great care must be taken over the wording of such a deal.

Gifts between husband and wife are tax free as long as they are genuine. This can help you to take advantage of two amounts of annual exemption rather than one. The gift cannot be made after the sale of the asset. You can also take advantage of your children's annual exemptions (even if they are babies), but the rules are more tricky; once again, the gifts must be absolutely genuine.

Capital gains that you make through inflation are given 'indexation relief' to take the decreasing value of cash into account. In addition, if you are selling an asset which you bought before 31 March 1982, the gain is calculated on the difference between the 31.3.82 value and the sale value, and then you can claim indexation relief on top. There is also some indexation relief for capital losses but the government are tightening up on the rules.

If you are a higher-rate taxpayer, you can reduce the amount of CGT payable by transferring an asset into a trust that can then sell it and pay CGT at the lowest rate. The proceeds can go to your children, for example, but not to you or your spouse, or the CGT will be charged at your tax rate, not the trust's.

> **There is also some indexation relief for capital losses but the government are tightening up on the rules.**

Your main residence and up to half a hectare of its garden is exempt from CGT. If you move and have trouble selling your old house, you have up to three years in which to sell it without losing any CGT relief. If you normally own two houses, you can switch main residences from time to time, which can reduce CGT when you combine it with the three-year rule.

Suppose your house has grounds that are much larger than half a hectare. You may still obtain exemption on the excess if you can show that it is necessary for 'the reasonable enjoyment' of the house.

If you use part of your house as an office or other business premises, you may be claiming some of the running costs against Income Tax. This can cause a problem when you sell, since the Inland Revenue may claim that the business part of your house is subject to CGT. If, however, you can show that no part of your house was used exclusively for business, you will be exempt from CGT.

If you own a business and sell it, the proceeds are usually subject to CGT, but if you are over 55 you can get retirement relief. Otherwise, you could transfer the business from the company to a new one and then sell it, which can reduce the amount of CGT.

Another relief for businesses is 'rollover relief'; if you sell certain categories of business assets and use the money to replace them, you can deduct the gain on the old asset from the price you paid for the new one. The new assets could be for a completely different kind of business – they don't have to be identical to the ones you sold. If you sell a business to your spouse, you will not have to pay CGT on the money you receive, while your spouse may claim rollover relief on the price paid. Groups of companies are like husbands and wives in this respect; you can transfer assets from one company to another, avoiding tax and getting rollover relief. To obtain rollover relief, the new assets must be bought between one and three years after the old ones were sold. If you are planning to move abroad permanently, rollover relief can be used to buy foreign assets, delaying CGT until you have become exempt from it as a foreign resident.

CGT on stocks and shares

You must keep complete records for all your share dealings. If you buy shares in the same company at different times, the indexation and CGT is worked out on the cost of the 'pool' of shares (i.e. the total number of shares you have bought). Get your accountant to show you how this works and, in particular, the tricky calculations for enhanced scrip dividends, where a company buys back scrip issues at a good price.

For the sale or gift of unquoted shares, the Inland Revenue will accept your valuation of any 'arm's length' deal where the two parties are not closely associated, but otherwise they may insist on valuing the shares themselves.

You can use your annual exemptions to the full if you own shares by selling enough of them at the end of each year to realise a CGT-free gain and then immediately buying them back at the beginning of the next year. This technique is called a 'bed and breakfast operation'.

Some securities, such as gilts, are exempt from CGT.

If you are married, take full advantage of your exemptions by dividing your shares accordingly.

INHERITANCE TAX (IHT)

If you care at all about the people you will leave behind when you die it is extremely selfish not make a will. Intestacy, or dying without a will, causes a great deal of expenditure and unnecessary suffering for your heirs – the state and the professionals will profit at their expense. Despite this, a very large number of people with assets die intestate, often because of a superstitious feeling that making a will may somehow hasten death. Making a will is inexpensive – there are even standard forms you can buy that will do the job – so it is really inexcusable not to make provision for how your possessions will be divided up after your death. It is advisable to use a solicitor when drawing up a will, because it is easy to make a mistake which renders it technically invalid; the fee should not usually be more than £100.

The key points to remember when drawing up a will are:

- Choose executors whom you trust. An executor is a person who agrees to take the responsibility for seeing that the legal formalities of dividing an inheritance are done properly. I believe that you should never appoint a solicitor, bank, or some other professional as an executor; their fees are likely to be out of all proportion to the value of the work they do, and in the despair of bereavement no one will want to fight them over their fees. It is quite extraordinary how often estates are shamelessly ransacked in this way. Any reasonably responsible person can do the executor's job, and a solicitor can always be engaged (at a much lower rate) to advise on technical matters. Have at least two executors, to avoid problems if one dies at the same time as you, or is too busy to do the work.

- Think long and hard about who you want to leave your money to. Don't try to play God, punishing the 'bad' ones of your family and rewarding the good – this often results in disputes. If possible, leave everything to one person, such as your spouse, whom you can rely on to care for the others whom you want to help.

- Plan carefully to avoid legally as much Inheritance Tax as possible. This is discussed in more detail below. The main point to remember is that proper planning can massively reduce the bite the state will take out of your money. Regularly review your will with an accountant and a solicitor, and adjust it to take any new legislation into account.

- Have a substitute beneficiary in your will in case the first ones die at the same time as you do – in a car crash, for example.

A dead person's assets (the 'estate') is taxed in three ways: through Inheritance Tax (IHT), Income Tax and Capital Gains Tax. Inheritance Tax must be planned for; it is a tax not only on the 'final disposal', which is the amount you leave when you die, but also on some gifts made during your lifetime. It's no good handing over all your money to your heirs on your death bed to avoid IHT – it won't work.

Inheritance Tax is currently charged at 40 per cent on disposals totalling more than £200,000. If your estate, including chargeable lifetime disposals, comes to less than this, no IHT is payable. Valuations of property must be agreed with the Inland Revenue, and the rules are complex. Woodland and agricultural property get special relief, as can the transfer of an interest in a business.

Lifetime gifts

- Gifts up to £3,000 per year are exempt and can be carried forward for one year.

- Gifts of up to £250 per year per donee are also exempt, in addition to the £3,000 mentioned above. Thus, you can give away £250 a year to, say, ten people.

- Gifts between spouses are exempt if both are domiciled in the UK.

- Normal, regular spending out of income is exempt.

- Wedding gifts of cash up to certain limits are exempt.

- Charitable and political gifts are exempt, with no upper limit.

- Family maintenance payments are exempt.

- Gifts, however large, which are made more than seven years before your death are exempt.

- Some gifts and payments into some kinds of trusts are exempt only if the donor lives for seven years after the gift is made. These are called Potentially Exempt Transfers (PETs). There is a sliding scale of tax rate depending on the length of time between the gift and your death if you die within seven years.

- Gifts into discretionary trusts are fully chargeable.

- Gifts with a Reservation of Benefit (GROBs) can catch people out; if you give away your house but go on living in it, it is a GROB, and chargeable. The rules governing GROBs are nightmarish, so professional help is necessary.

Estate planning

For people with assets far above the threshold for IHT, estate planning can be extraordinarily complex. It is therefore worth paying for the best advice you can get. Trusts may play an important part in the plan. Becoming resident in a tax haven with no death duties is desirable.

> Becoming resident in a tax haven with no death duties is desirable.

Most people are reluctant to give away large sums long before they die; inflation, the increased health expenses and lack of earning power in old age can easily get you into trouble when you are at your most helpless. One doesn't know when one is going to die, so it is foolhardy to budget at retirement age for one's own death at, say, 85, when one might hang on until the age of 93. In addition, you may well feel reluctant to give control of large sums to family members who are not mature enough to handle them. Human development being what it is, many people don't really 'grow up' until their parents die.

Trusts and IHT

Trusts separate the control over assets, the entitlement to capital and the entitlement to income. You must appoint trustees of complete integrity as they will be responsible for the administration of the trust's assets, and you can instruct them on who will get the income and who will get the capital.

If you own a company, employee trusts can be used to avoid IHT. If you create an employee trust through your will after you have died, you can leave your shares to employees, who can be family members, provided that they each own less than 5 per cent of the company already.

If you own a company whose value you expect to increase, you could transfer up to £147,000's worth of shares into a discretionary trust; there would be no IHT to pay, and you could get a CGT benefit on the gain as well.

Reservation of benefit

GROBs (mentioned above) offer a few loopholes. For instance, although you may not reserve a benefit for yourself when you give something away, you can reserve a benefit for your spouse in the gift without it being subject to IHT. Another wrinkle is to give a lease on your house to your spouse, or to yourselves jointly, and give away the freehold, which will have a much lower value during the term of the lease, and thus reduce the amount of tax.

'HIDDEN' TAXES

As well as Income Tax, Capital Gains Tax and Inheritance Tax, there are also all kinds of taxes on things that you buy, such as VAT. They don't seem to be taxes because they are included in the price, but they are. Spend your money in lower tax countries where possible.

TRUSTS

Trusts were invented centuries ago to protect assets from the depredations of the Inland Revenue and other undesirables such as irresponsible or immature beneficiaries. The Victorian man of property would go to great lengths to make sure that his assets would be managed by responsible business people after his death, while the proceeds could be enjoyed by his unworldly descendants. Today, the main advantage of trusts is their use in reducing the amount of Inheritance Tax.

> .....The trustees have a legal duty to act in the best interests of the beneficiaries and have many other heavy legal obligations. ....

The players in a trust are the settlor, who is the person transferring the assets, the trustees, who administer the trust, and the beneficiaries, who receive the benefits of the assets. Trusts are normally set up to run for about 80 years.

The settlor can retain some control over a trust by retaining the right to appoint new trustees, or by making the trustees get consent before taking certain actions. The trustees have a legal duty to act in the best interests of the beneficiaries and have many other heavy legal obligations. A settlor can be a trustee, but this can give rise to tax liabilities. A settlor can also be a beneficiary.

Bare trusts

With bare trusts, the trustees act as nominees who hold assets for someone else, who still legally possesses them. They can be useful to higher-rate taxpayers who want to accumulate money for their children; a child can possess the assets, held by the trustee who re-invests the income. Because

> ..... A child can possess the assets, held by the trustee who re-invests the income. ....

this income belongs to the child but is not paid to the child, it is tax free up to £3,445, and taxed at 25 per cent above this figure.

Fixed interest trusts

In this kind of trust, the beneficiaries receive income from the trust which is liable for income tax. If the trust deed allows it, the settlor or trustees can cancel this if the beneficiaries behave in a way that they don't like.

Discretionary trusts

This is where the trustee has the power to decide the amount of money a beneficiary can receive. The trust's income is taxed at 35 per cent, but a beneficiary who is a lower-rate taxpayer can get part of this back from the Inland Revenue.

Accumulation and maintenance trusts

This is for beneficiaries up to the age of 25 and has special advantages for Inheritance Tax.

Capital Gains Tax on trusts

Trusts pay CGT and have a lower annual exemption than people do, unless the settlor or the settlor's spouse has an interest, in which case their own exemptions come into play. Trusts pay 25 per cent CGT unless some or all of their income is liable to Income Tax at 35 per cent, in which case CGT is charged at the higher rate. Cash held by trusts is exempt from CGT.

STARTING A COMPANY

If you are not business-minded, it may never have occurred to you that forming a limited company to hold some or all of your assets, including shares, can be a a useful way of reducing taxes. Company law is complicated and cannot be dealt with in full in this book, but here are some of the advantages.

Changing from being self-employed to having a company

If you are self-employed and your earnings are increasing, there may come a point when it becomes worthwhile to transfer the business into a limited company to keep profits taxed at 25 per cent, which is the 'small companies' rate of corporation tax on profits up to £300,000, rather than having to pay Income Tax at the higher rate. Another advantage is that because self-employed people are taxed on a preceding year basis, it is possible, with careful planning, to choose to cease trading as a self-employed person at a time when you are making large profits and avoid paying tax on a large proportion of them due to the 'drop out' effect. Get your accountant to explain how this works. You can then transfer your business to your new company.

Tax relief on borrowing

If you withdraw a large sum of money from your company and it then borrows the same amount from a bank, the company's borrowing attracts tax relief on the total interest paid, which makes it cheaper than if you borrowed it personally. You have to do this in the order described; it's no use having your company borrow the money first and then withdrawing it for your own use as the Inland Revenue may deny you the relief.

Working abroad

If you work overseas for part of each year and make yourself an employee of your own limited company, you can obtain a 100 per cent deduction for your foreign earnings, so long as you stagger your trips abroad carefully over a 365-day period; you need not be working for all of the time that you are abroad – holidays can be inluded, for instance, due to a genuine loophole in the rules. Once again, get your accountant to explain how this works.

Ex-gratia payments

Otherwise known as golden handshakes, ex-gratia payments made by a company to employees when they leave the company are tax free up to £30,000. Such a payment must be entirely separate from any contractual obligation that a company has to the employee.

Bibliography

Attitudes of Companies in Britain to Fraud (Consensus Research), Ernst and Whinney, 1987.

The Bank of England: A History from its Foundation in 1964, John Guiseppi, 1966.

Be Your Own Stockbroker, Charles Vintcent, Pitman Publishing, 1995.

Common Stocks and Uncommon Profits, Philip Fisher, John Wiley, 1996.

Competition in the Investment Banking Industry, S.L. Hays, A.M. Spence and D.V.P. Marks, Harvard University Press, 1983.

The Control of Commercial Fraud, L.H. Leigh, Heinemann Educational Books, 1982.

Corporate Cultures, Richard Eels and Peter Nehemkis, Macmillan, 1984.

The Financial Times Guide to Business Numeracy, Leo Gough, Pitman Publishing, 1994.

Fututre Stock, Alvin Toffler, Random House, 1970.

The General Theory of Employment Interest and Money, J.M. Keynes, Harcourt, 1936.

The Great Crash, J.K. Galbraith, Penguin, 1975.

The Hacker's Handbook, Hugo Cornwall, Century Hutchinson, 1989.

100 Minds that Made the Market, Kenneth Fisher, Business Classics, 1995.

The Intelligent Investor, Benjamin Graham, HarperPerennial, 1973.

Inside the Gilt-edged Market, Patrick Philips, Woodhead-Faulkner.

The Money Game, Adam Smith, Vintage, 1976.

Offshore Investment, Leo Gough, Pitman Publishing, 1995.

One Up On Wall Street, Peter Lynch, Penguin, 1989.

Parkinson's Law, C. Northcote Parkinson, John Murray, 1958.

Preserving Capital and Making It Grow, John Train, Penguin.

The Profit of the Plunge, Simon Cawkwell, Rushmere Wynne, 1995.

A Random Walk Down Wall Street, Burton G. Malkiel, W.W. Norton & Co., 1991.

Reminiscences of a Stock Operator, Edwin le Fevre, John Wiley, 1994.

The Rich and the Super Rich, Ferdinand Lundberg, Thomas Nelson & Sons, 1969.

The Rockefeller Millions: The Story of the World's Most Stupendous Fortune, Jules Abel, 1967.

Security of Computer Based Information Systems, V.P. Lane, Macmillan, 1985.

The South Sea Bubble, J. Carswell, Cresset Press, 1960.

Tolley's Tax Guide, Tolley Publishing Company, Annual.

Too Good to be True, Rowan Bosworth-Davis, Bodley Head, 1987.

Where are the Customers' Yachts?, Fred Schwed Jr., Simon and Schuster, 1940.

White Collar Crime, Edwin H. Sutherland, Dryden Press, 1949.

Useful addresses

Association of Investment Trust Companies (AITC)
Park House, 16 Finsbury Circus, London EC2M 7DJ
0171 588 5347

Financial Intermediaries, Managers and Brokers Regulatory Association (FIMBRA)
22 Great Tower Street, London EC3 5AQ
0171 929 2711

Financial Times
1 Southwark Bridge, London SE1 9HL
0171 873 3000
UK company information – 0891 123001
UK stock market information – 0891 123002

Investment Management Regulatory Organisation (IMRO)
Centre Point, 103 New Oxford Street, London WC1A 1QH
0171 379 0601

Leasehold Enfranchisement Advisory Service
1st Floor, 6–8 Maddox Street, London W1
0171 493 3116

Life Assurance and Unit Trust Regulatory Association (LAUTRO)
Centre Point, 103 New Oxford Street, London WC1A 1QH
0171 379 0444

Personal Investment Authority (PIA)
3–4 Royal Exchange, London EC3V 3NL
0171 929 0072

Securities and Investment Board (SIB)
Gavrelle House, 2–14 Bunhill Row, London EC1Y 8RA
0171 638 1240

Security and Futures Authority (SFA)
Cottons Centre, Cottons Lane, London SE1 2QB
0171 378 9000

Stock Exchange
Throgmorton Street, London EC2N 1HP
0171 588 2355

Unit Trust Association
65 Kingsway, London WC2B 6RD
0171 831 0898

Addresses for gilt market investors

Bank of England
Gilt-edged and Money Markets Division, Bank of England, Threadneedle Street,
London EC2R 8AH
0171 601 4540

Bank of Ireland
1st Floor, Moyne Buildings, 20 Callender Street, Belfast BT1 5BN
01232 329507

Central Gilts Office and Central Moneymarkets Office (CGMO)
Bank of England, 1 & 2 Bank Buildings, Princes Street, London EC2R 8EU
0171 601 3978
0171 601 4782

HM Treasury
Accounts Division, HM Treasury, Parliament Street, London SW1P 3AG
0171 270 5137

National Savings Stock Register (NSSR)
National Savings, Blackpool FY3 9YP
01253 697333

Registrar's Department, Bank of England
Southgate House, Southgate Street, Gloucester GL1 1UW
01452 398718

Addresses for commodities investors

Chicago Board of Trade (CBOT)
LaSalle at Jackson, Chicago, Illinois 60604–2994, USA
00 1 312 435 7217

Chicago Board Options Exchange (CBOE)
400 South LaSalle, Chicago, Illinois 60605, USA
00 1 312 786 5600

Chicago Mercantile Exchange (CME)
30 South Wacker Drive, Chicago, Illinois 60606, USA
00 1 312 930 1000

Deutsch Terminborse (DTB)
Borsenplatz 6, Postfach 10 08 11, 6000 Frankfurt am Main 1, Germany
00 49 69 2197 0

Hong Kong Futures Exchange Ltd
New World Tower, 16–18 Queens Road Central, Hong Kong
00 852 526 5747

Kuala Lumpur Commodity Exchange
4th Floor Citypoint, Dayabumi Complex, Jalan Sultan Hisamuddin, 50740 Kuala
Lumpur, Malaysia
00 60 3–2936822

Marché à Terme des Instruments Financiers (MATIF)
176 rue Montmartre, 75002 Paris, France
00 33 1 40288282

New Zealand Futures and Options Exchange (NZFOE)
PO Box 6734, Wellesley Street, Auckland, New Zealand
00 64 9 309 8308

Singapore International Monetary Exchange (SIMEX)
1 Raffles Place, #07–00 OUB Centre, Singapore 004
00 65 535 7382

Sydney Futures Exchange
30–32 Grosvenor Street, Sydney 2000, Australia
00 61 2 256 0555

South Africa Futures Exchange (Safex)
PO Box 4406, Johannesburg 2000, South Africa
00 27 11 836 3311

Tokyo Commodity Exchange for Industry (Tocom)
Tosen Building 10–8, Horidome 1–chome Nihonbashi, Chuo-ku, Tokyo
00 81 3 661 9191

Winnipeg Commodities Exchange
500–360 Main Street, Winnipeg, Manitoba, Canada R3B 0V7
00 1 204 949 0495

Stock Exchanges outside the UK

American Stock Exchange (AMEX)
86 Trinity Place, New York, NY 10006, USA
00 1 212 306 1000

Korea Stock Exchange
33 Yoido-dong, Seoul 150–010, Republic of Korea
00 82 2–780 2271

National Association of Securities Dealers (NASDAQ)
1735 K Street, Washington DC 20006, USA
00 1 202 728 800

New York Stock Exchange (NYSE)
Eleven Wall Street, New York, NY 1005, USA
00 1 212 656 3000

Paris Bourse
Palais de la Bourse, 4 Place de la Bourse, 75080 Paris, France
00 331 4927 1000

The Stock Exchange of Hong Kong Ltd
1st Floor Exchange Square, PO Box 8888, Hong Kong
00 852 522 1122

Stock Exchange of Singapore Ltd
1 Raffles Place 24–00, OUB Centre, Singapore 0104
00 65 535 376

Taiwan Stock Exchange Corporation
7–10th Floors City Building, 85 Yen-Ping South Road, Taipei, Taiwan
00 886 2–311 4020

Tokyo Stock Exchange (TSE)
2–1 Nihonbashi-Kabuto, Chuo-ku, Tokyo 103
00 81 3 666 0141

Glossary of terms

ACCOUNT – fortnightly, or sometimes three-weekly, trading period on the Stock Exchange.

ACTUARY – A statistician, usually employed by an insurance company, who calculates risk.

ADVANCE CORPORATION TAX (ACT) – A basic-rate tax paid by companies on dividends distributed to shareholders, who can sometimes set ACT tax credits against other tax liabilities.

ADVISORY BROKER – A stockbroker who advises clients on their investments as well as buying and selling on their behalf.

AGENCY BROKERS – In the UK, broker/dealers who act as agents between market makers and investors.

ALLOTMENT PRICE – In a tender for gilts, the price allotted to successful tenders. In a gilts auction, non-competitive bids are allotted a price which is the weighted average of successful competitive bids.

ANNUAL CHARGE – Management fees levied on investments, often as a percentage of their value.

ANNUAL PERCENTAGE RATE (APR) A standardised way of expressing interest rates which make them comparable with one another, and include hidden charges and other extras.

ANTI-TRUST – Anti-monopoly legislation, originally aimed at US trusts used to create monopolies.

ARBITRAGE – Taking advantage of the difference in price of the same product or rate in different places.

ARBITRAGEURS ('ARBS') – Speculators who practise arbitrage or buy shares in a company in the hope that it will be taken over.

ASSET – Anything which has a monetary value.

AUCTION – For gilts, an auction is where new issues are bid for in one of two forms – competitive or non-competitive.

AUDIT – The process of inspection of a company's books by independent accountants.

AVERAGING – 'Averaging' the average price you have paid for a share holding is achieved by buying more on a fall or selling some on a rise in value.

BACK TO BACK LOAN – Hedging against interest rate changes by borrowing in one currency against the security of a deposit in another currency.

BACKWARDATION – This is when the spot or near-term price of a commodity is higher than its forward price, sometimes caused by shipment delays.

BALANCE OF PAYMENTS – The difference between the total value of money entering a country and the total leaving it in a year.

BALANCE OF TRADE – The difference in total value between a country's annual imports and exports.

BALANCE SHEET – A statement of a company's financial situation at the end of the last financial year.

BARGAIN – A transaction on the Stock Exchange.

BASKET CURRENCY – An invented currency based on several national currencies, such as the ECU and Special Drawing Rights .

BEAR – Someone who thinks the share market will go down.

BEARER BONDS – Bond certificates which can be held anonymously and used almost as freely as cash.

BED AND BREAKFAST OPERATION – Selling shares and then buying them back to mitigate Capital Gains Tax.

BELL WEATHER SHARE – A share in a company that is regarded as likely to move in line with market trends.

BENEFICIAL OWNER – The true owner of a security who may not be named in the register of ownership.

BID PRICE – The price at which a unit trust manager or market maker is willing to buy shares.

BLUE CHIP – The top 100 or so companies on the stock market, reputedly stable investments.

BOILERHOUSE OPERATIONS – Firms who use high-pressure tactics to obtain investments of doubtful value.

BONDS – Securities, usually paying a fixed rate of interest, which are sold by companies and governments.

BONUS ISSUE – The issue of additional shares by a company to its shareholders at no cost; also called a 'scrip issue' or a 'capitalisation issue'.

BRETTON WOODS – The place in New Hampshire, US, where the post-war system of foreign exchange was agreed in 1944.

BULL – Someone who thinks the share market will go up.

BULLDOG BONDS – Bonds issued by governments in sterling, other than British government gilts.

CALL OPTION – The right to buy shares at an agreed price within a certain time.

CAPITAL GAINS TAX (CGT) – A tax on the increase of value of assets realised in a particular year.

CAPITALISATION – The total value at the market price of securities issued by a company, industry or market sector.

CAPITALISATION ISSUE – *See* 'bonus issue'.

CASH AND CARRY – When a dealer buys a commodity for cash and sells the futures contract at a profit, possibly when the spot price is more than the forward price, interest, storage and insurance costs.

CENTRAL GILTS OFFICE (CGO) – The Central Gilts Office is where trade in gilts is processed on computer.

CENTRAL MONEYMARKETS OFFICE (CMO) – The Central Moneymarkets Office is where trade in money market instruments is settled on computer.

CHARTIST – Someone who studies charts in the hope of predicting changes in stock market prices.

CHINESE WALLS – The attempt to keep confidential information from passing from one branch of a securities house to another.

CHURNING – Trading with a client's portfolio in order to generate dishonestly extra commissions.

CLEAN PRICE – The price of a gilt, not including rebate interest or accrued interest.

CLEARING HOUSE – A system for making sure that buyers and sellers meet their obligations.

CLOSED-END FUND – A fund where the size of the total investment is fixed. All investment trusts are closed-end.

COMMERCIAL BANK – A 'high street' bank which deals mainly with the public.

COMMODITY – Any raw material.

COMMON STOCKS – The US name for ordinary shares.

CONCERT PARTY – An informal group of investors who try to obtain control.

CONSIDERATION – The value of a share transaction before the costs of dealing are paid.

CONTANGO – The normal situation in the futures market where the spot price is less than the forward price.

CONTRACT NOTE – Written details of an agreement to buy or sell securities.

CONTRARIANS – Investors who act against consensus views.

CONVENTIONAL OPTION – Options which are not traded.

CONVENTIONAL STOCKS/BONDS – Bonds with fixed interest rates and repayment dates.

CONVERTIBLE LOAN STOCK – A security paying a fixed rate of interest which may be changed in the future for ordinary shares.

CORPORATE GOVERNANCE – A jargon term for the fashionable issue of how companies should be run, in the context of society as well as the law and best practice.

CORPORATE ISSUE – A bond issued by a company.

COUNCIL OF LLOYD'S

COUPON – The nominal interest rate on a fixed-interest security (bond), or a warrant which is detached from a bearer bond or bearer share certificate to be used to claim interest.

CUM – The Latin word for 'with'. For instance, 'cum dividend' means 'with dividend'.

CURRENCY HEDGING – Trying to reduce or eliminate exchange rate risks by buying forward, using financial futures or borrowing in the exposed currency.

DEALING COSTS – The cost of buying and selling shares, including the broker's commission, stamp duty and VAT.

DEBENTURE – A bond issued by a company, paying a fixed rate of interest and usually secured on an asset).

DEEP DISCOUNT – Bonds which have been issued in the UK after 14 March 1989 at a discount of more than 1/2 per cent per annum or 15 per cent in total are said to have a 'deep discount', and the discount is to be taxed as income. No such bonds have yet been issued.

DERIVATIVE – An investment which is tied to an 'artificial' concept, such as a stock index, rather than to stocks and shares themselves.

DESIGNATED TERRITORY – The UK's Department of Trade and Industry (DTI) terms certain tax havens 'designated territories', meaning that they operate proper controls over their financial industries. They include the Isle of Man, Luxembourg, Jersey and Guernsey.

DEVALUATION – The formal reduction in the value of a currency against other currencies.

DIRTY FLOATING – The practice of a state intervening to influence or manipulate exchange rate movements.

DISCOUNT BROKER – A stockbroker who deals for clients but gives little or no advice and charges low commission rates.

DISCOUNTED CASH FLOW – A way of estimating the value of an investment in today's money by adjusting future returns to get their present value.

DIVIDEND – A regular payment out of profits by companies to their shareholders. Dividends are currently taxed in the UK at 20 per cent.

DIVERSIFICATION – The act of spreading capital across different investments in order to reduce risk.

DOMICILE – The country where you are resident for tax purposes; it is difficult, but not impossible, to change your domicile.

DOUBLE DATED STOCK – UK gilts which can be redeemed by the government between two specified dates.

DOUBLE TAXATION TREATY – Treaties between countries to offset a person's tax liabilities in one country against those in another.

DRAGONS – The economies of Thailand, the Philippines, Malaysia and Indonesia.

EARNINGS – The net profit of a company that is distributed to its shareholder.

EARNINGS PER SHARE (EPS) – The profits of a company, after tax, divided by the number of shares.

ECU – *See* 'European Currency Unit'.

EMS – *See* 'European Monetary System'.

ENFACEMENT – The process by which a UK bond passes from a CGO member to a non-member. *See also* 'Central Gilts Office'.

EQUITIES – Another name for shares.

EUROBOND – A stock which is issued by a syndicate of banks and is usually bought and sold outside the country in whose currency it is denominated.

EUROCURRENCY – Deposits of a currency which are held outside the country in which the money is denominated.

EURODOLLAR – US dollars held outside the United States.

EUROMARKET – The market in currencies and securities outside the countries in which they are denominated.

EUROPEAN CURRENCY UNIT (ECU) – A basket currency of weighted amounts of the currencies of the EC countries.

EUROPEAN MONETARY SYSTEM – The exchange rate regulation system used between European Community member countries, begun in 1978.

EUROWARRANT – A certicate linked to a Eurobond which entitles the holder to buy a given number of shares at an agreed price and time.

EXCHANGE RATE MECHANISM (ERM) – The system by which European Community countries give a central exchange rate against which their currencies' fluctuations are regulated.

EX DIVIDEND DATE – The date when a holder of a UK bond receives the next interest payment.

EX DIVIDEND STOCK – UK bonds which are sold to a buyer who does not receive the next due interest payment because the deadline for registration of the transfer has passed.

EXTERNAL BONDS – Bonds issued in the market of one country which are denominated in the currency of another.

EXTERNAL NAMES – Names at Lloyd's who do not work there.

FEDERAL RESERVE – The central banks of the United States.

FIXED ASSETS – A company's assets which are not being processed or bought and sold, such as buildings and machinery.

FLAT YIELD – Also called 'running yield' or 'interest yield', it is the income you earn in a year if you bought £100's market value of a bond. The figure is calculated by dividing the coupon by the market price and multiplying by 100).

FLOTATION – When a company first issues its shares on a stock exchange.

FLOATING CHARGE – A right to priority payment from the assets of a person or company.

FLOATING EXCHANGE RATES – Currency exchange rates which change their rate according to the activity in the market.

FLOATING RATE NOTE – Bonds and other debt instruments which carry a variable rate of interest, usually linked to a reference rate such as the London Inter-Bank Offered Rate (LIBOR).

FORCE MAJEURE – A supplier usually has a clause in delivery contracts allowing him to break the contract when there is *force majeure* – a major external event such as a strike or major catastrophe.

FORWARD EXCHANGE CONTRACT – An agreement to buy an amount of a currency at an agreed exchange rate on a fixed date.

FT ACTUARIES ALL-SHARE INDEX – A stock market index, divided into forty sections, covering all shares quoted in the UK.

FT INDUSTRIAL ORDINARY SHARE INDEX – An index of the ordinary shares of 30 top companies.

FT-SE 100 INDEX – The 'Footsie', the principal index for the price of shares quoted on the London stock market.

FT-SE STOCKS – The 100 companies whose shares are represented in the FT-SE 100 Index. Generally regarded as 'blue chip'.

FUNDAMENTAL ANALYSIS – The assessment of the value of a share on a company's actual earnings, assets and dividends.

FUNGIBLE STOCKS – UK bonds which are issued after an identical issue and merged with it.

FUTURES – The right to buy or sell a financial instrument at an agreed price at some future time.

GEARING – The ratio between a company's share capital and its borrowings. High-gearing means a proportionately large amount of debt and low-gearing means a small amount of deb).

GEMM – A Gilt-Edged Market Maker.

GENERAL AGREEMENT ON TARIFFS AND TRADES (GATT) – A group representing most nations which supervises international trade.

GILT-EDGED – Securities issued by the British government, usually at a fixed interest rate. US gilts are called Treasury bonds.

HOLDING COMPANY – A company that controls one or more other companies.

INDEX FUND – An investment fund that invests in all the shares used in a given market index, mimicing the performance of the index.

INFLATION – A general increase in prices.

IN PLAY – When a company is thought to be the target of a bid, it is said to be 'in play'.

INSIDER DEALING – Trading in shares when in possession of price-sensitive information which is not known to the market. Insider dealing is illegal to some degree in most markets.

INSTITUTIONS – The large, managed investment funds, including pension funds, insurance funds, unit and investment trusts are known as institutional funds and are the major players in the stock market.

INTERNATIONAL MONETARY FUND (IMF) – The international lender of last resort, set up by the Allies in 1944.

INVESTMENT BANK – Called a 'merchant bank' in the UK, a bank which works as a financial intermediary, offering such services as takeover and merger assistance, and the placing of new share and bond issues.

INVESTMENT TRUST – A company which manages share portfolios and whose own shares are quoted on the Stock Exchange.

JUNK BONDS – Company bonds which are not rated by credit-rating agencies. They are 'low quality' and offer a higher rate of interest than other bonds.

KERB TRADING – Trading that occurs after a stock market has officially closed for the day.

KONDRATIEV WAVE – A theoretical economic cycle lasting approximately 60 years.

LESS DEVELOPED COUNTRY (LDC) – A polite way of saying a poor country.

LIQUIDITY – The degree of ease with which an asset can be turned into cash.

LLOYD'S OF LONDON – An insurance market.

LONDON INTER-BANK OFFERED RATE (LIBOR) – The rate of interest offered by commercial banks to other banks on the London Inter-bank Market.

LONGS – British government securities which are to be redeemed in 15 or more years' time.

MANAGEMENT CHARGES – Fees taken by fund managers to cover their overheads. These can be too high.

MARGIN – In the market, a cash deposit against a sum invested on credit.

MARKET MAKER – Formerly 'jobbers', these are dealers in securities in their own names on the Stock Exchange.

MARKETABILITY – The degree of ease and speed with which a security can be sold.

MEDIUMS – British government securities which are to be redeemed in between 5 and 15 years' time.

MERCHANT BANK (see investment bank).

MONEY SUPPLY – The available money in a system and the rate at which it circulates.

MUTUAL FUNDS – The US name for unit trusts

NAME – An investor at Lloyd's of London

NATIONAL SAVINGS STOCK REGISTER (NSSR) – the cheapest way to buy gilts.

NET ASSET VALUE (NAV) – The net assets of a company divided by the number of shares it has issued gives the net asset value per share.

NET MARGINING SYSTEM – Used by some stock exchanges in the United States, this system reconciles the total margins due to each broker so that the difference, rather than the total, is passed to the clearing house.

NET PRESENT VALUE (NPV) – A figure which represents the total of future cash inflows from a project, less cash outflows, inflation, and/or a required rate of return.

NET WORTH – The value of an individual's assets after all debts have been subtracted.

NIC – A newly industrialised country, for example South Korea.

NOMINAL VALUE – The value of a security printed on its certificate. Also called 'par' or 'face value'.

NOMINEE – A person or company that is registered as the owner of a security in order that the true owner's identity is kept secret, or to make dealing easier.

NON-COMPETITIVE BID – In a gilts auction, a bid for between £1,000 and £500,000's worth of stock which will receive an allotment at a price which is the weighted average of the successful competitive bids.

OFFER PRICE – The price at which a unit trust manager or market maker will sell a stock or share.

OPEN-ENDED – A fund which has a variable amount of capital and doesn't have to match its buyers with sellers (see unit trusts).

OPEN OUTCRY – A system of face-to-face trading where brokers shout their bids and offers out loud; used in most commodity and derivatives markets.

OPTION – The right to buy or sell a security at an agreed price within an agreed timespan.

ORDINARY SHARE – The most usual type of share, called 'ordinary' to distinguish it from other kinds, such as 'preference' shares which pay a fixed dividend.

ORGANISATION OF PETROLEUM EXPORTING COUNTRIES (OPEC) – An association of some of the major oil-producing countries which tries to regulate oil production and prices, thus affecting the world oil market.

OVER THE COUNTER (OTC) – Any market which does not work through an exchange-based system.

PAR VALUE – The nominal value of a share or bond, as stated on its certificate. This is not its market value.

PARI PASSU – Latin for 'at the same rate', 'equal ranking'.

PERSONAL EQUITY PLANS (PEPs) – A tax-free shelter for UK taxpayers.

PIT TRADER – A dealer who works on the floor of an exchange, usually a futures exchange, that uses the 'open outcry' system.

PORTFOLIO – A collection of securities held by one investor or fund.

PREFERENCE SHARES – Fixed dividend shares giving preference, as a creditor, over ordinary shareholders but behind bond holders.

PRICE/EARNINGS RATIO (P/E) – The market price of a share divided by its earnings (e.g. profits) gives the p/e ratio, which is the most commonly used measure of the 'value' of a share.

PRIOR CHARGES – Interest paid on loan stock and debentures that is settled before the distribution of dividends to shareholders.

PRIVATE PLACING – An issue of new shares to institutions and large private clients rather than to the general public.

PROGRAMMED TRADING – Investors who give standing instructions to their brokers to buy and sell at pre-ordained price or growth levels.

PROXY – A person who votes, with permission, in the place of a shareholder at company meetings.

PUT OPTION – The right to sell a security at an agreed price within an agreed time limit.

QUOTATION – The price of a security currently fixed by a stock exchange market maker.

RATING OF BONDS – This is done according to risk: the least risky bonds are rated AAA and the highest risk bonds are rated D. Junk bonds are too risky to be rated.

REDEMPTION YIELD – Any one of several methods of calculating what interest rate is necessary for the market price of a bond to equal the net present value of the remaining interest payments and redemption value.

RESERVE CURRENCY – The currency which is most used by governments and institutions for holding cash reserves. Currently, it is the US dollar.

REVERSE AUCTION – When a bond issuer invites bond holders to sell their bonds back to the issuer.

RIGHTS ISSUE – When a company offers new shares pro rata to its own shareholders, usually at a discount.

SAITORI – Members of the Tokyo Stock Exchange who work as intermediaries between brokers. They are not allowed to deal on their own accounts or for non-members of the Exchange.

SAVINGS AND LOAN (S&L) – The US equivalent of British building societies.

SCRIP ISSUE – *See* 'bonus issue'.

SEAT – Having a seat on an exchange means being a member of the exchange.

SECURITIES – These are any financial instrument traded on a stock exchange, such as shares and bonds.

SELF-REGULATING ORGANISATIONS (SROs) – These are financial organisations which regulate, with varying degrees of effectiveness, the activities of their members.

SHARES – *See* 'equities'.

SHELL COMPANY – a quoted company which has few or no trading activities.

SHORTS – Short-term bonds.

SPECIAL DRAWING RIGHT – A basket currency used by the International Monetary Fund (IMF) which consists of weighted amounts of sterling, French francs, deutschmarks, yen and US dollars.

SPECULATION – Gambling on the change in the price of a security.

SPREAD – The difference between the prices of a share at which a market maker will buy (bid) and sell (offer).

STRADDLE – Making contracts to buy and sell an option or future at the same time in order to protect against big price changes.

SWAP – An agreement to exchange a stream of future payments.

TAP ISSUES – In the UK, the name for an issue of government bonds that is not fully subscribed. In such cases, the broker keeps the remainder and 'dribbles' them into the market slowly.

TECHNICAL ANALYSIS – The attempt to predict share price movements on the basis of past patterns of movement.

TIGERS – The economies of Hong Kong, Taiwan, Singapore and South Korea.

TOMBSTONE – A newspaper advertisement that sets out the details of a bond issue or major loan, and the banks that have underwritten it.

UNDERWRITER – One who provides insurance cover or guarantees a financial transaction.

UNIT TRUSTS – UK savings schemes run by specialists for small investors; funds are invested in securities. In the United States they are called mutual funds.

WARRANTS – A certificate, usually attached to a bond, which gives the holder the right to buy shares at a given price and date.

WIDOWS AND ORPHANS – Mythical creatures symbolising clients who are very risk averse and financially unsophisticated.

WORKING NAME – An investor at Lloyd's who also works as an agent or underwriter there.

YEARLINGS – These are short-term bonds, usually with a one-year life.

YIELDS – The annual return on an investment, excluding capital growth.

ZAIBATSU – The Japanese word for 'financial clique'; the original *zaibatsu* was a group of powerful families who industrialised Japan in the last century.